THE CHUTES OF THE VYNE

First edition (rev 1.0)
published in 2005 by

WOODFIELD PUBLISHING
Bognor Regis, West Sussex, England
www.woodfieldpublishing.com

ISBN 1-903953-92-8

THE CHUTES OF THE VYNE

edited by

FRANCIS CHALONER CHUTE

PART I
THE VYNE AND THE PORTRAITS

PART II
900 YEARS OF THE CHUTE FAMILY

Woodfield Publishing - 2005

FOREWORD

This book is in two parts, designed:

First: To help visitors to The Vyne who want to know something about the people behind the portraits. The bold typeface should be legible in a darkened room, and the stories are short enough to read while you stand.

Second: To trace the rise and spread of a family of gentry from small beginnings to national eminence in England and Ireland, focusing (from 1500 onwards) on a few remarkable characters who are interesting in themselves or for their place in history, but did not live at The Vyne. In each part, the narrative is designed for easy reading, but there are notes/appendices for those with stronger stomachs.

This is not a description of The Vyne; there is no substitute for the National Trust's expert guidebook, nor for the first "History of the Vyne" written by Chaloner William Chute in 1888. (The latter can be seen in Hampshire Records Office at Winchester.) The writer records his warm thanks to the National Trust for their stewardship of the house, for help to him, especially that of Douglas Whyte and Kevin Rogers, while preparing this book, and for their permission to use the photographs on pp. 3, 7 & 50.

He gratefully acknowledges help from the staff of County Records Offices at Chichester, Ipswich, Lambeth, Maidstone, Norwich, Taunton and Winchester, from Taunton Castle Museum and the Drama Library of Bristol University, and the respective permissions to reproduce the following owned or copyright material:

Photographs: `Country Life`: p.9; Thames Television: p.10; Victoria and Albert Museum: p.50 (top 2 images); Mrs Freydis Welland; p. 53; Mrs Guy Moreton of Pickenham: p. 54 (lower); James and Rosemary Chute: pp. 55, 99, 202; Somerset County Records Office: p.168; Mrs Susan Faulkner: p.171; National Portrait Gallery: p.173.

Documents and Articles; Hampshire Chronicle: pp.69-71; Basingstoke Gazette: pp.89-90; "Hampshire" magazine pp.91-94; Dr Mark Page: map on p.107; Lambeth Records Office: p.137; Messrs Constable and Robinson for the extract from Mark Bence-Jones's "Twilight of the Ascendancy" on p.152; Mr Don Carleton and the Bristol Branch of the Historical Association: p.176.

Grateful acknowledgements also to: the Friends of Strawberry Hill for their pictures and for their mission to preserve Horace Walpole's fragile house into the future; to Mr Colin Macfadzean and Mr David Manners for material on Fr. Desmond and the Bristol Chute lineage; to Messrs Chaloner, James and Richard Chute, Mrs Guy Moreton and the late Mr Desmond Chute in England, Mr Gerard Chute in Ireland, and Mr Steven Chute in Canada for documents and essential family information, and notably to Miss Jacqueline Chute in New York for generously sharing items from the database of her heroic project to document worldwide Chutes, past and present. It was her great-grandfather William E. Chute who compiled the first `Genealogy & History of the Chute Family in America` in 1894, and her own `Chute Family Index` is kept up to date on Internet.

Where he has been unable to find the copyright holder, the writer apologises, and will gladly give acknowledgement as soon as practicable. He took most of the photographs himself, and craves pardon for their quality and for the lapses in computer handling - which are his fault and not the publisher's, he being too old to know any better.

His greatest appreciation goes to his dear and patient wife Rosamund, who got him started with her own researches, but has paid for it ever since in countless miles travelled, parking places fought for, steeples chased, tombs examined and proofs checked. All remaining faults are his, and as there are, inevitably, errors and omissions in the `Register of Chutes In/From Europe` (p. 209ff), he and Jacqueline will be happy to receive confirmation of missing names and family connections.

CONTENTS

PART ONE: THE VYNE AND THE PORTRAITS

PART TWO: NINE CENTURIES OF THE CHUTE FAMILY

A Tradition from the Conquest to 1956

THE CHUTES OF THE VYNE

Day after day in an English summer, hundreds of visitors come to the Vyne - described in `England`s Thousand Best Houses` as **"the classic house of the English gentleman down the best of ages ... and the loveliest mansion in Hampshire"**. Indeed, after seeing the Oak Gallery, the Tudor Chapel, the Staircase Hall and the Tomb Chamber, people often leave with the feeling that they have experienced something more than ordinarily beautiful.

In the National Trust handbook they have an excellent guide to its art and architecture, both for reading on the tour and for a souvenir to enjoy at home.

NTPL/Oliver Benn

But if we treat it as a museum we miss the point; it is a minor miracle that the house still stands. As a family home until 1956 it had a rough ride - downsized, repeatedly mortgaged, threatened with a gothick makeover, left near to collapse. The handbook mentions its forced sale by the Sandys family after the Civil War; but what about its ups-and-downs under the Chutes who took it on and owned it for 300 years?

Why was it that the eminent lawyer who bought the Vyne left his heirs in a position to be locked out of it for 25 years ? Who mortgaged it in the full knowledge that he could never repay? Which resident was used as model in a Jane Austen novel ? Which MP wore a powdered pigtail when hunting, ordered a portrait of his foxhound, and let the ceiling rot over his head ? Who, on gouty legs, chased his prospective heiress to stop her eloping with an Irishman, who ended in an asylum ? The Chutes in the portraits are anything but a dead lot. Their stories can enliven your enjoyment of the house.

Apart from those who lived at the Vyne, you may also notice a striking portrait of Philip Chowte, who saved Henry VIII in a French attack, governed a castle and ran an estate for Queen Anne of Cleves. His son was an endearing failure, and his grandson was thrown into the Tower. Who, you may wonder, were this curiously-named family? Without noble blood, how did they come to occupy this Tudor palace and social position ? How was it that for a season in 1659 Chaloner Chute of the Vyne became (in the words of Cromwell`s former deputy) "the greatest man in England"? In Part Two we trace their rise from a Jutish sailor in Norman service, selecting the stories of some Chutes whose adventures in war, Tudor spin-doctoring, radical politics, theatre, priesthood, arts and crafts, etc. helped to make England what it is.

THE VYNE'S OWNERS SINCE 1653

The estate came to the Chutes in 1653 by purchase from the Sandys family, who had built the house in Tudor times but were impoverished by supporting the late King Charles I against Parliament.

Chaloner Chute, who in 1659 became Speaker of the Commons, established a family dynasty at The Vyne which lasted three centuries. Since some date in the Middle Ages his ancestors had borne heraldic arms of three swords, and Chaloner Chute displayed them prominently on the classical portico which he added to the Vyne in the course of simplifying it for family use.

He and the successive Chute owners and their wives are listed below, with portrait faces and the page number where you can find each one's story.

A. THE LINE FROM CHALONER CHUTE

owned the Vyne
between dates

CHALONER CHUTE, THE SPEAKER (1595-1659) p.18-22   1653-1659
his 1st wife **Anne Skory**   his 2nd wife **Dorothy Lady Dacre**

p.22   p.22ff   p.77ff

CHALONER CHUTE M P, ("CC II") (1630-1666) p.22   1659-1666
his wife **Catherine Lennard**

p.22

CHALONER CHUTE, ("CC III")   (1656-1685) p.23, 81   1666-1685
.   (unmarried)

EDWARD CHUTE   (1658-1722) p.25, 27-9   1685-1722
(no known portrait of his wife
Katharine Keck, p.26)

ANTHONY CHUTE, M P   1691-1754) p.30-31   1722-1754
.   (unmarried)

JOHN CHUTE (1701-1776) pp. 30,73   1754-1776
. (unmarried)

meanwhile, John`s uncle **Thomas Chute** and his wife **Elizabeth Rivett**
had bought Pickenham
Hall in Norfolk, and their
daughter Elizabeth Chute
had married Thomas Lobb
and had a son Thomas;
when John Chute died
childless, this young Thomas
Lobb took the name Chute
on inheriting the Vyne.

THOMAS LOBB CHUTE   (1721-1790) p.37   1776-1790
(no portrait survives of his
wife Ann Rachael Wiggett)

WILLIAM JOHN CHUTE, M P (1757-1824) p.38   1790-1824

his wife
**Elizabeth
Smith** p.41

her father
Joshua Smith
M.P.

Caroline Wiggett
whom the
Chutes adopted; pp.44,81,85

REV. THOMAS VERE CHUTE (1772-1827) p. 45   1824-1827
. (unmarried)

when, in turn, these last two brothers died childless, the estates
passed to Caroline Wiggett`s brother - a cousin in the family of
Thos Lobb Chute`s wife Ann Rachel Wiggett -

B. THE WIGGETT CHUTE LINE

WILLIAM LYDE WIGGETT CHUTE, M P   p.47   1827-1879
(1800-79)

his wife **Martha Buckworth**
and their son Chaloner, who
succeeded to the Vyne

CHALONER WILLIAM CHUTE (1838 - 1892) p.55   1879-1892

his wife **Eleanor Portal**

Sir CHARLES LENNARD CHUTE, Baronet
                    (1879-1956)   p.57,59   1892-1956

his wife **Joan Baker**

Sir Charles and Lady Chute - the last Chutes of the Vyne, died childless; the Wiggett Chute lineage continues today through cousins, as does the original Chute blood-line in many parts of the world.

OTHER NOTABLE FAMILY PORTRAITS

PHILIP CHOWTE
(or Chute), ancestor
of the Speaker; M.P.
Standard Bearer
to King Henry VIII
pp.104, 122

ARTHUR CHUTE
grandfather of the
Speaker (in a double
portrait with his wife)
                    p.160-1

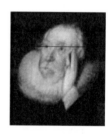

FRANCIS CHUTE
F.R.S., M.P.,
18th C. barrister
and wit; brother of
Anthony and John
pp.26, 31

CHARLES CHUTE, M.P.
father of the Speaker
                    p.160-1

FAMILY TREES:
Diagrammatic family trees for the Chute and Wiggett Chute owners of the Vyne, and their lineages, will be found on pages 160 (Chute) and 74 (Wiggett Chute)

THE CHAPEL AT THE VYNE

"of a magnificence not recorded outside the royal palaces of Tudor England".
The 16th century stained glass is brilliant in colour and clear as a jewel;
it was removed for safety during the 17th century Civil War
but restored by Edward Chute in about 1700.
The superb carved stalls are comparable to those in Winchester Cathedral.

Among the delights of The Vyne are the many majolica tiles on the Chapel floor.
They are thought to have been made by Guido di Savino (locally known as Andries)
who was working in Antwerp by 1513, and may have sold them from his workshop
direct to Sir William Sandys about 1522

THE OAK GALLERY AT THE VYNE

It is dated to about 1520 from the heraldic badges carved on the panelling
which refer to King Henry VIII and his current Queen, Catherine of Aragon,
also to the families of Sandys, their associates at Court and relations by marriage.
It is said to be the oldest such gallery surviving in its original state in England.

Long galleries were first created so that ladies could take exercise in wet weather
but the fashion developed for using them to display
pictures or other treasures, to glorify the family

JOHN CHUTE`S STAIRCASE HALL AT THE VYNE

16TH CENTURY CARVED PANELLING IN THE OAK GALLERY

WITH THE ROYAL ARMS ABOVE THE DOOR WHICH KING HENRY VIII
USED TO REACH HIS BEDROOM WHEN HE VISITED THE VYNE. THE PRESENCE
OF CATHERINE OF ARAGON`S ARMS AND OF HER SYMBOLS (POMEGRANATE,
ETC.) DATES THE PANELLING TO THE PERIOD WHILE SHE WAS QUEEN.

THE COATS OF ARMS AND MOTIFS CARVED ALONG THE GALLERY
PROVIDE A "WHO`S WHO" OF FAMILIES RELATED TO THE SANDYS AND
THEIR ASSOCIATES AT COURT AND IN THE CHURCH IN THE 1520s.

THE VYNE ON THE MAP IN 1632

This section of Saxton & Speed's Map of England 1632 clearly shows "The Vine" (top left)

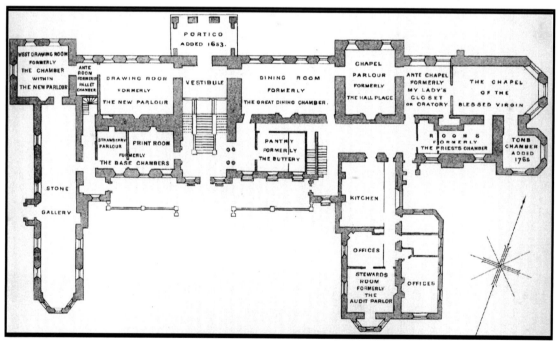

Diagram from C W Chute's `History of the Vyne` showing the Tudor names for each of the ground floor rooms, according to an inventory of 1540, and their names in 1888. The Tudor palace not only extended to the water with a Base Court, but was also fronted by a high, crenellated curtain wall with an ornamental moat at its base.

THE UPS AND DOWNS OF A GREAT COUNTRY HOUSE

A Tudor Palace

The Vyne was built around the year 1510 by William, 1st Lord Sandys, chamberlain to King Henry VIII. The rules of the day were that a wise man carefully avoided the sort of pretentious edifice which would provoke the King's suspicions and get his head cut off; so he built in a low-lying style in a low-lying site. In Tudor England, all the same, a courtier did need space in his house in case he had to play host to a royal visit, with the immense retinues this could involve.

Henry VIII brought Queen Anne Boleyn to the Vyne with a large party, but the blockbusting visitor was Queen Elizabeth, whose meeting with the French Ambassador at the Vyne involved the Sandys family putting up no less than 400 people for two nights. For miles around every bed was commandeered; carts full of hogs, venison, chickens and pheasants churned up the muddy tracks to the Vyne to victual the royal progress.
To house and feed these people, you needed a huge floor space, and it is presumed that Sandys originally built the house on a mediaeval courtyard pattern, with a big "base court" lying across what is now the slope towards the lake. This was typical of earlier, more dangerous days, when an unfamiliar visitor, once admitted past the outer gate, was obliged to dismount in an enclosed yard in full view of surrounding rooms - in case he was up to no good.

17th Century - The Chutes Move In

Now we advance a century. The Sandys have backed Charles I and are impoverished in a lost cause. So in 1650 the nobility moved out of the Vyne; the middle gentry moved in, paying £30,111. 17s. 4d to buy it. The Chutes were urban intellectuals in favour with both King and Commonwealth. The buyer, Chaloner Chute, was a successful London lawyer and in later life a Member of Parliament, where he was conspicuous as a negotiator. For 3 months towards the end of the Commonwealth he was Speaker of the House of Commons. At that date nobody was interested in keeping a huge country home in waiting for a royal visitor - not when England had just beheaded its king.

Chute intended the Vyne to be a family home, not an extension of the royal court. He therefore knocked down the bulk of the Tudor palace; but to give a focus to the north facade after removing the base court, he built on the Classical portico. This enabled his new wife, who had been Lady Dacre, to tell everyone that she had added the first classical portico to any house in England. She lived to over 90, and could enjoy seeing her fashion spread across the country.

We too can be thankful that the house was reduced at that time; this surely saved it from the fate of many oversized houses that have since been demolished.

One Leg on the Land

In 1650 therefore we find a family of lawyer-politicians, who kept London houses, planting a leg into the depths of rainy Hampshire, at a place so remote from a decent road that you could barely reach it (as Horace Walpole said) on stilts, and where the local peasants were so cut-off that their dialect was a language of its own.

Note: The design at the head of this page is taken from a carving in the Vyne Chapel

But life did not run smoothly for the Speaker's heirs. Within months of his death, his widow proclaimed that her stepson was cheating her of her entitlements. She took him to court and obtained a sequestration order on the Vyne. Hence the extraordinary fact that for some 25 years the Chute heirs were barred from living in their own country home. During that period they had no incentive to learn how to run a rural estate - even if the idea had occurred to them.

Attitudes to the country

In the 17th century, town and country were different worlds. Gentlemen found it much more comfortable to live in London than on their country estates. In truth, most of them actively disliked the countryside as such, apart from the prestige of owning a huge acreage like an ancient baron. You left the estate management to a steward, and if he was not reliable, your stately home could be a financial drain - as well as being draughty, uncomfortable and isolated.

The Chutes were among many families who held what we would call a 'townie' attitude until well after 1800. For more than 150 years at the Vyne they lived off London incomes or rich marriages and made little effort to turn its estate to profit, even though generally in the 18th century, English farm incomes soared.

18th Century Improvements

The Chutes did however have a feel for art, and when the Speaker's younger grandson Edward Chute inherited the Vyne in 1685, he carried on the process of modifying its Tudor core with updated styling. After three centuries their family home would be described as "*the epitome of changing fashions in architecture ... representative of almost every major development in the tradition of country house society*"*

This of course required money, which was not forthcoming from a backward agricul-

---

* Avray Tipping, quoted in Barry Turner's "A Place in the Country" (Thames TV 1972)

tural estate. Edward and his younger brother Thomas were therefore careful to make 'prudent' marriages; these enabled Edward to keep race horses as well as improve the Vyne, and Thomas to buy a large estate in Norfolk.

But Edward's wife had 12 children, which spread the inheritance thinly, and the two of their artistic sons who inherited the Vyne - Anthony and John - were not the marrying kind. As will be seen in the course of this book, Anthony's ownership, with no paid employment, no rich wife, and an obligation to house his unmarried sisters, was clouded by persistent financial anxiety and was the nadir of the Vyne's fortunes. John lived in Italy and never expected to inherit the Vyne, which he shunned as a "mouldering estate"; indeed the house was feeling its age, and the damp from its mediaeval foundations made it cold and unhealthy to live in.

John Chute, designer and gentleman-architect, is the most celebrated of the Chute family. He was a close friend of Horace Walpole and designed much of Strawberry Hill for him, and he gave the Vyne its Tomb Chamber and Classical Staircase, the two post-Tudor features which visitors most admire today.

John faced a range of problems when he unexpectedly inherited the Vyne in 1754 - not the least being Walpole's insistence that he should embellish the Vyne with Gothick fantasies. We can follow with fascination how, with no ready money from the Vyne estate, he contrived to fund his great classical designs and to secure the long-term future of the ancestral home. (This is too detailed a story for our main narrative, but can be read in an Appendix on p 83.) John Chute's portraits may look like 'High 18th Century Camp' but in the history of the family, his talents, good nature and *savoir faire* make him one of our most admirable figures.

Foxhunting Tories in the Saddle

John, however, did not touch the basic structure of the house - its roofs, walls and foundations. Nor did the Lobb Chutes, the cousins who succeeded him. Their background was neither agricultural nor artistic. They came from a `sporting estate` in Norfolk, backed by income from the law. On inheriting the Vyne in 1776 they were so delighted with it that for half a century they would not change a thing, indoors or out. They scorned the idea of making money from the farms. For them, the one priority was foxhunting. A hound had its portrait painted; hunters grazed on the unkempt lawn and stuck their heads in the windows while people sat at meat; foxes nested trustingly under the floor until fetched out for the chase.

After 1800 William John Chute went on affecting 18th century fashions by wearing a powdered wig. This kind of behaviour earned the Chutes acid comments from their neighbour Jane Austen, but they were much loved by everyone else, and the Vyne, even as it crumbled away, probably never heard so much laughter before nor since.

Victorian Energy

The final phase of family occupation came with the Wiggett Chutes in 1827 - cousins who became the second family to take the Chute name for the honour of owning the estate. Its new owner found the house in dangerous disrepair; the ceiling of one room was so rotted that its whole weight was supported on a few wall panels. The farms were stuck in mediaeval methods, even though, in the outside world, England's burgeoning population was crying out for food.

But now the Vyne had the man it needed - an earnest youth from a country rectory with more energy than cash. William Wiggett Chute was one of the visionary Victorian improvers. He freed the house of a coat of ivy 2 feet thick, and restored it in the form we see today. For the next hundred years it needed no major repair.

He dredged a century`s mud from the lake. The local roads were a disgrace, so he built new ones, and then new village houses, school and rectory. He tackled unemployment, re-organised his farms and boundaries and turned the estate into profit, probably for the first time since the Sandys owned it.

His wife was an artist, and her interior paintings have been used by the National Trust to guide their arrangements of several rooms. Despite years of living in a virtual building site, she bore him eleven children.

Cold

The first piped heating at the Vyne was installed in the Stone Gallery in the 1850s for the children`s games. (From there, one son went on to play cricket for Essex.) But the family still had to live with its mediaeval foundations, whose clammy cold has been blamed for killing off each new wave of the family. Only one of those eleven Wiggett Chute children produced grandchildren, and he was the one who escaped in his youth to a Norfolk rectory.

Conclusion

The Wiggett Chute lineage were hard-working, scholarly and artistic with a high proportion of clergymen; but they were so taken up with voluntary public services that they made little income. Land began to be sold off. With some extra heating installed in the 1920s, the Vyne was let to a girls` school, to make ends meet. Then in the `39-`45 war, a boys` school was invited to share the house, its owners still having no children of their own.

Finally, the rise in Death Duties forced Sir Charles Chute - created baronet for his unprecedented life of service and leadership to Hampshire - to bequeath the property to the National Trust. He died in 1956, since when the Trust have owned the Vyne and have dedicated their resources to researching its history and restoring its fabric, so that thousands of visitors can enjoy it today.

PATRIARCHS OF THE CHUTE FAMILY

CHALONER CHUTE, M.P.
1595-1659

Speaker of the Commons in 1659

PHILIP CHUTE (or CHOWTE), M.P.
1506-1566

Standard Bearer to the King in 1544

above: painting of the Speaker, in the style of his day

below: sculpture made c. 1765 by Thomas Carter for the Memorial Tomb to Chaloner Chute at the Vyne, designed by his descendant John Chute

PUTTING THE CHUTES ON THE NATIONAL MAP

The family achieved national status in the very different persons of **Philip, the King's Standard Bearer** (1506-1566) and **Chaloner, the Parliamentary Speaker** (1595-1659). Both their portraits can be seen at the Vyne, but their worlds were in sharp contrast. Philip Chowte (as he spelt the name), a soldier, saved Henry VIII from public humiliation and had to keep his act of valour secret. His story comes in our Part Two, as he never knew the Vyne. From the spying and 'spin' of the dictatorial Tudor Court it is a world away to the democratic public argument which characterised the Commonwealth - the scene of Chaloner Chute's election to the Speaker's Chair.

There are two images of 'the Speaker', a tall dark painting in the Drawing Room and the luminous marble effigy in the Tomb Chamber. Which one is the better memorial for the great man who preserved the Vyne for us? Admittedly, only the painting was done from life, but it is formal and tells nothing of his character. In fact, Chaloner was moral, intellectual and open; and these qualities are celebrated in the face of the marble figure, sculpted a century after the Speaker's death. It is of course idealised, but a lot of thought went into it. The sculptor had proposed a specifically 'Cromwellian' image (p.50); the model is fine, but its limited message would not have done justice to Chaloner's breadth of character. The chosen image is surely a truer icon for the original Chute of the Vyne.

We will now examine his career, but on the way it is worth noting why the Vyne displays a large copy of the **1651 Seal** *(below)*. Back in 1634, Saxton's Map of England had showed "Vine" as one of few place names in Hampshire; at that date the (Royalist) Sandys family still owned the house. Fifteen years later, the King was beheaded, the Sandys were out of favour and their house might well have been expunged from the map.

On the contrary; Cromwell's Great Seal of England 1651 - which was affixed to give legal force to an Act of Parliament - again shows "Vine". At that date, Chaloner Chute had contracted to buy the estate, and the future Protector's extraordinary gesture proves the respect in which Chute was held. Oliver Cromwell, we deduce, had seen Chute as a key political figure in the making, a man with the moral and intellectual authority to help him consolidate the Commonwealth.

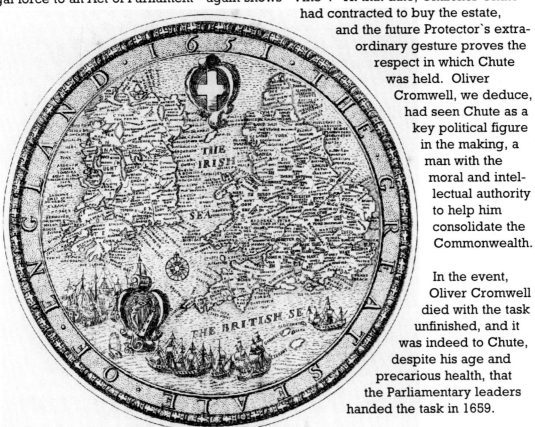

In the event, Oliver Cromwell died with the task unfinished, and it was indeed to Chute, despite his age and precarious health, that the Parliamentary leaders handed the task in 1659.

CHALONER CHUTE - THE LAWYER AS HERO

In honouring him as "The Speaker", his family have echoed the popular acclaim with which, in 1659, the House of Commons chose Chaloner Chute to lead them. Even the French ambassador reported home that "*the Parliament proceeded to elect its Speaker, who is one of the most celebrated lawyers in the nation, and there appeared to be no diversity of opinion regarding his election*".

It is no disrespect to him if we make two comments: 1. that every important achievement in Chaloner Chute's life took place before that event; 2. if there is ever a good time to enter full-time politics, this - the dying gasp of the Protectorate - was surely one of the worst. Indeed it was due to his previous successes in public life that Parliament, virtually leaderless after Oliver Cromwell's death and disillusioned by a succession of elections, de-selections, purges, dismissals, etc., looked to this ageing barrister to cut through their problems, restore their prestige and guide their revolution to the Promised Land. Nobody can claim that Chute became a great Speaker; he never had a chance. He was ill when he took the Chair and died of overwork within 3 months. (In fact, two Speakers died in office in that same year.)

Lawyer Rising Above His Profession

Chaloner Chute followed his father Charles into the Middle Temple, and was called to the Bar in 1623 at the age of 28. He married Ann Skory four years later; it seems that he loved her, and put his private life above the pursuit of wealth. This astonished a younger lawyer, Roger North, who remembered: "*one instance of his loftiness, even while he practised in Chancery. It was, in short, but this: if he had a fancy not to have the fatigue of business, but to pass his time in pleasure after his own humour, he would say to his clerk, `tell the people, I will not practise this term`, and was as good as his word, and then no one durst come nigh him with business.*

But when his clerks signified he would take business, he was in the same advanced post at the Bar, fully redintegrated as before, and his practice nothing shrunk by the discontinuance.

I guess that no Chancery practiser ever did, or will do, the like. It shows a transcendent genius, superior to the slavery of a gainful profession."
(Roger North; Lives of the Norths: Vol 1, p.13)

That sounds like a most refreshing attitude to work. But he was certainly no idler. It is recorded that he was so disgusted with the traditional arrangements for suits in Chancery that he stayed at his desk through a summer's Long Vacation formulating better rules for their conduct.

A Man of Courage

As arguments increased between King and Parliament, Chute's mettle was tested by an attempt of the Commons to impeach the Bishops of England, on the pretext of their issuing canons without Parliament's consent. The Bishop of Rochester sought the best counsel at the bar for their defence; but none of those retained had the courage to appear, with the exception of Chute "who, being demanded of the Lords whether he would plead, `Yea`, said he, `so long as I have a tongue to plead with`". The defence he drew up was so powerful that it even surprised an ex-lawyer among the bishops. The Commons withdrew the attack; his reputation was made.

Other great trials he was engaged in included that of Archbishop Laud (1643) for whom he "and Master Hearn were assigned to be of counsel, and were permitted to have free access in and out to him". In 1647 he defended the 11 MPs whom Cromwell charged with high treason as enemies to the army and evil counsellors to parliament. (*For further legal examples see C W Chute: History of the Vyne, 67 ff.*)

A Safe Hand at the Tiller

The distinction of Chaloner Chute is not so much that he became the Speaker, nor that he brought the Vyne into the Chute family, as that, in a time of near-anarchy, he had won national respect for being not only a brilliant and fearless advocate, but also far-sighted and moral.

His superior skills and diplomacy made him rich, and this enabled him to buy the Vyne. But it is interesting to find one of his bedside books at the Vyne, "A Treatise on the Immortality of Reasonable Souls", inscribed with the words *"sum e libris Chaloneri Chute praecipuis"* (I am one of CC's principal books).

Chute entered Parliament as Knight of the Shire for Middlesex in 1656 and again in 1658. But as he was not chosen Speaker for his politics, we will not try and summarise here the tangled political situation of the Commonwealth and Protectorate at that time. A larger question - one which faced Chute at every session - was **how to make democracy work**. What rules must govern policy and debate in order that Parliament can reasonably be expected to reach a decision? The legal profession has its rules, which avoid a court's time being wasted on matters which are irrelevant, erroneous, or not within the court's competence. Chute knew these and presumably hoped to enforce them in the House. Unfortunately, at that date, Parliament was composed of a multitude of sects whose only concern was to shout their case louder and longer than the next man.

There had been a shattering of authorities. The King had been executed. A citizen no longer felt obliged to bow to Pope or Archbishop. The age-old 'wisdom' of the Roman Church had been discredited by Bacon and Galileo; the Established Church of England was under attack from Puritans who considered it a vessel of the King and too close to Popery. But religion was still passionately felt; it was simply that you, the modern man, now felt free - indeed morally obliged - to decide your own form of Christian socialism. You interpreted the Scripture for yourself and joined either the C of E or whichever Dissenting sect suited your own conscience. Everyone boasted his own moral-cum-social vision, and a Puritan was likely to hold it with egalitarian self-righteousness. Alongside the country squires and independent gentlemen, Parliament had included from time to time: Diggers, Ranters, Quakers, Anabaptists, Presbyterians, and the extreme Levellers and Fifth Monarchists.

"The Greatest Man in England"

One of the more delightful traditions at Westminster is that when a Member is elected Speaker of the House of Commons, he or she is expected to put up a struggle while being led to the Chair. This has its origin in the real historical hazards of taking on that office. For the good of Parliament, you surrendered the comfort of the benches and took on an unpaid job that might be dangerous and was certainly taxing, in two respects:

1. The "Speaker" was so called because he was the **mouthpiece of the Commons** in petitions to the king. Kings always resented the power of the Commons, and on a famous occasion in 1642, the Speaker was confronted by Charles I in person and a troop of soldiers who entered the Chamber to arrest five Members. Mr Speaker Lenthall, braving possible violence, outfaced the King with dignity.

2. The Speaker is **above party politics**. His daily meeting organises the business of the House, and every speech in the Chamber is addressed to the Speaker's Chair. This is supposed to prevent Members shouting at each other and reminds them that decisions must be reached.

But in 1659 Chute not only 'refereed' debates. He also was expected, as a learned lawyer, to succeed where the great Oliver Cromwell had failed; to know how to steer Members into agreeing a lasting constitution for England - one which was republican (for which no blueprint existed in northern Europe) and would satisfy the puritan conscience.

Chute was an older man than Oliver Cromwell and in fact was reluctant to become Speaker. When called by unanimous vote of the Commons on 27 January, it is recorded: *"Mr Chute endeavoured to excuse himself on the ground of ill health and debility, as well as his want of experience of the rules and orders of the House, but although the statement as to his bodily infirmities was unfortunately correct, the House insisted upon his taking the chair."* Indeed on 9th March he came to the House pleading that "he found himself grow weaker and weaker". (Manning's `Lives of the Speakers`, pp 334-6)

We must recognise what a commanding personality Chute must have been, for the Commons to insist on him, in spite of his age and poor health, in preference to others who had already served as Speaker and won respect. The shortness of his tenure is not the point. His distinction is to have been the man of the day whose brains and prestige offered the Commonwealth a hope of permanence. Haselrig, the heir of Pym, Hampden and Cromwell at the head of the Parliamentary party, said openly to Chute: *"I say...you are now the greatest man in England".*

Last Chance for the Commonwealth
Haselrig was well aware of the poisoned chalice he was offering. By 1659 the eyes of England were glaring critically at Parliament. After twenty years of civil strife - murder of the King, puritanism forced on every community at the point of a sword, wars and executions, impoverishment and tyranny - where was this promised "second coming of Christ" proclaimed by Fifth Monarchists? The charismatic Oliver was dead. The army was moving on London, short of pay, full of resentment at slights received, and ready to impose military rule. *(In fact the army did stage a coup, a few days after Chute's death.)* Those who saw no other hope, secretly intrigued for the King's restoration.

What was urgently needed was a disciplined decision in the ranks of MPs to negotiate a new republican constitution, in enough detail to convince the public that Parliament knew where it was going.

Ironically, if it had been left to Chute and his colleagues to work out a solution in the quiet of his office, he might have lived longer and Parliament might have been offered a constitutional framework it could accept. But the Speaker's job is to guide, not command Parliament, and Chute's task (we see now) was virtually impossible.

First, the list of accumulated grievances was enormous, ranging from taxation to law enforcement, from the privileges of the Lords to the position of the altar in church; in open debate they would have taken years to resolve.

Second, there were too many factions in Parliament, some more pragmatic than others but each with its own political priority. Today, such groups sort out their differences in `smoke-filled rooms`, make the inevitable compromises and unite behind broad party banners.

In 1659, Parliament had no idea how to make democracy work. Every faction argued passionately for its own idealised programme, convinced it had God's blessing and yielding not an inch.

Promising Start
When Chute took the Chair, things began surprisingly well; another MP said *"he had so much gained the affection of the House that he swayed much with them".*

But by bad luck, the next business raised a point of principle which has proved emotive over the centuries - whether and how to continue the House of Lords*; and on a point of principle no politician can be kept quiet. `Parliamentary History, Vol. 21, 1656-1659` pp 264- 295 records

---

* The question of how a Government should set up external checks on itself is a matter of endless debate. The House of Lords was restored in 1660 and gradually became part of the checks and balances needed for good government. Its aristocratic origin was tolerated so that independent experts, both legal and political, could be entitled, within our unwritten constitution, to scrutinise proposed legislation and prevent a dictatorship of the Commons enacting bad law. In 2000 the New Labour Government emasculated the Lords because of its partly hereditary element, but after four years has failed to agree a workable substitute [Ed.]

one speech as typical of the debates in February/March 1659 - an hour-long tirade by a furious republican against recognising any Upper House; after exhaustive arguments from English & continental history he put the matter beyond doubt by a series of analogies from the Bible. That pattern of argument went on, late into every night.

By March 9th Chute had to appeal for sick-leave saying: *"that he came to the chair with a great desire to serve the House, but their sittings had been so extraordinary, and their business such, and so requiring it, that he was utterly disabled to serve them as he would for the present".*

After a month a group of leading parliamentarians came to visit him at his Chiswick home - officially *"as a great honor to him"* to express their hope for his recovery, but perhaps primarily to pick his brains. (Had he any new ideas on how to make progress in parliament; or even, perhaps, could he begin privately drafting ideas for a compromise constitution?) By now, however, it was too late; in mid-April 1659 he died.

Within days, the army had forced out the elected Parliament. It reinstated tame MPs who had been ousted years before. They of course had not heard Chute's pleas for orderly rules of debate, and achieved nothing. Within months an invitation was drafted for Charles II to be restored as King.

What If ?
It may be pointless to speculate what might have happened if Chute had been younger and healthier, and if Parliament had cooperated with him and agreed a lasting constitution. But when we stand back to consider the historical status of Chaloner Chute, and the prize available if he <u>had</u> had that combination of success and luck, it is surely fair to claim that he could have become, eventually, the first President of the first democratic republic of the modern world.
His stature as conciliator, and the nation's relief at a positive outcome to a generation's turmoil, would have made Chute, not Cromwell, the ikon of the 17th C. Revolution.

Still a Hero to English Republicans?

In today's world some people still seem to revere his place in history. A surprising tribute from the political far-left came in the 1990's, when Lambeth Council named a set of housing blocks after its revolutionary heroes. There, beside Hampden, Pym, etc., a block is named Chute House. (Chaloner Chute of the Vyne would have scratched his head at that - the idea and the building.*)

Chute House, Stockwell, London

Civil War Shatters a Family
Parliament's long contest against the Stuart Kings, and the damage it did to English families, will be a recurring feature of our story. In the family of the Speaker's mother, the Chaloners, the split was deadly.

His cousins, Thomas and James Chaloner, who had absorbed revolutionary ideas in France, served on the court which condemned Charles I to death. James was Cromwell's military governor of the Isle of Man. Thomas was a "rebellious and drunken" MP until the Restoration in 1660. By the end of 1661 both regicides had died violent deaths.

The irony is that their father had been the loyal Chamberlain and tutor to King Charles's elder brother Henry, the prince who died young and full of promise, and who, had he lived, might have saved England its blood-bath.

(* And still more at the local headline "**Al-Qaeda at Chute House**" in 2002, when an amateur terrorist who failed to explode a shoe-bomb in a transatlantic airliner was found to be a council tenant in that building.)

LINEAGE OF CHALONER CHUTE
AT THE VYNE 1653-1776

CHALONER CHUTE, THE SPEAKER (c.1595-1659)

As the leading lawyer of his day, he earned sufficient wealth to buy the Vyne estate from the Sandys family in 1653. His mother Ursula **Chaloner** had married Charles **Chute**, lawyer from East Anglia (Wrentham, Suffolk & Kelvedon, Essex), one-time M.P. for Thetford and friend of Sir Walter Ralegh. Chaloner Chute married twice:

A young widow, **Ann (née Skory)**, who died leaving 3 Chute children; and
An ageing widow, **Dorothy, Lady Dacre.** (She was born of the North family, lawyers and politicians whose portraits adorn the Vyne. Their descendant was the Lord North whose gentlemanly but fatal deference to King George III led to the American War of Independence.)

Lady Dacre, an arrogant lady whom Chaloner Chute married in his fifties, brought with her a Dacre-born daughter, **Catherine Lennard**, who grew into adulthood in the Vyne, in company with the Speaker's children by Ann Skory. Eldest of these was

CHALONER CHUTE, the second (1630-66).

In due course he and his step-sister Catherine were married. (We will call him "CC II".)

All the Chutes mentioned above have portraits at the Vyne. Catherine looks repressed, her husband looks anaemic and rather ill at ease in his ceremonial armour; one knows the problem of growing up under dominating parents.

CC II was no soldier, and the Civil War armour which he wears is reputedly Roundhead mail given him by Richard Cromwell, associating his memory with the Parliamentary cause. He was, however, a forceful and well-balanced MP who, both under the Commonwealth and after the Restoration, assembled pressure groups of young Members to challenge illiberal measures in Parliament. In 1656 Oliver Cromwell tried to purge him for being "unfriendly to the Protectorate" and in 1662 the House of Commons had him arrested for speaking out publicly against its "Honour and Justice, and Privileges".

A Stepmother from Hell?

Dorothy, the wife of Chaloner Chute I's declining years, is always remembered as "Lady Dacre". The only aristocrat in our ancestry stares out defiantly from her portrait `after Van Dyck` at the Vyne (in contrast to the vulnerable Ann Skory), and frankly she was a disaster for the Chutes. We may wonder why on earth the Speaker married her; even her own family wrote that she was "scurvy", foolish and relentlessly vindictive. The unlucky CC II, in turn, was persuaded to let his stepmother become his mother-in-law as well. After the Speaker died she was a cuckoo in the nest for 25 years, ousting two generations of Chutes from the Vyne and no doubt contributing to the early deaths of CC II and CC III, aged 36 and 29.

Our Appendix `Dorothy, Lady Dacre` (p.77) gives the full story from House of Lords MSS; but, in a nutshell, she mounted a legal case that the Speaker had promised her far more in his lifetime than the bequests she received by his Will. Young CC II, a lawyer, declared her claims ill-founded; in any case, certain assets had been trapped by the widespread revision of property law at the Restoration. She however had nephews who were influential lawyers, and won a Bill in Chancery awarding her £5000 (roughly £250,000 in

CHALONER CHUTE   1595-1659

PURCHASER
OF THE VYNE
IN 1649-53, and
SPEAKER OF THE
COMMONS
IN 1659.

HIS FIRST WIFE
ANN SKORY (right),
MOTHER OF
HIS CHILDREN

HIS SECOND WIFE
(left) DOROTHY,
LADY DACRE
(widow of 13th
Baron Dacre)

MOTHER OF
CATHERINE LENNARD
                    (right)

WHO MARRIED
HER STEP-BROTHER
CHALONER CHUTE II

CHALONER CHUTE II
1630-66 (left)

SON OF THE SPEAKER
AND ANN SKORY,

AND FATHER,
BY CATHERINE
LENNARD,
OF CHILDREN
INCLUDING

CHALONER CHUTE III
1656-1685   (right)

YOUNGER GRAND-CHILDREN OF THE SPEAKER

EDWARD 1658-1722 (left)
THOMAS c.1660-1702 (right)
ELIZABETH d. 1711 (below left)

on the early death of Chaloner Chute III, Edward inherited The Vyne; Thomas married

ELIZABETH RIVETT (right) and they bought the Pickenham, Norfolk, estate;

Elizabeth Chute married Sir L. Cottrell of Rousham Park (the famous garden)

—————————— *EDWARD CHUTE'S SONS* ——————————

ANTHONY 1691-1754 (r.)
JOHN 1701-1776 (below)
who owned The Vyne in succession

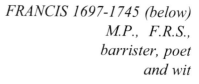

FRANCIS 1697-1745 (below)
M.P., F.R.S., barrister, poet and wit

(No portrait survives of Edward's wife, Katharine Keck)

today's money) plus damages against her step-son. Ignoring his success in getting her Chiswick house restored to her, she actioned CC II for default, got the Vyne sequestrated and put her bailiff there in his place. In his death-bed Will (1665) CC II cried to heaven that he never tried to do Lady Dacre injustice, and she should be touched with mercy and not pursue the vendetta against his children. No such luck! She revived all her claims and the sequestration order against her 10-year-old grandson CC III, and stripped the Vyne of timber for 19 more years until his early death. She lived to 90.

The Speaker appointed Lady Dacre trustee for the younger grandchildren who were not due to inherit the Vyne. It was said that she "favoured" CC III's brothers Edward and Thomas; in fact, out of her £6000 loot from selling Vyne timber it was a niggardly fraction (£1250) that she spent on their education and a start in their professions.

Indeed she never relaxed her vendetta until the Chutes found new money to buy her off. In time Edward got engaged to an heiress whose rich father, Sir Anthony Keck, liked the idea of a daughter at the Vyne. In the marriage settlement (*see under Edward below*) he and Edward paid off Lady Dacre's long-standing claim with Keck money. In 1685 the sequestration order was lifted and Edward sailed into possession of the Vyne - the first Chute able to do so for 25 years!

If all the detailed legal arguments had survived, we could better understand this extraordinary business. But it became so complicated that the House of Lords heard appeals and counter-appeals, and finally got tired and threw the case out.

Two young Chutes died under the lash of Lady Dacre. Alas for Catherine, her daughter caught in between, whose portrait looks so tight-lipped and hopeless.

CC II died and was buried at Chiswick in 1666, leaving Catherine a young widow with four children (Benjamin having died young). Their eldest son -

CHALONER CHUTE the third (1656-1685) was probably brought up in a house near the Law Courts. When he inherited the Vyne at the age of 10, Lady Dacre promptly renewed the sequestration order, and not until about 1684, when he paid her £2000 on account, did she let him actually live in the Vyne (though with her bailiff still in charge). Despite the big wig in CC III's portrait, we read of him serving in adulthood not as a lawyer but as a soldier in an imperialist French army in the Netherlands.

---

1. Patriot or Traitor?

It is astonishing to find that in 1684 this heir to the Vyne, a descendant of liberal Protestants, served with the army of Louis XIV in a Catholic campaign to intimidate the Protestant Prince of the Netherlands, which had only recently been freed from Spanish rule. CC III, in a letter of July 1684, called himself **"a kinde of a poor common soldier in a French army"** who would be glad to "desert the French service", like other "examples every day of those that desert because they cannot starve". He reported:

"we still talke of peace with Holland and consequently with the Spaniards in these parts, but we have a greater assurance that it will not be if the Prince of Orange can hinder it. There has been no town besieged since the taking of Luxembourg, altho` we have an army here of five and fifty or threescore thousand men, an army great enough to take whatever towns they please".

- *For a brief review of the historical background see overleaf:* -

Given this volte-face in England's policy towards Louis, it seems lucky for the Chutes, in a sense, that their 'fellow-traveller' with the French army happened to die before William came to England as king. CC III was back at the Vyne by Feb. 1685 and his last recorded action, in June, was to go to see the Duke of Monmouth beheaded at the Tower - a Protestant Patriot condemned as a traitor. In October began the massacre of Protestants in France; in November 1685, CC III died at Park Privett, Basingstoke of causes unknown.

2. An Unwelcome Marriage Suitor

Writing from France in 1684, CC III had addressed his letters to the Countess of Rutland. This was part of his long-term campaign to marry her sister Bridget Noel*. He was obsequious to the Earl, sending him presents of wine, 'curious outlandish partridges' and barrels of Colchester oysters. Despite all, he was not well received at Belvoir Castle, the Rutlands' home. In 1681 Bridget's mother wrote of him as a "fool" who "brags of the correspondence that he keeps with Belvoir". (This could be shorthand for "he is not in our league; in any case my spies report that he is gravely short of income".)

---

*The first of the Chute enterprises to marry money?

She complains to the Countess (in her eccentric spelling): "I am much vexed at Mr Chute, for, whatever he pretends to the contrey, he declares heare, that ever one salutse me with the newse he is to have Bridget"; and "most in Town conclude that Bridget is to marry Chute, which vexes me mightily, and nobody now thinks of her"
(April 18/20, 1681).

For four years Chute had sent letters and presents to Belvoir, but the wedding never took place. He died at 29, and the noble Bridget (who has given us no record of her feelings for him) was left to her basset, picquet, dice and cribbage - where "her wagers grew alarmingly high"- to her smart parties and mining speculations, and an unmarried life to the end of her days.

What a story, indeed, lies between those portraits - of the famous Speaker, of his anaemic son in fancy armour, and of that young man in a heavy wig whom the Speaker had dandled on his knee as a baby. Not to mention the hapless Catherine, torn every way in a venomous family quarrel.

All within 27 years of the Speaker's death, his son and his eldest grandson suffered short, frustrated, and dishonoured lives. For them, the Vyne was anything but a happy place. If CC III had lived to have his way, those grandiose portraits of Lady Dacre would surely not have been left to hang on its walls.

Chaloner Chute III`s siblings were:

Edward (1658-1722), who next inherited the Vyne - see below;
Thomas (c.1660-c.1702), Clerk of the Crown in Chancery, who married a Suffolk
      heiress Elizabeth Rivett and bought a sporting estate at Pickenham in Norfolk;
Elizabeth who m. Sir Charles Lodowick Cottrell, knight, Master of Ceremonies to
      Queen Anne and the owner of Rousham Park, Oxfordshire (a famous garden).

EDWARD - A WHIG COUNTRYMAN

Edward`s portrait looks confident and agreeable. For good reason; he had charm, ability and fantastic luck. As a boy he charmed the vindictive Lady Dacre; as a graduate he won a fellowship at New College, Oxford, and the North family got him a clerkship to Charles II`s Secretary of State. The best known tribute to his luck is the silver `Basingstoke Monteith`, on show in the Victoria and Albert Museum, his fabulous prize for a win at the local races in 1688. It was luck for him that his older brother died and left him the Vyne. But his greatest luck was to love and be loved by Katharine Keck, to see her suddenly widowed so that he could marry her, and to find her father Sir Anthony able and willing to pay off the Chute family`s 25-year-old debt to Lady Dacre.

Political Prudence

Edward, quite by accident, had kept his nose clean politically. His elder brother, as we saw, somewhat compromised himself by joining the French army against William of Orange and, if he had lived beyond 1688, might have been an embarrassment to the Chutes when William became England`s king. But CC III unexpectedly died in 1685 and Edward thankfully took over the Chute estate; promptly quitting government service, he escaped any taint of having worked under the Catholic James II.

From then on he was careful to hold an uncompromising Whig, pro-Hanoverian, position* as against the Scots and Tories who yearned for a Catholic restoration. He became High Sheriff of Hampshire in 1699, and his sons Anthony and Francis later entered parliament in support of Sir Robert Walpole. Their brother John, close friend of the Prime Minister`s son, was of the same mind, and in 1745 went to Rome to argue the English government`s case in smart Italian society, which adored Bonnie Prince Charlie for his romantic attempt on the throne.

Property and Marriage

Edward had never expected to inherit The Vyne. Only eight weeks before CC III died, their cousin Roger North wrote to the new King`s Secretary of State proposing Edward for a government job. Being a fluent French speaker, Edward was promptly assigned to Paris; his luggage was half-way there when he suddenly inherited the Chute estate. North`s letter of September 1685 is rather interesting, for he comments that Edward in youth was:

"left an infant without provision, and by the kindness of Lady Dacre, his grandmother, he was brought up at Winchester through all the severities of that school, and from thence preferred to New College..."

We might have taken this as a damning criticism of their father if we did not know that (a) North was related to Lady Dacre and took her side in the dispute; and (b) she, having sequestrated the Vyne estate, was the only one of the family with disposable income. (His word "kindness" rings hollow. She made over £6000 by selling Vyne timber, but told the House of Lords she spent £1,232 on "the younger children")

---

* as we learn from a Horace Walpole letter remarking on John Chute`s upbringing

Katharine, Edward's wife, was a daughter of Sir Anthony Keck, whose properties included the famously picturesque village of Great Tew, Oxfordshire; five of its church bells were his gift in 1709. Being a wealthy lawyer *"that had raised himself by his wits"*, he saw social advantage in having a daughter seated at the Vyne, but only consented to the marriage <u>after</u> Edward had inherited the Vyne and a raft of legal protections were in place. First, Lady Dacre's grip on the estate had to be removed so as to allow the Chutes to live there; part of the deal was that the Kecks would pay off all her claims. In exchange however, Sir Anthony insisted on the Marriage Settlement incorporating a mortgage of the Vyne to the Keck family as bond for Edward's conduct as husband. Sir Anthony's benefactions to the Chutes bear out his description as *"a man of polite merry genius"* - when not in pain from the gout. He paid for a Bill to lift the sequestration order, so that Edward could enter the Vyne and marry his bride.

Profitable Romance

Katharine brought Edward capital as well as happiness. On her death, he and their children came into Keck property, such as three Nottinghamshire estates. She left her children lands at Great Tew (whose leases John Chute re-sold in the 1750s to help finance his first phase of architectural work at the Vyne). And when her brother Francis died without children, the Chutes received manorial land which includes the site of to-day's Rownhams Service Area on the M27.

In the Vyne and Sherborne St. John Church we find the Keck arms in several places (more than any arms other than the Chutes) though Katharine's portrait is unfortunately missing. Edward was showing gratitude to Sir Anthony as best he could, short of leaving us a Chute drinking song on the lines of:

> *" All praise to Keck,*
> *The mover and shaker,*
> *Who freed our neck*
> *From the vampire Dacre"*...

In this serendipitous marriage, the only possible 'downside' for the Chutes was that:
(a) Katharine's sister Anthonina (perhaps handicapped in some way?) came to live and be supported for her lifetime at the Vyne, and
b) Katharine was the widow of one Ferdinand Tracy and brought with her to the Vyne two Tracy children. A letter of Horace Walpole (1754) tells us that the Tracy family, sons of Edward's step-son John, claimed a right to succeed to the Vyne; perhaps he feared that John Chute might be obliged to 'buy them off'.

> Their claim is obscure. John Tracy seems to have been Edward's god-son (as well as step-son) and he might have had 'expectations'; but in his Will, all that Edward legally bequeathed to his "dearest friends" John and Ann Tracy was "twenty of my whole peices of Broad Gold".

Edward and Katharine went on to have a huge family - 10 Chute children born 1687-1701. From the portraits of Anthony and John we infer that she had a rather 'Roman' nose.

Children of Edward and Katharine Chute

Edward, b. 1687, died in childhood.
Chaloner (1688-1705), he died aged 17 while studying commerce at Rotterdam.
Anthony (1691-1754) M.P.;
  owner of the Vyne 1722-54
Catherine, b. 1690; married her cousin Thomas Chute (junior) of Pickenham.
Mary, b. 1693
Thomas, b. 1695

Francis (1697-1745), Chancery barrister and wit, much admired by Horace Walpole. Fellow of the Royal Society. Recorded in a "register of English poets" in 1723. Briefly M.P. for Heydon, Norfolk.
Margaret, b. 1699
Ann, b.1700; d. after 1747
John (1701-1776), architect;
  owner of the Vyne 1754-76

Clatter of Tiny Feet

Although Edward was the first Chute able to live in solid comfort at the Vyne, he and his wife were so fertile that the quart overflowed the pint pot*.   The Vyne now seethed with bodies: - up to ten little Chutes, two young Tracys, his sister-in-law, all the nurse maids, house servants. Plus the children's clothes and clobber; toys scattered around and perhaps 50 muddy shoes; their hobby-horses, hoops, drums, pet animals and so on.

Since there was no upstairs corridor at that date, there was no privacy in the bedrooms which all ran into each other. Thankfully there was play-space in the Galleries and the area of 'offices' beyond the kitchen, but how often Edward must have regretted his grandfather's demolition of the "base court".

Katharine herself was almost incessantly pregnant, and died in her forties. The Chute children therefore had no mother-love in their later childhoods. Was an awkward foster mother called in, or did Edward become withdrawn and drive them into themselves? Something is needed to account for the despair we see in the portraits of Ann and Mary, for Anthony's lifelong antagonism towards John, and the oddity that only two out of the ten Chute children ever married.

A Legacy of Beauty

However, Edward and Katharine's example to their children at the Vyne began almost a century-long tradition of art and decoration. They unearthed the precious stained glass and restored it to the Chapel. They collected fine furniture and tapestries; and see how they decorated the outdoors plumbing in 1696.

As Rupert Willoughby observes: **"At The Vyne, even such mundane objects are beautiful."**

---

* A Stops-and-Starts Genealogy

We may note how the Chute 'family tree' over the years is actually a series of population explosions followed by dreadful silences. This happened 4 times, after:

- <u>Katharine and Edward Chute had 10 children</u> - but their only grandchild
was Catherine's son by her cousin at Pickenham, who died without issue;
- <u>Anne Rachael, wife of Thomas Lobb Chute, had 10 children</u> - but only one
grandchild, who eloped in her teens and was disinherited;
- <u>Martha, wife of Wm. Wiggett Chute, had 11 children</u> - but only one of these
had grandchildren;
- <u>Eleanor and Chaloner W Chute had 4 children</u> - but again no grandchildren.

ANTHONY CHUTE - THE MISFIT

A Comely Gentleman

As eldest surviving son, Anthony inherited the Vyne in 1722. He kept on his father's racehorses and evidently enjoyed his food since, after he dined with Sir Robert Walpole in January 1742, Horace Walpole reported him (at first meeting) as being a "fat, comely gentleman".

He was, however, the kind of cranky mis-fit who will keep on being re-evaluated. The Vyne History tactfully says "little is recorded" of him. But its author, C W Chute, grew up with that revealing portrait which clearly shows Anthony's spitefulness; and it is evident that nobody liked him.

Monster or Artist?

On further acquaintance Horace Walpole called him a "capricious monster" of "vinegary temper". He was (in today's terminology) 'de-selected' by his constituents once they had experience of him as MP. He antagonised Lord Bolton of Hackwood, the local grandee, who urged electors not to vote for him again. He trespassed on lands of his Brocas neighbours, and on refusing to settle amicably, he was summoned to Assizes. Proud, obstinate, resentful, you see it in the portrait. And yet...

Anthony was undoubtedly a man of taste. He subscribed (in company with Walpole, the poet Gray, and others) to the London publication of Palladio's "Four Books of Architecture". An expert wrote him up in 'Country Life' as
the underestimated figure in the history of the Vyne", whose work reveals
"*a remarkable example of the sensitivity of a Rococo eye*".

He rearranged the rooms in the North Front, sashing the windows and installing the fine panelling in the Dining Parlour. Floor tiling, classical busts and fine furniture were due to Anthony. Even his colour schemes (later overlaid) earn the praise of connoisseurs.

Bitter and Twisted?

One could shrug and say - what would you expect when a sensitive man is deprived of his Grand Tour because he inherits a great estate, and therefore must become Sheriff and go into Parliament against all his inclinations? Any bachelor with that background, suffering painful gout, and living amid Hampshire mud at the Vyne for 30 years with three maiden sisters and all the bills to be met, might well become bitter and twisted. Especially when one younger brother (Francis) was a popular wit in London society and the other (John) seemed to be living like a 'milord' in Florence with company to his taste and not a care in the world.

Well, that was part of the problem; but let us step back and consider contemporary attitudes to the countryside.

Townsmen in the Country

It is curious how some townsmen who acquired country estates seem to have wilfully refused to manage them for profit. Anthony failed to exploit the Vyne farms; his successor John employed as bailiff an Italian who (so we are told) could scarcely add two figures together; and after 1790 we will find William John Chute M.P. scoffing at his bailiff's failure to make a profit.

Incredible! The Chutes in the 1600's were indeed urban intellectuals whose house in the country was a symbol of professional success and not (yet) an economic enterprise. As lawyer-politicians they kept afloat by earning fees in London and marrying heiresses. But Anthony was unmarried. The injection of Keck wealth had been diluted between many children; he made little professional income and his country life became a penance.

The consequences are all too clear in his inventories & financial accounts which survive in Hampshire Records.

Anthony had all the expenses of being High Sheriff and 13 years as MP (a Newport Election alone costing £84.7s) on top of his living costs, frequent excursions to Town, the maintenance/embellishment of the house, obligations as local squire and support to his sisters, some **£700 - 800 a year expenditure** in all. We do not find him having a London income beyond his parliamentary allowances, and - this is the crucial point - **the 4000 acre Vyne estate produced on average less than £400 a year.** (For comparison the Walpole estate in Norfolk, before Sir Robert aggrandised it, made £1,300 p.a. profit). Anthony must have been running down his capital at a fearful rate.

The Chutes had missed a great opportunity to secure long-term income. In the early 1700's a surge in England's population clamoured for food; farmers nationally enjoyed boom conditions. Yet in Anthony Chute's accounts (of which we print an extract below), where there should have been a rich cash flow, we see an anxious analysis of his personal expenditures - the *"avoidable"* and *"unavoidable"*;
"£450 in the whole year ... I think verily will be with management sufficient, though ye year 1742 I spent above a hundred more"

It was a depressing period for the Vyne. From Italy, his brother John called it a "mouldering estate which has no hope of being repaired", and which he personally had no wish to inherit. Small wonder that Anthony left no Will; in 1754 there was nothing beyond the real estate to bequeath.

Since all his brothers had now died, John, the youngest, inherited by default. The house was in far better order than he had feared, but Horace Walpole warned him to hunt through the wainscots in case Anthony had maliciously hidden a Will leaving the Vyne to someone else. Even in death, Anthony won no credit.

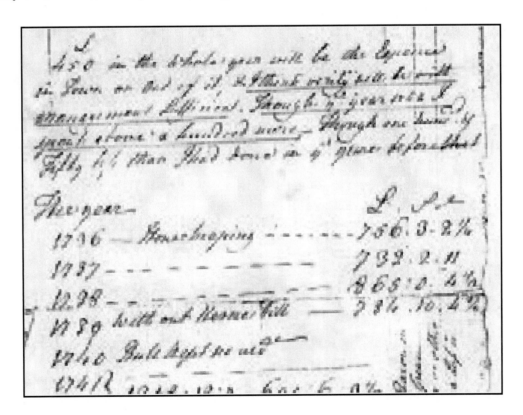

JOHN CHUTE - THE ARCHITECT

John, great-grandson of the Speaker, is the most widely known of the Chutes of the Vyne: - in the history of taste, for his friendship with Horace Walpole and his contribution to the Gothick Revival; in the history of the Vyne, for his Classical Staircase and Tomb Chamber; in Chute family history, for the elegant deal with his Norfolk cousins which rescued the family fortunes.

But who would have expected it ? He was the youngest child of ten; he had weak eyesight and suffered painfully from gout; he was a solitary aesthete in his teens and not the marrying kind; he wore flamboyant clothes and carried a fan; he was suspected of keeping bad company; he was kept away from the Vyne by his hostile brother Anthony; after many years in Italy he was ready to settle permanently in Florence.

It was only by default that he inherited the Vyne in middle age. This sudden opportunity to embellish his ancestral home needed such prolonged thought and preparation that he did not live to see his works completed. At his death in 1776 the male Chute line in England expired.

John Chute figures repeatedly in Walpole`s Letters (which in the Yale edition run to over 30 volumes). His artistic achievement is spelt out in many articles in `Country Life`, `Apollo` etc. on the Vyne and on Strawberry Hill, the house he helped design for Walpole. For his Grand Tour to Italy, see a full chapter in "Originals Abroad" by Warren H Smith, a colleague at Farmington, USA of W S Lewis who edited Walpole`s Letters. There are portraits of John Chute at the Vyne and hundreds of his drawings at Hampshire Records Office.

Given so much published information, and an illustrated chapter on John in the National Trust guide-book which you can get at the Vyne, we will limit ourselves here to the highlights of his life and work.

Grand Tour

In 1739 John, with his sister Ann, his barrister brother Francis and his wife, and a young cousin Francis Whithed, went to France to begin a Grand Tour - the 18th Century gentleman`s cultural exercise.

Only John and his cousin went on to Italy. Whithed was deaf, shy in company and untravelled, so John took charge of the itinerary, which took them to Florence. There, staying in the English Resident`s quarters, they met the Prime Minister`s son Horace Walpole and the poet Thomas Gray who had just arrived. Chute and the three much younger men `did the sights` and struck up a friendship which was to last a lifetime. Chute, who seems not to have had a student period at university, joined warmly in their somewhat juvenile humour in Florence,

and even sported a dazzling jacket, eyeglass and fan - to the horror of other visiting Brits. Whithed contributed none of the wit but paid a generous share of expenses; he also took an Italian mistress and fathered a child.

But behind all the frivolity Walpole respected Chute`s common sense, relying on him, as an Italian-speaker, to chase after antiques - to keep prices down but get the goods. And because the Chutes were Whigs and a continental war was in progress, he asked John to send intelligence reports to London (on ship movements, local politics & public opinions, etc.) via Horace Mann, the Resident. When Walpole asked Chute to go to Rome in 1745 to bargain for an antique eagle, he also asked him to get into Roman society, where Bonnie Prince Charlie's adventure in Scotland was the thrill of the season and had wild support, and publicly argue for England's official Whig case against Stuart restoration.

Walpole and Gray had returned home in 1740, but Chute and Whithed stayed on for five years. Letters streamed between Chute, Walpole and Mann covering social gossip, art criticism, politics, even the love-life of their dogs. Chute thought of settling in Florence for good, but fate intervened with his brother Francis's death.

Death of Francis
Francis was an 18th century all-rounder - a wit, a recognised poet, a Fellow of the Royal Society (of scientific luminaries), a barrister and a fine speaker, briefly being MP for Heydon, Norfolk in the Whig cause. He was the only one of Edward's sons to marry, but had no children. When he suddenly died in 1745, his youngest brother John found himself heir presumptive to the Vyne in the event of Anthony's death. With little enthusiasm for that "mouldering estate", John returned slowly to England with Whithed in 1746 to sort out his own finances and meet Walpole again.

The latter was now about to buy a cottage at **Strawberry Hill, Twickenham,** with the dream of turning it into a Gothick castle. Valuing John's architectural skill and taste, he recruited him with another architect Richard Bentley on to a "Committee of Taste" to devise designs and collections for the new 'plaything'. Walpole and Chute proceeded to tour southern England to draw, measure and memorise examples of gothic style.

When Walpole finally bought the house, he largely adopted Chute's designs for his private Tribune and the great Gallery; these can be seen today. John went on to design other houses as well, e.g. Donington Hall for which some drawings are on view at the Vyne. It is noteworthy that their gothic decoration (just then coming

into fashion) does not interfere with the classical symmetry of structure which John had learned to love in Florence.

John Inherits the Vyne
In 1754 Anthony Chute died, after such frigid and capricious behaviour towards John that Walpole feared he would be disinherited. However, no will was found and John automatically succeeded; Walpole's letter of ecstatic delight is surely the most unusual letter of 'commiseration' ever sent to a bereaved brother!

Horace leapt at the chance of gothicising the Vyne. He led his Committee through muddy Hampshire lanes, and villages in which folk still talked a strange mediaeval language, into the bitter cold of John's house, where he wrote out a long 'Inventionary' of projects which would give it the proper Gothick air and surround its new owner with portraits of his Strawberry friends. (There is still a "Strawberry Parlour" at the Vyne with 18th C. pictures commemorating their meetings.)

But John would not be bullied. He let the Committee do nothing more serious than affix some pseudo-mediaeval strapwork on to the walls of the Ante-Chapel, of which, says the guidebook, *"the gothickness can deceive no-one"*.

The Gothick Question
It was also possibly to humour them that John had his 'official', large scale, portrait painted in flamboyant costume with a diagram in his hand showing a gothicised version of the Vyne facade. But he holds this gothick elevation at arm's length and the solid architecture in the portrait is a classical portico.

The ambiguity of this picture, and the fact that hundreds of John's sketches have been preserved showing possible classical or gothic versions of the Vyne exterior, have led commentators to conclude, lamely, that *"Chute was never to resolve his conflicting impulses"* towards either a gothic or classical solution. Certainly there is room to speculate, but if one recognises John's artistic integrity and the adult analysis that he would apply to Walpole's juvenile and escapist enthusiasms, the issue is scarcely in doubt.

There is not space in this chapter to examine the question in depth, but an Appendix on page 83 reproduces a talk given to the Friends of Strawberry Hill in 2002, offering a detailed explanation why Walpole's life-long friend refused to do any significant gothicising at the Vyne. Here one need only remark that despite years of nagging from Walpole to get on with his gothick plans, Chute almost wholly adopted classical inspiration for his two major works of architecture at the Vyne, the Great Staircase and the Tomb Chamber.

These are resounding successes, and rank with the Tudor Oak Gallery and Chapel as the highpoints of any visit to the house. Moreover, by maximising the use of light-weight material John triumphed over the building's architectural defect - its weak foundations over the mediaeval moat. He also avoided having to reconstruct miles of rough roadways from the house to the turnpike so as to import heavy loads of stone and marble.

Paying the Bills
John had all the expenses of a Chute of the Vyne including a year as High Sheriff, and he cannot have improved the flagging income from its farms by appointing as steward the innumerate Martelli, his former valet from Florence who came to live in the Vyne with a wife and 12 children. To complete the construction projects, John stretched his financial credit to the limit and left unpaid bills for his successor to pay, as key-money on inheriting the Vyne. This was a descendant of his uncle Thomas Chute in Norfolk, one Thomas Lobb, who now took the name Chute.

To have persuaded this rich cousin to leave his comfortable home and underwrite the Vyne in its parlous financial condition, is John's diplomatic triumph. He had always been liked and respected by the Norfolk cousins, and if he used the argument that it would boost them socially to live in the Vyne, and help them to win a seat in Parliament, then he was certainly right; for that is just what followed.

Epitaph and Assessment
John Chute's death upset Horace Walpole profoundly. His letter to Sir Horace Mann on 27 May 1776 shows that by then they were visiting each other every few days, and that Chute had become *"a friend to whom one speaks as confidentially as to one's own soul ... He was my counsel in my affairs, was my oracle in taste ...the genius that presided over poor Strawberry ... His sense decided me in everything, his wit and quickness illuminated everything"*.

In assessing this long friendship, it is worth remembering that Walpole was not merely a brilliant letter writer, wit and social commentator. He also grew up among England's greatest private collection of paintings, those gathered by his father into Houghton Hall, Norfolk and in London; and it was Horace whom Sir Robert asked to write the detailed inventory and description of the collection (published as *Aedes Walpolianae*). So there was aesthetic authority as well as friendship behind Horace's retrospective (1793) assessment of John Chute as *"an exquisite architect & of the purest taste both in the Grecian and Gothic Styles"*.

The purity and skill of his Great Staircase at the Vyne, and in the Tomb Chamber his timeless blending of baroque stained glass, gothic ceiling and Ionic plinth with heraldic shields, appeal to visitors today as convincingly as Walpole's emotional epitaph.

HORACE WALPOLE ON THE VYNE

" In October you will find it a little difficult to persuade me to accompany you there on stilts" (29 August 1754)

" Mr Chute is at the Vine, but don`t expect to hear from him. No post but a dove can get from thence" (6 Jan. 1756)

" I don`t believe that the Vine is within the verge of the rainbow - it is too damp for you" (To John Chute,1 Feb. 1759)

".. to let you alone till you die at the Vine of mildew, goes against my conscience. Don`t it go against yours to keep all your family there till they are mouldy?  Instead of sending you a physician, I will send you a dozen braziers; I am persuaded that you want to be dried and aired... for God`s sake don`t stay there any longer..." (13 March 1759)

HORACE WALPOLE ON CHUTE AS DESIGNER AND ADVISER

" Well, how delightful! how the deuce did you contrive to get such proportion? You will certainly have all the women with short legs come to you to design high-heeled shoes for them. The cloister [at Strawberry Hill], instead of a wine-cellar, has the air of a college. It has already passed the Seals....

" I assure you, Mr Chute, you shall always have my custom. You shall design every scrap of the ornaments; and if ever I build a palace or found a city, I will employ nobody but you. In short, you have found a proportion and given a simplicity and lightness to it that I never expected. (4 November 1759)

" If I were to say all I think of Mr Chute`s immense honesty, his sense, his wit, his knowledge and his humanity, you would think I was writing a dedication" (to Mann, 2 Oct. 1747)

JOHN CHUTE`S MANUSCRIPT DESIGN FOR THE
CHUTE FAMILY SHIELD ON THE MEMORIAL TOMB

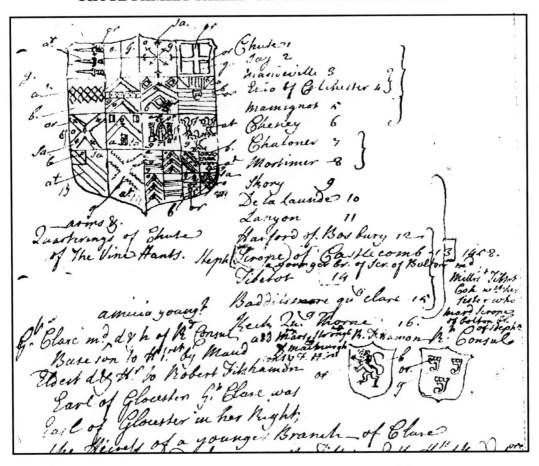

My Dear Brother

I am glad you like the arms, they are as follows, Chute, Gee (who was great Grand mother to the Speaker) Chaloner, Thorp, De la Launde, Lanyon, Westford; these three last Quarterings of the Thorps; Keck, Thorne, this last was my Grandmothers Keck's arms, who was an Heiress, and accordingly I remember to have seen them Quarter'd with the Kecks, in Escutcheons used at the Funeral of my Uncle Keck.

the Enclos'd list, is a set of Busts in plaister which I have met with, at a Painter's in Town which are exactly as good as any we could have got by sending for them on purpose from Italy, those I have mark'd are the principal only and are very well ... off, that number would compleatly furnish the ... 2 between each two windows, & the Jamb beyond the farthest window, and 1 on each side the Door in all 11. the Prices are as reasonable as we could get them at Florence and one avoids the Risque of many of them being broke in coming so far, a thing which frequently happens. I would not fix upon them, without acquainting you, and if you approve of having these also or any number of them, I will beg you to let me know by the return of the Post, for ... they should be sold if we use any longer Delay, the man not promised to stay for ...

(SECTION MISSING)

that you are in a ... than when she wrote to me before, I beg my kindest love to her, and thanks for her kind Epistles, and am

My Dear Brother's

most truly affectionate

J. Chute

Argyle Buildings Ap. 3d 1753.

At this date, John had no expectation of ever returning to live in the Vyne himself.

He is disinterestedly proposing adornments for the Vyne: (a) his designs for heraldic arms of Chute ancestry to go on the mantelpiece now in the Tapestry Room & (b) letting Anthony know of 10 plaster busts of Greek & Roman worthies which he has `met with at a Painter's in Town` and could be had for a good price if Anthony would send his approval by the return of the Post - they are only being reserved for John until Saturday. The busts were duly acquired.

Considering how little love was lost between them, it must have been through gritted teeth that he dutifully subscribed the letter

"My Dear Brother's most truly affectionate J.Chute"

(preserved by C.W.Chute in a scrapbook now held at Hants Record Office)

~ 36 ~

An Inventionary of

Alterations to be made at the Vine

Within the House.

The Staircase, to have four flights. +

The little Strawberry parlour.

a Commode. a couch, & two fly tables.

The great parlour?

Two large pictures, one at each end.

The two lesser doors to be stopped up.

Two half length portraits of Lord & Lady Dacre on one side of the chimney

On the other side, half lengths of Mr J. Chute & the old Lady Dacre.

Over the doors, heads of Mr Whithed, Mr Gray, Mr Bentley & Mr Walpole.

Drawing room within great parlour.

To be hung with green.

Over the Chimney, view of Matland.

A Bedchamber & Alcove to be within that

The Chimney piece of the stone gallery to be carried into

is to be a billiard room.

The great Hall to be quite plain.

for the old parlour

Two large settees, & two coins.

The Antichapel.

To be finish'd as the End is.

The Windows to be painted by Price with the pedigree.

The Chapel.

3 pictures under the Windows, of the Lord's supper, christ in the garden & christ
walking on the sea. The 4 Evangelists in the long pannels on each side.
A rich purple & silver altarcloth, with handsome old embossed plate.
A brass Eagle for a reading desk.
The Walls above to be painted in a Gothic pattern: & a closet with a screen in the
same pattern.

The great Drawing room one pr of Stairs.

To be hung with the Chinese Tapestry.
The Chimney piece to be alter'd.
Two Views of Strawberry hill over the Doors.

**HORACE WALPOLE'S "INVENTIONARY" OF WORK FOR JOHN CHUTE TO
CARRY OUT AT THE VYNE (PAGE 1)**

After 2 months Walpole wrote to Bentley "Mr Chute is at the Vine, where I cannot say any
works go on in proportion to my impatience" (18.9.55)   Two years on: "I see Mr Chute will
never execute anything. The very altarpiece that I sent for from Italy is not placed yet. But
when he could refrain from making the Gothic columbarium for his family, which I propose,
and Mr Bentley has drawn so divinely, it is not probable he should do anything else. Adieu!"

To be a Drawingroom with a bow Window.   *The Green bedchamber,*

                                      The Gallery;

To be finish'd at the Ends with canvas's Wainscot.

To have two more whole lengths.

                              The Library

to have the Antiroom laid into it, to be finish'd with old Wainscot, & gothic Window

                              Without doors.

A semicircular court, with a Gate like Caius College.

a Sheep paddock of 30 acres.

Two Towers added.

The new Walk continued cross the meadow to Morgason.

Opposite to the House, a Roman Theater, with an Obelisk, two Urns, Two

Cypresses & Cedars.

The old garden to be an open grove.

The hither Wall of the kitchen garden to be pulled down, & the garden to be

A Spire upon the Barn.

Cypresses about the Summer house & the House.

Two Lanes of flowering Shrubs, without the Garden.

The Water, to be done what one can do with it.

                           a Triumphant Arch instead of Pallas.

Above: page 2 of Walpole's Inventionary

Right:
Detail from John Chute's portrait showing a gothicised elevation of the Vyne

'LOBB CHUTES' AT THE VYNE 1776-1827

Come Over, Cousin, We Need You

After John Chute died in 1776, the "Chutes of the Vyne" were kept in being for two generations by descendants of the Speaker in the female line. His great-grand-daughter Elizabeth, living in Norfolk, had married a Thomas Lobb, and their offspring, the **Lobb Chutes**, owned the Vyne until 1827. The connection was as follows.

Back in the 1680's when Lady Dacre was harassing the young Chaloner Chutes, she kept a soft spot for her youngest grandson **Thomas Chute**, and helped him into a Clerkship to the Crown in Chancery. This sounds like a remunerative post, but after Thomas held it from 1694 to 1701 he was still owed many of his fees, and had to petition his superiors - even King William III - for back-payment. They all turned him down. But Thomas did succeed in winning a rich Suffolk heiress for bride. **Elizabeth Rivett**'s father had died and her guardian was persuaded to let her marry at the tender age of 18. Together they acquired in 1700 a large sporting estate at Pickenham, near Swaffham, in west Norfolk.

> **Pickenham Hall** remained in Chute hands until 1844. Twice re-modelled, several times re-sold, the house is not open to visitors. Its owner in 1900, a button millionaire with social ambitions, completely rebuilt the house to give it proper dignity for the Prince of Wales to visit for a weekend's shoot!
>
> **South Pickenham Church** is a little gem with one of the delightful East Anglian round-towers, perhaps first built as signal-beacons. Under its altar and on the chancel walls, you can see Chute and Wiggett memorials.

The Lobb family in Norfolk

Elizabeth, Thomas Chute's daughter, married into a family of jovial hunters/shooters. This could be described as a 'prudent' marriage, since the Lobbs (of Cornish origin) owned the adjacent manor of Great Cressingham. They had incomes from London practices in architecture, law and drapery. When her brothers & nephew all died unmarried, Elizabeth inherited the Chutes' Pickenham estate, which by law became her Lobb husband's property.

THOMAS LOBB CHUTE
looking down from above the
mantel in the Strawberry Parlour
at the Vyne

Their eldest child **Thomas Lobb (1721-1790)** was recorded as being "*short of build and red of face. He stumps about his estate in black breeches too tight for his legs, which are very stout. He begins every conversation with 'Ahem!'.*"

In 1776 he took the additional name **Chute** on entering The Vyne as John Chute's heir. He "*developed a fondness for servant girls. This caused his long-suffering wife some unhappiness.*" But "*he disliked seeing servants around Pickenham Hall, and everyone from the parlour maids to the footman and on to the Butler, Jorkins, were instructed to have completed the main tasks of the day before 11 a.m. Any domestic caught around the corridors ... after this hour was sent off to work on the farm for the day, this arbitrary rule applying to men and women alike, regardless of rank*".

The 'Chute Ellis' cousins in Australia

Lobb Chute blood did not only migrate to the Vyne. Thomas Lobb Chute's sister Elizabeth married the Revd. James **Ellis** of North Repps near Norwich, and their descendants went to Australia after 1827 with the help of £16,000 in legacies from Thomas Vere Chute - the last Lobb Chute of the Vyne. Their talents won them prosperity there in trade, farming and local administration. They of course inherit the blood of CC I, the Speaker, and to this day they take the middle name Chute.

THE BURDEN OF TWO ESTATES

John Chute's 'deal' with his cousin, to take on the Vyne and pay off the debts, left Thomas Lobb Chute with two large and expensive properties on his hands in 1776, when his sons were still too young to share the responsibilities. Pickenham, a sporting estate, was on thin dry soil. The Vyne had better potential for farming but was poorly managed and barely yielded a profit. To finance them both, substantial funds were needed after 1776. In addition to the Lobb family wealth, help was to come unexpectedly from the father of Thomas Lobb Chute's wife **Ann Rachael Wiggett**.

William Wiggett, solicitor, was Mayor of Norwich in 1742, where his massive and well-fed portrait still hangs in St. Andrew's Hall. He and his wife loved Pickenham, retired there and, Ann Rachael being their only child, they put money into enlarging the property*.
(See p.198 ff for more detail on Pickenham.)

Thomas Lobb Chute wears a velvet coat and magnificent waistcoat in his portrait; he was, after all, the 'angel' who rescued the Vyne from debt. He added his arms to John Chute's plinth in the Tomb Chamber, but his heart was still at Pickenham, where in

When the Pickenham estate was up for sale in the 1990's, it contained over 3500 acres of prime shooting country including the Hall and a whole village.

1790 both he and his wife died. Their sons William John and Thomas Vere took the name Chute and one estate each.

William John (1757-1824) moved to the Vyne and, as perhaps John Chute had suggested, used his new status to enter Parliament. He became one of the Vyne's most colourful characters.

Thomas Vere (1772-1827) never married (*p.47 below*). After he inherited Pickenham, England found itself in serious danger of invasion by Napoleon, and its Lords Lieutenant assembled an oddly amateurish militia to protect the coastline. Thomas loyally enlisted, and scanned the horizon from Folkestone. But after Wellesley's continental campaigns put Napoleon on the defensive, Thomas demobilised and took Holy Orders (the first English Chute to do so). As Rector of Pickenham, he often relaxed by riding over to the Vyne and hunting with his brother, to whom he was always very close. They were famous for their extrovert humour.

When William John died in 1824 Thomas inherited the Vyne as an addition to his Pickenham estate. But as William's widow Elizabeth was still in residence, Thomas never lived at the Vyne, his brief ownership being marked only by the rebuilding work he did in Sherborne St. John village.

WILLIAM JOHN CHUTE AT THE VYNE

Pleasure Before Business

William John Chute was probably the most casual landlord the Vyne ever had; yet he was such fun that everyone loved him, and when he died, the shops in Basingstoke all shut for a day as a mark of regret. On leaving Pickenham in 1790, he seems to have treated the "Vine" (so spelt in his time) as a refuge from reality.

The Vine Hunt

His passion was hunting; he hunted hare until 1795 but, finding foxhounds faster than harriers, he then founded 'The Vine Hunt' with 18 couple of hounds . At his own expense he maintained it until his death. He had his wife paint a portrait of New Forest Jasper, chief ancestor of the Vine Pack, arguing that "as great families have the portrait of their distinguished ancestor, the judge or the general or the statesman, in their room, he did not see why the dogs should not have their family picture also." But apart from Emma Smith's oval miniature (*p.52*) we only find a pencil portrait of William himself.

New Forest Jasper

At the back of the picture is the Latin couplet he composed, praising the hound's pedigree and skill at the chase:

"Hic bene apud memores veteris stat gloria gentis,
Hinc plus quam solito robore vulpes eget."

Animals turned up in odd places at the Vine; in 1822 a old hound bitch whelped in the copper hole in the Brewhouse, and saw off a young man who had been told to get her out. Guests said that during dinner a horse might poke its head in at a window. Foxes had similar hospitality; on one famous run (where a hound was missing for 5 days but was eventually found safe, wedged in an earth with the dead fox between its paws) the fox in question was from a litter born in a drain under the Vine drawing-room floor.

Chute M.P.

William John Chute served as one of two MPs for North Hampshire from 1790 to 1820, with a brief interlude in 1806 when the Whigs were in power after Pitt's death. Lord Palmerston called him "a hospitable squire (who) preferred entertaining his friends at the Vine to mixing with much zeal in Parliamentary disputes". This is an understatement. Chute never made a speech in the House, and there is no record of his ever holding a constituency meeting or a 'surgery'. However, elections were a huge party, with slogans shouted - *"Heathcote and Chute for ever. Huzza"* (Jane Austen thought that very vulgar.)

His wife's letters show that on days he had vowed to attend the House, he was slow to get up in the morning. Having ridden an hour or more towards London, he would ask for news whether he was needed for a vote at the House; if not, he would promptly turn round and come home.

During one hunt, he had trouble getting out of a wood; he slipped while leading his horse, and the horse trod on his thigh. His neighbour said: "Egad, I thought we were going to lose our Member". "Did you?" said Mr Chute, rubbing his leg. "Well, I can tell you I thought I was going to lose mine."

Many anecdotes are told of his whimsical humour, notably in a memoir of the early days of the Vine Hunt by "Sexagenarian"

(i.e. James Edward Austen-Leigh, Jane Austen's nephew and first biographer). Chute was most affable to to all he met out hunting and many people preferred having a middling day with him rather than a better day with others.

" Sturdily built but never a great horseman or well mounted, he could well stand long days in the saddle. He was not fond of jumping but preferred to dismount in good time and, catching his horse by the tail, allowed the horse to pull him over an obstacle."

Cultured 18th Century Gentleman
" A strict Churchman* and a staunch Tory, he was a fine type of a cultured 18th Century gentleman, in no way affected by the lax standards of the Regency Bucks."
" He was quite one of the old school" and " the very personification of cheerfulness and friendliness. No one ever saw him out of temper, out of patience, or out of spirits; no one ever heard him utter an ill-natured remark...
" He did not wrangle in Parliament or in the field, in fact, he was never heard to use a coarse expression, but he was able to make a suitable and witty reply to his Radical neighbour, Sir John Cope. This worthy baronet had sent Mr Chute a note saying that he had a litter of five dogs in that year's entry, whose names had all pretty much the same meaning, for they were Placeman, Parson, Pensioner, Pilferer and Plunderer.
" Mr Chute's retort was quick and apt; he told Sir John that he could show him a litter of which the names were equally synonymous, being Radical, Rebel, Regicide, Ruffian and Rascal."

He spoke fluent French (having lived for a time at Angers) and could write reasonably good Latin verse. "His taste in books was naturally good. He ate sparingly but was most particular what he ate; his bread and butter had to be spread by a maid, never by a man". He liked good port wine in moderation and abhorred claret, saying that old Bush, his butler, "could make as good stuff as that out of the washings of his port wine glasses".

Pigtail
He affected the style of the fictional squire, the jovial Sir Roger de Coverley, and wore a powdered wig and pigtail in 18th century mode. He was not deterred by the tax which Government imposed in 1795 to help pay for

the war against Napoleon. Hair powder was then so popular that every Englishman wearing it was taxed a guinea a year. It is said this tax raised £200,000.

Austen Leigh remembered Chute with affection. He "had a fair round face with a most agreeable countenance, expressive of good humour and intelligence. He was rather short, but remarkably well made, with full, well-rounded limbs, indicating both strength and activity. I wish I could make others see him, as I fancy that I see him myself ... sitting rather loose on his horse, and his clothes rather loose upon him - the scarlet coat flapping open, a little whitened at the collar by the contact of his hair powder and the friction of his pigtail; the frill of his shirt above, and his gold watch chain and seal below, both rather prominent, the short knee breeches scarcely meeting the boot tops."

In time his pigtail hung on by only a few hairs, and in his last season "a momentous event occurred. Mr Chute was induced, after a great struggle, to allow Fox the hairdresser to remove his pigtail. Mr Fox won the battle by demonstrating that only five hairs remained, all the rest was ribbon. This must have been one of the very last pigtails in the county."

His god-son William Wiggett went to church with W J Chute, and recalled that once, as the latter was offered a pew while everyone else was left standing, he turned to WW and whispered: "See what it is to look like a gentleman".

Duke of Wellington
The victor of Waterloo became Chute's neighbour when he moved to Stratfield Saye. Though idolised by the nation, he did not over-awe the Chutes. A letter from the Duke (March 23, 1820) was delivered to the Vyne after he had spent a long and fruitless hack trying to find the Hunt:
" My dear Sir, I went out this morning to meet your hounds, having ordered my horses to Clarken Green, as I had settled

---

In truth, his churchmanship was probably for appearance's sake; he was known to mutter about "obsolete mythology".

with your huntsman. I went on as far as Dean, but could not find my groom, and I then returned to Clarken Green, thinking it probable that he had gone to the covert-side. From there I went to Ebbworth, and not finding or hearing anything of you or my horses, I have returned home. I regret this exceedingly, particularly as I feel you will have waited for me. I shall be much obliged if you will let me know on what days and at what places you will go out next week. Ever yours most faithfully,
WELLINGTON"

Is this not a model of politeness between gentlemen, considering that the Duke had just had a very annoying and wasted morning as the result of Chute changing the venue without giving him notice.

Hundred Guinea Oak

It was all very well being flamboyantly conservative. We noted earlier that the Vyne farms made no profit, and may be surprised that William John refused to update farming practices there or sell any trees from his extensive woods. He even gloried in making no profit from the estate, and mocked his steward`s efforts to sell his own entitlement !

Visitors to the Vyne are shown "The Hundred Guinea Oak". This tree caught the eye of a man from the Admiralty seeking oaks for shipbuilding, and offered Chute a hundred pounds for it. Chute refused. Next morning the man came back with an offer of a hundred guineas (5% more); Chute supposedly answered that a tree which gained so much value in a single night was too good an investment to lose!

William John was so bored by estate management that his god-son, on inheriting the Vyne, found "the state of the roads ... little better than driftways and generally impassable by anything but carts and waggons ... I have seen Mr W. Chute`s carriage stick in the mud on the hill by the side of the present rectory Glebe". In the house in 1827 he found roofs to have become positively dangerous. "Over the front staircase... the principal tie beam was rotten at the ends and had very litle, if any, support but the ornamental plaster ceiling." In the south-west tower "the heavy floor was found to have no support but the shutter boards of the present billiard room beneath it, which was then used by Mr and Mrs Chute as their sitting room." "The Chapel Hall I found used as a place for coal and wood, the floor being of stone; a not very appropriate place..."

It was to such a happy-go-lucky lifestyle that, back in 1794, William John had brought the wife of his choice.

Eliza Chute

Chute became engaged to Elizabeth Smith in the belief that she would "make a good domestic wife" and even perhaps enjoy his hunting talk. She did her best, but it was an odd match. Eliza was a talented artist (see  her flower paintings on view upstairs at the Vyne), literary and fashionable, and wrote with wit. Her father was a wealthy MP for Devizes, and she was brought up nearby with lively sisters at a grand house Stoke Park (now, alas, turned into a prison).

Whenever her husband went to Parliament Eliza seized the chance to escape into London. There she could visit art galleries, study painting, and be back in the Smith family`s social whirl.
When her sister, the Marchioness of Northampton, and the cream of county society visited the Vyne, their talk was naturally of London.
Apart from that, her diary was her constant companion.

Eliza's diaries (which for many of the years 1793-1840 survive in the Austen-Leigh collection at Hants. Records Office) give brilliant snapshots of social life. For example, **her wedding to William John Chute in 1793:**

15th October 1793: London.
"White frost, sunny unclouded sky. May it be a happy omen.
"I was married at St Margaret's at half after 9. - Lord and Lady Arden, Sir John and Lady Burges,
. Mr and Mrs D Smith, Mr G Smith, Mr Vere Chute, Mrs Norman, Lord and Lady Compton,
. Papa, Mama, Augusta & Emma present. Mr Atwood the clergyman.
"We all returned to breakfast in George St. Set off at quarter before 12, stopped 20 mins at Bagshot & arrived at the Vine half after 5."

16th. The Vine. Very fine and sunny. Received from Mr Chute £49.19.6.
Mr Vere Chute to dinner; he returned to Mr Bramston's [his brother in law at Oakley Park] in the evening.
17th. The Vine. Fine, no sun, pleasant. Mr & Mrs Bramston & Miss Chute [sister in law] in the morning as a visit.
18th. The Vine. Pleasant. Papa, Mama, Augusta Emma & Ld and Ly Compton came about 3 to spend a few days. Much joy on all sides.
19th. Mr & Mrs Bramston came in the morn to spend two days. Mr C & Ld Compton went out shooting....

This was a fashionable wedding. Only 5 guests, plus the priest, from outside their immediate families; 10 from the families; no mention of her (or anyone else's) dress.
If the service lasted, say, half an hour, they only had an hour and three-quarters to get home, have the wedding breakfast, and be ready to climb in a coach at 11.45.
No honeymoon. His brother came to dinner the next day. Two days later, her parents and sisters and in-laws thronged in, to "joy on all sides", and stayed for four days.

After they left, it did not take long for William to get back to hunting with his male friends.
On the 22nd her family left, except sister Augusta who stayed with her.
On the 23rd "Mr Chute hunted for two hours". On the 30th the newlyweds went to Stoke, her family home, for a week, and returned on 7th November. On both the next 2 days "Mr Chute hunted" and "I walked". The day after that, they began reading "together" Laure de Germoran, and she began reading "alone" the Life of Petrarch.

What Chute expected in a "domestic wife" we can only guess. She pored over Parliamentary Bills with him (e.g. "the evening was spent in reading newspapers and this new Bill, which we endeavored to understand"), she read an immense amount in private (preferring this to receiving casual visitors), and she wrote of an evening "spent with some degree of chearfulness; as proof of it, I send you some verses of Mr Chute's". They both spoke French, and several quotations in her diary are in Italian.
She herself was a good country rider for pleasure, who would take a house guest on a full day's "ramble" on horseback to see Silchester and visit friends. But his passion for the hunt, and for talking about it, bored her stiff.

The Diary shows how deeply she missed the social whirl of London. She was no flighty "deb"; quite as important as parties were the concerts, plays, opera and picture galleries, on which her diary comments in detail.

Accounting. As a wife she was serious and conscientious, as befitted an heiress of her grandfather's self-made timber business. William was born in a family of rich lawyers where a young man's priority was hunting, and he was surely bowled over by her meticulous accounting, which tells us - more than 2 centuries later - a lot about their respective characters.

In passing housekeeping money to her he seems to have been tiresomely irregular. She accounted to the last half-penny. Then he got into the habit of borrowing from her; one January she notes down that he has repaid her the (huge) sum of £100 as backlog for the previous year; in other words, he borrowed something like a year's working capital from her pocket. Her diary makes a clear distinction between what "Mr Chute repaid me" and what "Mr Chute says he repaid me"!

She, by contrast, was a fount of generosity to the poor, the unemployed and the ex-soldier; we even find her giving alms "to a Turk"! (How ever did *he* get there?)

She founded a local school and ran soup kitchens in winter for the parish poor. Whereas William's interest in the parish church at Sherborne St. John was mainly social, she paid, after his death, for the restoration of its tower and the addition of a spire.

Neighbours and Visitors

Eliza was somewhat conscious of her social status and used to go to Stratfield Saye to provide conversation to the Duchess of Wellington who, she noted, was "unfortunate" and was looked down on by society.

Like Jane Austen (some of whose remarks on the Chutes we will meet below) Eliza has a sharp eye. In one letter she describes their noble neighbour Lady Bolton, as "extremely civil and willing to please, as far as her abilities will allow."

A Mr & Mrs Dyson are recorded as "unmeaning silent people, of whom neither good nor harm can be said. He seems abominably stupid; she is liked by those who know her intimately. Some think her pretty; I do not."

Lord and Lady Dorchester she reports as "carrying delicacy and refinement to a ridiculous and troublesome pitch. If he had not brought his valet with him, many things would have gone wrong... He always dresses and undresses downstairs, and never goes near her room until she is in bed.

"When I showed her her room after dinner, the first thing she did, was to throw

JOSHUA SMITH, M.P. father of Eliza Chute   (portrait at the Vyne) His father had established a timber importing business in Lambeth, on which the family fortune was based

the window open, for let the weather be what it will, frost or snow even, they always sleep with the sash open ... never shutting it but when the rain beats in violently. At this time of the year [end December] they rise by candlelight, go in the woods and walk about, and then come in to bathe...

"She makes a point that all her children should do the same.

"Oh how glad I am that I was not born a daughter of the family ... I fancy she is head of the house. Perhaps her motive for bringing up her children thus hardy, was to inure them to the cold of Canada ...
I never saw such stout ones of all ages, and such bones ...   Tom Chute calls them Dorchester bulls."

But Eliza keeps her end up with Lady Dorchester - "notwithstanding her rank, I feel a sort of superiority from having more acquaintance with the ways of the world; she consults me on little matters, and I do not consult her."

One's lasting impression from Eliza's Diaries is of a forceful and cultivated woman, bored to tears with the damp and loneliness of the Vyne, while her popular husband lived a carefree life among men friends. If only she had had children of her own...

Adoption of Caroline Wiggett

One day, after almost 10 years of childless marriage, William John received an appeal from an old college friend, the Revd. James Wiggett of Crudwell in Wilts, whose wife had just died leaving him with a flock of children. Could William John Chute, already godfather to baby William Wiggett (who had been named after him) see his way to adopting one of the girls? The Chutes took a deep breath and consented to adopt Caroline, aged 3, as "niece" (an odd concept, but her adoption as daughter could have caused problems if they later produced a Chute child). She was brought, a weeping little bundle, to the Vyne. It was thought best for her to have no more contact with her brothers and sisters, so for years she felt abandoned by them.

The **Memoirs of Caroline Wiggett**, written in later life, run to 50 vivid pages, describing life for an adopted orphan at a grand house in the early 19th century. The Chutes did their best for the child, giving her parties, an education and trips out. At a meet of the Vine Hunt it was:

CAROLINE WIGGETT

"*a very great excitement to see the gentlemen in their red coats, to hear the horn blow and George's [the huntsman's] melodious voice calling his hounds ... nothing daunted at the hearing of the bugle, out I was, over the hedges and ditches, tally-hoing at the top of my voice*". She describes domestic arrangements at the Vyne, her terrors as a child, the excitement of carriages arriving for parties, the visits to Eliza's sister Lady Northampton, adventures in a rowing boat, how Uncle Tom Chute fell in love, and the stream of jokes between the two brothers.

"*When at the Vyne, the old Hall resounded with our merry laughs, we were so joyous together. Children were real children in those days and the Vyne was called Liberty Hall by the Smiths.*" Perhaps the Smiths, as a family, were rather stiff, because Eliza could not muster up much maternal warmth for Caroline, and the girl felt herself becoming a mere `companion` to her adopted aunt. But Caroline loved William John: "*The very sound of his step upon the stairs was like music in the house.*"
She made many drawings of the Vyne and commented: "*The ground opposite the house ... contained magnificent trees which Uncle Chute called his picture gallery and took everybody to see them; he could not bear to take down a tree.*"

Among Caroline's childhood playmates was Jane Austen's nephew James Edward (later Austen-Leigh). Thomas Chute's Will implies that he expected Caroline and Edward to marry. However, Edward was to meet Emma Smith, Eliza Chute's artistic niece, and fall for her instead.

The Chutes cannot have made much effort to find Caroline a husband, and in time she married the family doctor Thomas Workman. The doctor was sickly, as were the children from his first marriage which Caroline had to take on. This marriage was considered socially 'beneath her'; her agonised letter to her brother confessing the engagement, and Aunt Chute's coolness towards it, can be read in an Appendix (*p. 95 below*).

Reunion with William

Though no child survived from her marriage, it had been Caroline's joy and vindication to see her adored brother inherit the Vyne. She and William were separated in infancy, but 12 years later he was sent to college at Winchester and his godfather invited him up to the Vyne. The young man played his cards right and became a regular guest, joining as much in the daytime hunts and shoots as in the evening's music and games.

Soon the childless Chute brothers decided (*see page 57 ff.*) that young William Wiggett would be the best man to inherit their estates.

Thomas Vere Chute

Though hunting-mad, Thomas was (more than the other Lobbs) ready to face life's realities and genuinely interested in people. He became a priest, was friendly with Jane Austen, and got on well with the young. When his niece Ann Hicks* ran off with Cromie in 1816, it was Tom whom her parents called for rescue. He came all the way from Norfolk, with painful gout in his legs, and ran the pair to earth in Cheltenham; but even his charm did

---

* it was her father who 'made terrible faces' (p.89)

not outweigh that of the Irish fortune-hunter. Cromie miscalculated; he married Ann but, not trusting him, her uncles disinherited her.

Tom himself never married, but contemporaries vividly recalled the "extraordinarily beautiful" Mrs Wheeler, who had been deserted by her husband and became governess to friends of the family. She had every virtue: "even ladies approved of her, and gentlemen fell in love with her". Falling ill of consumption, she was cared for at the Vyne: "Uncle Thomas had been with us all the winter helping to nurse our poor invalid, and I heard he became deeply attached to her" She might have become the love of his life, but he had to watch her die; she lies unmarked in the chancel in Sherborne St John.

The two brothers were very close. When William died in 1824, Tom found his pocket diary and made two touching entries.
<u>March 30</u>: "The last day of hunting. Poor Brother never went any more".
<u>December 13</u>: "At 5 1/2 in the morning my dear Bro. died, so beautiful, calm and quiet that we have reason to think his soul is now in Perfect Happiness".

Tom kept largely to Norfolk during his brief ownership of the Vyne, since Eliza was still living there. He died at Pickenham in 1827 from painful complications after falling from his horse. A memorial tablet set up by his heir can be seen to the right of the altar in South Pickenham Church.

THE VYNE IN THE TIME OF JANE AUSTEN

"William Chute called here yesterday. I wonder what he means by being so civil"

(14 Jan 1796)

Jane Austen did not appreciate William and Eliza Chute. She found his politics ("Chute for ever") overbearing, and avoided their company. Several of her letters show it; e.g.

"This morning we called at the Harwoods, & in their dining room found Heathcote and Chute for ever - Mrs Wm. Heathcote & Mrs Chute ... the second walked down from Oakley Hall attended by Mrs Augusta Bramston. They had meant to come on to Steventon afterwards, but we knew a trick worth two of that.

" If I had thought of it in time, I would have said something civil to her about Edward's never having had any serious idea of calling on Mr Chute while he was in Hampshire; but unluckily it did not occur to me."

(25 October 1800)

Unequal Neighbours

Jane grew up at Steventon, a few miles from the Vyne. Her brother James was appointed Rector of Sherborne St. John by William John Chute, and her father was sometimes invited to officiate there. The hearty masculinity of the families' relations must have hurt her mother, and perhaps irked Jane as well. The male Austens were invited to meals at the Vyne, to go hunting or in connection with church duties; Jane's young nephew James Edward came along, and played with Caroline Wiggett. But they were not in the social élite of 'county families', and Mrs Austen was rarely invited.

Relations did gradually get warmer. By the time of Jane's early death, James Edward was a regular guest at the Vyne for theatricals, and later he married Eliza Chute's niece Emma.

He was to write of Eliza as William's "excellent and cultivated wife". Her diaries confirm that she was a voracious reader, as well as a painter and music-lover, but we cannot find any mention of her taking an interest in Jane Austen's writings. So did Jane feel resentful that this cultivated lady took no trouble to recognise her talent?

The Original 'Fanny Price' ?

Novelists need plots, and it is said that Fanny Price, the heroine of 'Mansfield Park' is based on little Caroline at the Vyne. Fanny was 'adopted' as a child by rich relations and one of her miseries was to be continually reminded of her 'obligations' to them; the odious "Mrs Norris" is one of literature's great sadists, missing no chance to humiliate the helpless child.

It is not fair to conclude that, even in Jane's mind, the Chutes consciously humiliated their adopted niece, since in a letter of February 1817, written when the teen-age Caroline was ill, Jane supposes that Mrs Chute would feel like a mother in losing her. Caroline genuinely loved both her "Uncle Chutes"; we have seen that - once she had got used to separation from her own family - the Memoirs of her childhood are full of joys and treats at the Vyne.

But social tensions did emerge later on which the novelist, had she lived, might well have built into fiction. After her dear Uncles died, Caroline, still youthful and impulsive, gradually slipped into becoming the unpaid 'companion' to Eliza. And if (as was surmised) she had had the hope of marrying James Edward, she sadly lost him to Eliza's niece. But Caroline's brother was now legally the owner of the Vyne, and Eliza was well aware that he was merely biding his time in Norfolk until she herself died.

Caroline, of course, was entitled to help in finding a suitor of her social class. We wonder if it was wholly accidental that no such suitor presented himself - so that she had to fall back, in the social degrees of the day, on marrying Dr. Workman.

Such a scenario would have been meat and drink to Jane Austen; it is almost a pity that she never set her hand to it.

CHUTE HERALDRY

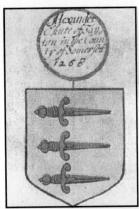

left: armorial which the Kentish Chutes credited to "Alexander Chute 1268"; *right:* later crest - mailed fist holding a broken dagger, over a Vyne doorway; *below right*: Chute swords reversed & on red field, in Chute/Keck hatchment; *below*: John Chute, whom Walpole dubbed "Strawberry King of Arms"; *bottom left:* John Chute's composite shield c. 1765 on the Memorial Tomb

WIGGETT CHUTE (1827 on)

John's portrait by Mathias shows his hand holding the pseudo-gothic elevation of the house, which he never built. His shield (*left*) of families who contributed genes to the Chute lineage includes (among others) Mamignot, Say, Mandeville, Cheney, Chaloner, Skory, Harford, De La Launde, Keck, Thorne.

(some of these are explained in our Part 2 below)

HIGH SHERIFF`S BANNER 1947

TWO MUSEUM PIECES AT THE VICTORIA & ALBERT

The "Basingstoke Monteith"

Presented to Edward Chute on 2nd October 1688 for his horse's win at the Basingstoke Races, this magnificent piece, a foot across and of solid silver *(hallmarked of Robert Cooper, London)*, is a form of punchbowl or ice bucket, with slots in the rim to hold the bases of drinking glasses which lie inwards. It is flat-chased with chinoiserie motifs and a Chinese figure presenting the Monteith; it also shows a jockey in contemporary costume spurring on his horse. (Silver Gallery, Room 65, on the first floor.)

`First Draft` of the Speaker's Effigy

The V & A Museum Sculpture Gallery holds a fine terra cotta maquette, offered by Thomas Carter to John Chute as design for the proposed effigy of Chaloner Chute on the Memorial Tomb. The preferred design, translated into marble after 1770, is more idealised, with the figure resting his head pensively on an elbow.

(author's photographs reproduced by permission)

THE CHOSEN IMAGE AT THE VYNE

Monument to the Speaker - designed by John Chute with sculpture attributed to Thomas Carter

(National Trust photo reproduced by permission)

NTPL/James Mortimer

JOHN CHUTE AT STRAWBERRY HILL

"If one man - apart from Walpole himself - can be called the architect of Strawberry Hill, that man is John Chute"

(Country Life articles on S.H. June 7th,14th,21st 1973)

Two of Chute`s designs are shown here.

portrait of John Chute by Muntz
at the Vyne

Right:
The Library, based on a
a design from Old St Paul`s

Below:
The Gallery

Strawberry Hill pictures reproduced by permission

WILLIAM JOHN CHUTE, M.P., M.F.H.
in the powdered wig he continued to wear
into old age when riding to hounds -
long after wigs fell out of fashion.

Right, the "**Hundred Guinea Oak**" which
he would not sell to an Admiralty agent who was seeking timber to build naval vessels,
around the time of Trafalgar. The agent's offer, after a refusal, went up overnight from
£100 to 100 guineas, which to W J C made it too high-growth an investment to let go.

Below, the "**Vine Hunt**" (in the earliest picture we can find - a newspaper of 1900) was
founded by W J Chute c.1795, run at his expense and enjoyed by, among others, the
Duke of Wellington, his neighbour. It enjoyed wide local support until the Ban in 2004.

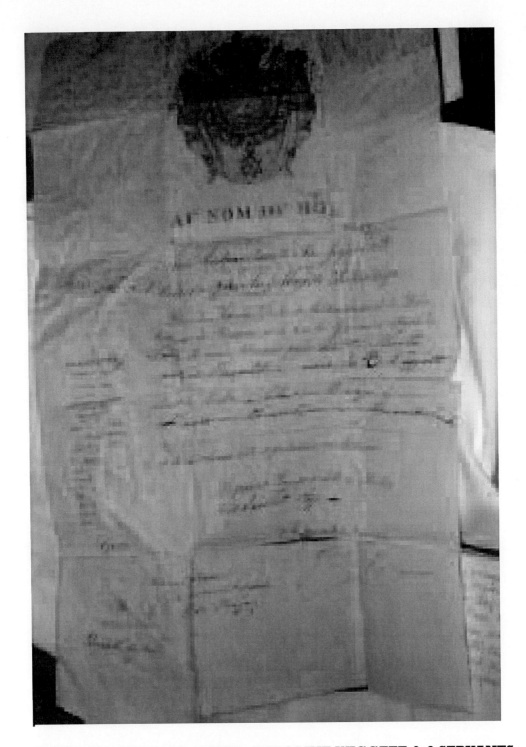

PASSPORT FOR ELIZA CHUTE, CAROLINE WIGGETT & 2 SERVANTS

to cross France on their way to Switzerland in 1827 - twelve years after Waterloo.
Issued *"AU NOM DU ROI"* by the French ambassador in London (calling himself
the *"Ambassador of his most Christian Majesty to His Britannic Majesty"*) who
requests the Interior Police of France and its allies to afford the lady travellers, with
a manservant and chambermaid, free passage, aid and protection in case of need.

Eliza`s signature is in bottom left hand corner. She was taking Caroline on their first
overseas holiday, for a change of scene after William and Tom Chute`s deaths

WILLIAM WIGGETT CHUTE (1800-79)

For whom the year 1827 turned up trumps.

"I had been working rather hard as a Student and Pupil in Chambers for 4 years and my health was yielding to the strain of sedentary employment & want of exercise.

"Like many other students at that time, I lived and slept in Chambers in the Middle Temple. Being soon tired of getting a bad chop or steak at a Pothouse, I engaged a respectable old Laundress to supply me with a dinner, which was not always hot or attractive.
"On Sundays ... I walked abroad and generally dined with ... my Uncle Humphreys."

In January 1827, he found himself willed into ownership of the two Chute estates - Pickenham and the Vyne.

"This sudden change in my prospects was as agreeable as unexpected ...
"I then went to live at Pickenham, and was obliged to nearly rebuild the house, which was old and much out of repair. I employed an architect [Donthorne] whose expenditure exceeded his estimate nearly threefold..."

Idealised picture which Donthorne gave to William Wiggett Chute, showing the Palladian mansion at Pickenham as it would be rebuilt to his design

(No other picture of the 1830`s house is known to exist)

THE VYNE UNDER WILLIAM JOHN CHUTE

This picture commissioned by his widow (c. 1833) shows the `antique` presentation favoured by its late, and arch-conservative, owner. He had chosen to ignore the building's deterioration under its mantle of ivy and creepers, and his successor William Wiggett Chute found parts of it - especially the central tower - near to collapse.

BOATING IN A TOP HAT

Everyone, in fact, seems to wear a hat in this delightful and relaxed image drawn by Martha Chute. The stream had been used as a series of Stew Ponds for fish until about 1760 when John Chute dammed the flow to make a lake. It was dredged and cleaned by Wm. Wiggett Chute a century later. To supply water to the house, a 'ram' pump was installed which made a ghostly thumping noise underground. The successors of the swans are still there.

THE WIGGETT CHUTES AT THE VYNE 1827-1956

In 1827, Chute blood at the Vyne died out for the second time. Neither William John (who died 1824) nor his brother Thomas (who died 1827) had children. They had had a problem in deciding who should inherit their two prestigious estates - Pickenham and the Vyne.

The Question of Succession

Ties of blood suggested that they choose either their niece Ann Hicks (daughter of their sister Ann Rachael and Sir William Hicks) or one of the flock of children produced by their aunt Elizabeth Lobb (also of Chute blood) and her husband Rev. James Ellis. As a fall-back, remoter cousins might be lured in from Chute Hall, Ireland.

The problems were that:-
(a) **Ann** had run off in 1816 with an Irish baronet Sir Lambert Cromie, a suspected fortune-hunter (who later ended up in a lunatic asylum), and had defied her uncles` efforts to bring her home;
(b) there were so many **Ellis`s** with equal claim that a choice would cause rancour, yet none had grown up in the `station in life` that seemed to qualify them to make a success of running prestigious estates;
(c) the **Irish Chutes** would not agree to move their principal home to England.

On the other hand, the brothers were conscious that their mother`s father William Wiggett, ex-Mayor of Norwich, had put a lot of money into the Pickenham estate, money which would have otherwise gone to Wiggett cousins; and that young William Wiggett, godson to W J Chute and brother of Caroline who had been adopted into the Vyne, seemed to show all the talent, energy and social graces needed to maintain the Chute estate and the family name.

So the Chute brothers decided that:
- Ann had put herself out of the running,
- the Ellis`s would on balance be better off by receiving a considerable cash bequest, which could be shared out between them; and that
- William Wiggett (then in his twenties and studying law) could be relied on to make the properties pay even if there was not much cash left for him.

Accordingly, when Thomas Chute`s Will was read out at Pickenham, young Wiggett was dumb-struck to find himself heir of a large Norfolk estate <u>and</u> another in Hampshire - neither of which had been kept in repair by its jolly foxhunting owners.

FAMILY ORIGINS - WIGGETTS AND BIGODS

The Wiggett family is older than the Chutes in that a Wigot de Saint Denis was named in a charitable deed in Normandy dated 1042, and some would claim (via one Ansfred Onofror le Goz) a 9th C. ancestor Rollo Bigod in Norway. The family`s Norman-English lineage was led by the **Earls Bigod of Norfolk**.

These Earls, "ruthless and scheming" governors of Norwich & Orford Castles, quarrelled ceaselessly with their kings, built themselves personal castles at Framlingham, Walton and Bungay, but did something to earn our gratitude by financing the magnificent church at **Tintern Abbey** on the Welsh border. Roger, 5th and last Earl, had no children and died in 1305. He hated his brother so bitterly that, to stop him succeeding, Roger resigned all the Bigod properties and earldom to the Crown.

The junior line to our Wiggetts included a Norfolk knight who fought in the Battle of Poitiers (1356). They could later claim royal blood, of a sort, through a mediaeval wife who was descended from the 10th C. King Hywel Dda of South Wales. Spelling their name Wygott or Wiggett, they lived at Guist near the popular shrine of Walsingham in Norfolk, and various descendants took the names Lytton, Earle and Bulwer. (Among them, the 19th century playwright and social reformer Bulwer Lytton had Wiggett blood.)

After Ann Rachael, daughter of Mayor Wiggett of Norwich, married Thomas Lobb, their sons William and Tom were at Clare College, Cambridge in about 1780 with Ann`s cousin James, and they all became friends. 20 years later James Wiggett, now Rector of the Wiltshire parish of Crudwell, asked William Chute to be godfather to his youngest son. The baby was duly baptised William, and it is he who eventually inherited the Vyne.

WILLIAM AND MARTHA WIGGETT CHUTE

Born in 1800 as William Lyde Wiggett in the rectory of Crudwell, Wilts (now a hotel) he was educated at Winchester and Oxford, and went on to London to study law. In the cold January of 1827 he was urgently summoned to Norfolk where Thomas, the brother of his godfather William John Chute, was dying after a riding accident. Nobody, it seems, had suspected that young William had been named heir by the Chutes; but he found himself, at the age of 27, possessed of a huge property split into two separate estates, each containing a great house which was starting to crumble from neglect.

As we saw, he did not inherit much cash with which to run them because of Tom's generous money bequests to his Ellis blood-cousins. (Indeed one Ellis came to England in the mid-1800s in the hope of buying the Vyne; but by then William had restored it, and it was his family's home.)

This **Ellis** family made good use of Tom's bequests, founding a successful business dynasty in Australia. There they flourish to this day, carrying the original Chute genes and still taking Chute as their middle name.

Conditions of the inheritance

William was required to take the name Chute; but he had to allow W J Chute's widow Elizabeth use of the Vyne for the rest of her life. Being therefore obliged to live at Pickenham for an indefinite period (which turned out to be 15 years), he gathered up whatever money *that* estate would yield and restored its dilapidated Hall, adding a Palladian facade.

(This was the house which, as mentioned above, a later owner of Pickenham pulled down in 1900 and rebuilt in gross Edwardian style, to make it "suitable for receiving the Prince of Wales" for a shooting week-end.)

Young though he was, William found himself appointed **High Sheriff of Norfolk**, which added to his unwanted expenses. Also, the local Tories made him promise to stand as parliamentary candidate; and when an Election was called for 1837 he had to go through with it, though he had just got engaged and would rather have been with his new fiancée.

He beat the Whigs against the odds on their own ground and was a **Norfolk M.P.** for the duration of the 1837-47 parliament.

Fin de Siecle at the Vyne

After Tom Chute died, Eliza took Caroline Wiggett with her on a trip to Switzerland; their passport for this journey recently came to light in Canada! From then on, Eliza endured 15 years of loneliness at the Vyne. Caroline left to get married, but Eliza must always have been conscious of her brother wanting to come and enjoy his inheritance. Eliza became much loved as a local benefactress, and started the 'social services' of the parish which William Wiggett Chute's building work was to continue so energetically.

Only after Eliza died (in 1842) could William fully examine the Vyne and realise the extent of its disrepair. Having just suffered in Norfolk from an architect who grossly underestimated costs and 'victimised' him, William saw that no-one could accurately estimate the cost of restoring the Vyne. But he already loved it and felt bound by his new Chute name to make his future there.

The Vyne's Great Improver

William Wiggett Chute is a key figure in the Vyne's history. He was one of the great Victorian improvers, a man of confidence, vision and tremendous energy. Without making any new architectural 'statement' he left the house much as we see it today, preserving its structure for well over a century, and he turned the estate into profit, for perhaps the first time in its long life. In this, he was supported by a remarkable wife.

They had youth and imagination, but not enough money to make a success of their responsibilities to both estates and their staffs. So they agreed to sell up in Norfolk; after 17 years' work at Pickenham he sold the Palladian house and estate in 1844.

Mother of many talents

On entering Pickenham, William had had the greatest luck in his 'girl next door'. **Martha Buckworth** of Cockley Cley was the ideal partner for a young 'improver', and their marriage proved one of the happiest events in Chute history. She was artistic, beautiful, and sweet-natured, letting herself be uprooted from Norfolk and raising eleven children at the Vyne in an almost permanent building-site. The mud and dust must have been ghastly, since the roads, when they came to the Vyne, were mere rutted tracks, and, as the roofs, walls and stonework were closely surveyed, ever more restoration was found necessary.

When it was finished, Martha took time off from the children to paint pictures showing how each of the main rooms and furniture were arranged. These have been accepted by the National Trust as guides for their 'authentic' arrangements of rooms on show - all bar the Stone Gallery, which Martha used as nursery-cum-playroom with a splendid rocking horse. Many other attractive drawings and oil paintings survive, both by Martha and her daughter Elizabeth.

The Enclosures

Unlike Anthony Chute a century before, who litigated obstinately with his Brocas neighbours over the boundary between their families' territories, but did little to make his farms actually pay, William had a friendly negotiation with them so that lands were exchanged for mutual economic benefit.

This is not the place to engage in dispute over the Enclosures, but as Wiggett Chute has received his share of abuse, it is fair to point out the condition of the Vyne when he inherited it. Some of the charges levelled against him depend on a fancy that the estate was some mediaeval paradise, where happy peasants should have been left in the sunshine, instead (as a sociologist would claim) of being disrupted by a bulldozing anti-social money-grubber. Especially one who, as a man, would naturally ride roughshod over his wife's more caring impulses!

Alas, the truth is that the house and estate were entering terminal decline, and for William to have done nothing would have been grossly irresponsible, as citizen, as landlord, and as head of a family.

First, one should remember that England's population nearly tripled in the century 1750-1850, from 6.25 to 18 million; this island could no longer be fed by mediaeval systems of agriculture, however much the individual peasant might want to retain his ancient pattern of life.

Drawbacks of Mediaevalism

Under the open-field system every farmer had to go at the same pace and follow the same methods as the rest of the village. Experiment was difficult, a go-ahead farmer was penalised and everyone wasted time in getting from one part of his holding to another. As William noted in his memoirs, the Vyne's tenanted fields were "in small occupations, rented in some case by tenants who lived in Basingstoke or elsewhere, there being no house on their farms; and very few of them had any capital or were able to pay their rents with any regularity." So by 1842 the mediaeval village community was already dispersed; and it was not only travel time which wasted productivity. He records that "the upper or field lands... were unenclosed ... and were divided by grassy banks or balks and occupied by different tenants in indiscriminate confusion ... After the crops had been gathered in, or at Michaelmas, the whole fields were open to all the various occupiers, so that the growing of turnips or any kind of winter crop was impossible, whereas thistles and weeds abounded."

After enclosures, however, each holding formed a compact area in which a farmer - whether landlord or tenant - could introduce new methods and try out new crops as he pleased; he knew that if he manured his land he would be in possession of the same land in 3 to 5 years time, and benefit from the expense and trouble. (It is for others to speculate whether the nation could have been fed under a different land régime.)

The Parish

Because of a general drift to towns, the local population fell by 150 between 1851 and 1871, though William (the conscientious son of a parish priest) did his best to improve village conditions. Many old buildings had leaking roofs, mud floors, rats, no water or sanitation. He built more and better farmhouses and cottages as well as a new schoolhouse, so that people could remain healthily in the parish.

More controversial was his provision of funds for two batches of villagers to emigrate to Canada, including "many of the worst and most idle characters of the Parish". Modern-day housing estates have the same problem from a handful of troublemakers. The practical question is: do you deal with them or pretend they are not there?

"Mouldering Estate"

The parish was the responsibility of the Chutes as lords of the manor, but we cannot judge from surviving records how much they had done for its welfare in the past. However if John was repelled by the "mouldering estate" in 1750, it had certainly not improved since then, with William John playing the 18th century squire in his powdered wig and cheerfully ignoring the passage of time. Almost every house from the Vyne itself to the humblest cottage needed emergency repair, if only to stop roofs falling on the Chutes` and all their tenants` heads. In page after page of his memoir, William lists the buildings he had to modernise. The alternative was no magical paradise, but rural squalor and the Vyne`s collapse.

The Human Cost of Saving the Vyne

Today`s sociologists feel obliged to brand any 19th C. landowner as a male chauvinist fat-cat who plundered the land and forced the deserving poor out of the parish. In reality, William & Martha were idealists with a priceless house and a village community depending on them, and a flock of children to bring up. They worked and worked, and for years were so short of money that they could not afford to invite guests, and therefore could not accept invitations (which would have to be repaid). He managed the building work himself and used home-grown timber and home-made bricks and tiles; there is still a`Kiln Lane` in Sherborne St John. To save the cost of governesses, she somehow gave all 11 children a good early education, while almost continuously pregnant herself. Though the boys went on to school, the girls had such little outside contact that none of them married. All this is a hidden human cost behind what we enjoy today.

INSIDE THE VYNE

Games in the Gallery

In the house, Martha`s family grew and grew. Chaloner, her eldest, recalled the cavalier way they treated the Stone Gallery, when they had grown beyond the age of playing with the rocking-horse. The Stone Gallery "was warmed and used very much as a play-room by the rising Chute family ... when it was the scene of many exciting cricket, football and afterwards badminton matches. It was also used for many seasons as a theatre, for which purpose it served admirably.

"The fine old map of London now [*i.e. in 1884*] on the vestibule at the head of the grand stair was hung here formerly, and was damaged by balls `hit to leg`; but I repaired it in 1880".

Cricket and Greyhounds

William loved cricket; the boys had a pitch near the great oak, grandly called `Lords`. When the girls grew older and became better players they demanded a larger pitch; father provided a better piece of turf - the `Oval`. A drawing of the `Vyne Cricket XI` is on show in the house. All this practice led to Theophilus Dacre Chute being once chosen to play for Essex County side. (An entry in Wisden proves it; there`s glory for us!)

Another of William`s enthusiasms was breeding greyhounds for the race track; and of course the family followed the "Vine Hunt", which other Masters continued after its founder, W J Chute, died.

Music and Theatre

When William first came to the Vyne in his teens, he played and sang for the Lobb Chutes with his sister Caroline. But now the whole family took part in music and uproarious theatricals with Martha`s painted scenery and proscenium arches.

Active Churchmen

Under W J Chute the Vyne Chapel was, so Caroline wrote, never used "except to show to visitors"; but Wm. Wiggett Chute, son of a clergyman, brought it back into regular family use*, and three of his sons became priests.

He reconstructed the floor of the Parish Church and left a mystery: *where are the old Chute tombs?* Edward/Katharine`s hatchments prove that they were buried there. Chute burials are on record from Anthony (1754) on. Two Lobb Chutes and Eliza were buried in a vault "on the south side of the chancel, under the communion rails". Wiggett Chute honoured his predecessors, but today the only visible Chute tombs are those of his family.

daily prayers continued there up to 1956.

Chaloner William 1838-92
pious lawyer, historian of the
Vyne, which he owned `79-`92,
solicitous for the estate tenants;
poor health kept him close to
home. Married Eleanor Portal.
Children: Rachel, Sir Charles,
Ven. Jack, Ven. Anthony.
No grandchildren

**Rev. Devereux Wiggett
1839-1929**
Rector of Sherborne St. John
over 60 years.
Married Mary Hunter, organist
of Sherborne, and had
daughters Maud and Norah.
(Maud m. H. de R. Walker)

Charles Thomas 1841-67
Royal Navy.
Died young and unmarried.

**ANCESTOR OF TODAY`S
WIGGETT-LINEAGE
CHUTES**

Elizabeth Martha 1843-1913
an artist, like her mother; some of
her paintings can be seen at the
Vyne, where she lived for most
of her life; unmarried.

Emmeline Mary 1844-1917
unmarried; she died of shock
on the death of her nephew
Russell during the Great War

Rev. Edward Russell 1846-89
Rector of Great Moulton, Norfolk.
Died at 43 of lung disease but alone
of this huge family, he had Chute
grandchildren. He m. Nina Firth.
Sons: Russell, Len, Vere, Mervyn

MARTHA HAD ELEVEN CHILDREN IN NINETEEN YEARS

Georgina Fanny 1849-1906
unmarried. Buried beside
her three sisters in the
churchyard of
Sherborne St. John

Maria Esther 1851-1936
unmarried; kept house in
Bayswater for her brother Arthur.

**Rev Theophilus Dacre
1852-1926**
Rector of Gt. Moulton, Norfolk
in succession to his brother
Edward Russell. Unmarried.
Once played for
Essex County at cricket.

**Lennard Buckworth
1856-72**
Died while still at school

MOTHER MARTHA
From 1838 to 1857 Martha achieved
on average a birth every 20 months.
She amply made up for the low sur-
vival rate of earlier Chutes & Lobbs
by raising 10 of her 11 children into
adulthood, and she also brought
artistic genes into the family. Endur-
ing years when the Vyne was under
restoration, she produced paintings
of lasting value and lived to 71.

**Arthur John Lyde
1857-1937**
London solicitor; unmarried

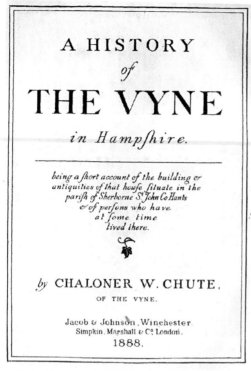

A HISTORY
of
THE VYNE
in Hampʃhire.

*being a ʃhort account of the building &
antiquities of that houʃe ʃituate in the
pariʃh of Sherborne St John Co Hants
& of perʃons who have
at ʃome time
lived there.*

by CHALONER W. CHUTE,
OF THE VYNE.

Jacob & Johnʃon, Winchester.
Simpkin, Marʃhall & Cº London.
1888.

Chaloner William Chute
(1838-1892) owner of The Vyne
1879-92.
Scholar, churchman,
lawyer and author of the
"History of the Vyne"

**His sons Charles, John and Anthony were also exceptional scholars at Eton
and Winchester.**

The younger sons
Jack *(left)* and
Tony in 1890

Both became
archdeacons
in the Church
of England.

Jack, sportsman,
mathematician
and artist was
for many years an
Eton housemaster.

Tony, Rector and
then archdeacon
of Basingstoke,
led a hospice of
celibate clergy.

Yet Again, a Huge Family Dwindles

Of the eleven children of William and Martha ten lived to adulthood. But none of the girls and only three of the boys married and had children. Then - as would so often happen at The Vyne - the family dwindled. Their known survivors today all descend from **Edward Russell Chute (1846-89)** the sixth of the eleven, who escaped in his youth from soggy Hampshire to Oxford and a Norfolk rectory. But even he had been so weakened by the dank environment of his childhood that he died of lung disease at 42.

The eldest son, Chaloner, was the fourth Chute of that name to be a lawyer and own the Vyne. But **Chaloner William (1838-92)** was deeply devout and shunned the limelight; he had weak health and died quite young. In due course, 2 of his 3 sons became parish priests and then brother-archdeacons.

When not at a desk in London, Chaloner was kept by his health close to home, where he was solicitous for his family and tenants, and wrote **"History of the Vyne"** (publ. 1888) which the National Trust has described as *"one of the most scholarly of late 19th century country house histories"*. Like his father, Chaloner married a beautiful girl next door who proved a perfect companion. **Eleanor Jane Portal**'s family was Huguenot, famous in England for making banknotes and for her cousin Viscount Portal's leadership of the RAF in the 1939-45 war. In the 1880s, Eleanor's Christian principles took her to the forefront of a new movement for women's welfare and legal rights. She was a founder member of the Mothers' Union and, for 24 years after Chaloner's early death, served as President of the Girls' Friendly Society.

ELEANOR PORTAL

Public Service

They had four talented children who also gave lifetime service to the community:

Rachel, activist for women's welfare and one of the first women JP's; unmarried;

(Sir) Charles (1879-1956) - see next page;

John ("Jack"), sportsman, artist, popular Eton housemaster, priest & Archdeacon of Sherborne - husband of the musical and irrepressible humorist "Mamie";

Anthony, priest, College Dean, and Archdeacon of Basingstoke; unmarried.

All were learned scholars but Rachel, being a woman, was not treated to a university education. This did not prevent her starting to learn Greek in her 80's after her brothers died, when, she said, *"I could no longer ask them for correct interpretations of the Greek Testament"*. In the Appendix we reprint some of her published articles which bring quirky events of Vyne history back to life.

None of the four had children; therefore on Sir Charles's death in 1956 the Vyne Chute succession expired.

**Chaloner and Eleanor
in the 1880`s with (from top)
Rachel, Charlie, Jack and Tony**

Schoolmaster Jack in the 1920`s

**Mamie, his wife, with Piccolo &
Luna. (Into her 90`s, the family
held birthday parties for her at
the Vyne, courtesy of the N.T.)**

(right) **Rachel in 1962
with her cousins
Francis & Russell**

SIR CHARLES CHUTE, BART. (1879-1956)

The last "Chute of the Vyne" trained as a lawyer, like so many of the name, but his baronetcy was awarded in 1952 for a long and outstanding public career. For a period he held concurrently, with all the crucial strains of wartime, three demanding positions in the county:-

Chairman of Hampshire County Council, **Chairman of Quarter Sessions**, and **Chairman of the War Agricultural Executive Committee**.

He also served part-time on Winchester Diocesan Finance Committee and was a pioneer for the Probation Service.

This exhausting schedule, to which he gave the full force of his energy and intellect, made Charlie seem unapproachable; it was also a great sadness to him and his wife Joan that they had no children to enliven the Vyne. But they twice invited whole schools to use the house. A girls' school occupied it through the 1920's, and in 1939 Charlie was rung up by the headmaster of a boys' school on the south coast, suddenly in danger of bombing; he promptly invited the entire school to live at the Vyne for the unforeseeable duration of war. Hence for five years, despite his full-time work for the county, Charlie became a fatherly host to over a hundred boys and masters. Among the 'archaeology' uncovered by the National Trust during their renovation of the house, were letters and schoolwork which boys had squeezed between the floorboards of the Vyne between 1939 and 1945.

For a fuller account of Sir Charles's career, see Obituary reprinted overleaf.

THE CHUTES BOW OUT

The Wiggett Chutes' lives - devoted over two generations to education, the church and voluntary public service - generated too little income to meet the crippling level of Death Duties in force when Sir Charles died. Nor, to be frank, could the family afford to continue maintaining the Vyne.

Sir Charles and his archdeacon brothers had hoped that a form of public ownership could be devised to make the house available to Winchester Diocese for the benefit of its clergy; but in the event this did not prove possible. As a result, after 303 years in Chute ownership, with the 'ups and downs' we have seen under different personalities, the house with over 1000 acres plus an endowment came to the National Trust in 1956, for public enjoyment as a national treasure.

The Trust have invested in the Vyne far more than could ever have been expected. It has now been thoroughly researched as an ancient monument, re-wired, re-plumbed, filled with safety equipment and staffed by professionals and volunteer stewards who make every visitor feel welcome.

This is a good conclusion, since - as this story shows - the Vyne has always been happiest when full of people.

author's photo at one of the summer evening concerts held at the Vyne

Sir Charles Lennard Chute
(1879-1956)
inherited the Vyne on his
father`s early death,
taking full possession on
his 21st birthday in 1900.

Scholar, lawyer and, after a lifetime of public service, described
as "Hampshire`s leading citizen".

Created Baronet in 1952.

The last Chute to own the Vyne.
He gave it to the National Trust
on his death.

Lady Chute (née Joan Baker) of the Vyne
who was hostess there to a girls` school in
the 1920`s and a boys` school throughout the
1939-45 War, and who contributed fine needle-
work to the house and the parish church.
They had no children.

"Digging for Victory"
- a national slogan
during the 1939-45 war

Charles Chute, an
indefatigable worker.
In 1943 while Chair-
man of Hants. County Council and of Hants. War Agricultural Executive Committee,
he `relaxed` by digging potatoes outside the small Drawing Room at the Vyne.

COMPLETION OF THE CHUTE PERIOD AT THE VYNE`: CAREER OF SIR CHARLES LENNARD CHUTE, BART. , M.C.

Charles Lennard followed his father at Eton and in the legal profession. He became a barrister at the Inner Temple, and, serving on the Western Circuit, he soon made a name for himself in the Courts. He was regarded as one of the most promising juniors on the Western Circuit Bar when he went off to the war. He became a Staff Captain and then a Brigade Major with the 164th Infantry Brigade in France and won the M.C. for gallantry in the field.

Upon his return from the war Mr. Chute (as he then was) did not resume his work at the Bar, somewhat to the surprise of some of his friends who had expected him to go far in the law. Instead he settled down to the life of a country gentleman and farmer to which he had been born, at his beautiful home at The Vyne and upon one of the most fertile stretches of Hampshire's agricultural land.   But village life could not hold for ever his virile mind. He became a Magistrate, and in the middle 1920's he began to take up the local government work in the county in which he was to find his real life's work.

County Council Work

In 1925 he went on to the Hampshire County Council and some seven years later he was raised to the level of Alderman. His 'grooming` for the greater duties which were to follow began when he took over the Chairmanship of the County Finance Committee, in many ways the policy-framing body of the county, from Sir Thomas Taylor. He inherited from him a financial policy of keeping as much of the county's capital expenditure as possible within the year-to-year income from the rates, in order to maintain the amount of borrowed capital as small as possible. It was a policy with which all on the Council did not agree, but it was one with which Sir Charles was himself very much in sympathy... As a result of the pre-war financial policy of the Council, Hampshire was able to enter into the post-war era, with all its tremendous financial obligations, better equipped and less encumbered by an overhang from the past than almost any other county.

The other main feature of his financial policy was his desire to get a standard rate established which should hold good for several years ahead - as long as possible, in fact - so that business men could plan their own budgets in advance. He was never in favour of small reductions one year when they had "windfalls", which would only have to be replaced and probably exceeded a few years after. Stability of the rate was ever his aim. Again, circumstances were against him and he happened to be in the chair during the most changing period of any local authority`s finances, the war and the post-war decade. Still, he struggled hard to carry through his policy, and in the face of the huge changes which fell upon the county with the new educational, health and other schemes of post-war years, one will find that the County Rate maintained a remarkable steadiness.   It rose of course at intervals, but when it went up it went to a figure which it was able to hold for several years ahead, and without fluctuations...

In the County Council Sir Charles was soon appointed Vice Chairman, and when the Earl of Malmesbury...retired, Sir Charles inevitably and almost automatically, it seemed, was unanimously voted to the chair. There he remained until his health broke down so suddenly last year (1955) and he retired to the position of an ordinary Alderman.

Agricultural Reorganisation

Soon after his taking over the Chairmanship of the County Council the clouds of war began to gather, and events moved fast: 1938 was indeed a year of crisis in Sir Charles's life. Munich came, and with it the decision of the Government to put the agricultural industry upon a war-time basis. The Minister of Agriculture, looking for someone to direct the industry in Hampshire into the channels needed by the nation, made the almost perfect choice. Sir Charles knew a good deal about agricultural landlording: he knew a good deal about farming. He knew, too, a great deal about Hampshire. Above all he had a mind trained to find out the truth despite smoke screens, a mind trained to look at both sides of a question before giving judgment, a man whose every action was impeccably fair.

Having assured himself of the technical assistance which he would be able to command, Sir Charles accepted the responsibility. Nor was that all, for that year Judge Barnard Lailey (Chairman of the Hampshire Quarter Sessions) died, and Sir Charles, who had already acted as a Deputy Chairman for some time and had already begun to show that his early training and promise had not rusted away with disuse, accepted the Chairmanship of the Quarter Sessions Courts in the county.

So, when the war broke in 1939, practically all the reins of local government in the county were assembled into the one pair of hands. The County Council responsible for keeping ordinary civil government going and, at the same time, developing all the new emergency services of Civil Defence and so forth; the Hants War Agricultural Executive Committee, charged with the superhuman task of turning a neglected agricultural industry (with thousands of acres of derelict downs, broken-down farm equipment and a shortage of manpower, machinery and stock) into the fourth line of defence; the administration of justice during a time when war-time conditions of bombing and black-out and the placement of people in strange places, far from their homes, presented temptations which normally would not have existed.

All these duties were accepted by Sir Charles in that spirit of loyalty, devotion to the country and the county which was the apotheosis of his traditions and his outlook on life.

Threefold War Task

How he carried through that three-fold task, only those close to him during the war years know. By a rigid and ascetic control of his time and his actions, not a moment was wasted. He attended practically every Committee of the County Council, forming the link between them all, and guiding them with the advice that came from experience. He travelled the county incessantly, ensuring that justice and fairness prevailed in the administration of the agricultural industry: he sat in the Courts often until nearly 10 o'clock at night to prevent jurymen, witnesses and others being kept away from their war-time duties in other places. The amount of work he could get through was amazing - though 10 years later it had its effect, when his health broke down, without question as a result of his superhuman activities during the early 1940's.

Appraisal

Some appraisement perhaps is due now of his work in each of these three-fold capacities. In the County... his interests were unlimited and his knowledge remarkable. On the matter of the survey of boundaries of the major local government authorities in this area, he fought for Hampshire's rights in other places with all the power he possessed, and he was indeed a tough negotiator on behalf of the county... As Chairman, he was a model in many ways.

Arriving at the best decision was paramount, and in order to do that, he was adamant in his determination to let every group in the Council provide its contribution; indeed minorities, no matter how small, received the most careful treatment and consideration. But time-wasting and "window dressing" he abhorred. In the agricultural sphere his task was probably the hardest, for he had no precedents to work on; but his judicial approach to the new problems saw him through. The agricultural re-orientation was carried through more completely in Hampshire - yet more fairly - than in many other counties. The only real difficulty which the Committee encountered was due to his belief in the strictest justice to all farmers, no matter how small or how big they were.

When the agricultural administration was put on to a peace-time basis following the Agriculture Act, he handed over to Mr. R. P. Chester. The record of food production in the county during the years which had gone before, and the completeness with which the agricultural revolution had been been effected here, was proof of the way in which he had led the industry through those difficult days. And he handed over a machine, built up in the most difficult conditions imaginable, which was, it is true, by no means perfect, but remarkably efficient and imbued with more than a touch of idealistic vision of the place agriculture could continue to hold in the county's life in the future.

Legal Reform

As Chairman of the Quarter Sessions he was very much responsible for the rapid development in recent years of the Probation Service. With his mind ever on reform rather than punishment, he saw in it a chance to revolutionise the penal system, and under his Chairmanship the probation service became a major feature of Court work here. He handed over the Courts to Mr. Ewen Montagu when he reached the age limit a few years ago (though he continued to act as a Deputy Chairman until last year) in a condition which enabled that

development to be carried still further to its present high efficiency.

Church Work

One other facet of Sir Charles' life deserves more than a passing reference - his work for the Church. He was a staunch churchman, of a staunch Church family. His two brothers are both now Archdeacons, one for Sherborne and the other for Basingstoke. He himself was patron of the living at Sherborne St. John ... In the diocese he was for many years a member of the Diocesan Conference, and he was a lay representative of the diocese on the Church Assembly. In the Diocesan Conference at Winchester his sound advice upon proper government and the proper administration of a diocesan financial policy was often invaluable.

Sir Charles had numerous other interests, mostly of a beneficent character. In the Basingstoke area such organisations as the old St. Thomas Home and its modern successor, the St. Thomas School for Deaf Children, enjoyed his continuous support. He was a Trustee of St. Cross Hospital at Winchester, and indeed a supporter of any cause of whose value to the local community he was satisfied. His beautiful home and garden were regularly open throughout each summer for various charitable causes.

Baronetcy

Recognition of Sir Charles's services to the county, and through the county, the country, came in 1952 when the baronetcy was conferred upon him. He had assiduously restricted himself to his work in Hampshire even when invitations to broaden his sphere of work were undoubtedly made. He believed that he could best serve the community here, and he followed implicitly what he believed to be right.

(Hampshire Chronicle, October 6, 1956)

HOT NEWS IN 1884 : THE LAST CHUTE BIRTH AT THE VYNE

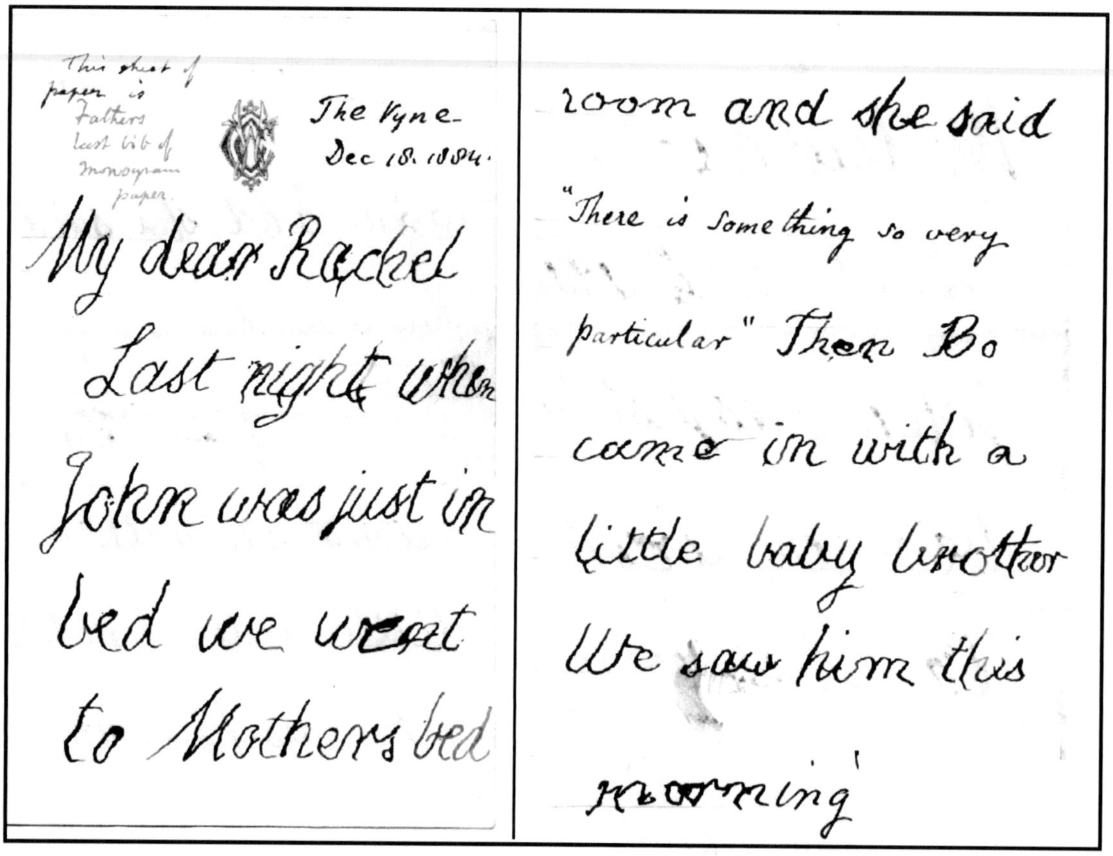

This sheet of paper is Fathers last bit of monogram paper.

The Vyne
Dec 18. 1884.

My dear Rachel

Last night when John was just in bed we went to Mothers bed

room and she said

"There is something so very particular" Then Bo came in with a little baby brother We saw him this

morning

Arrival of baby brother Tony

The earliest recorded letter of Sir Charles Chute (then aged 5) using up the last sheet of his father's monogrammed paper to send the news to big sister Rachel, then aged 8. Charlie's hand was "tired" after all that writing, so father Chaloner added the "difficult bit" and finished the letter with some faces.

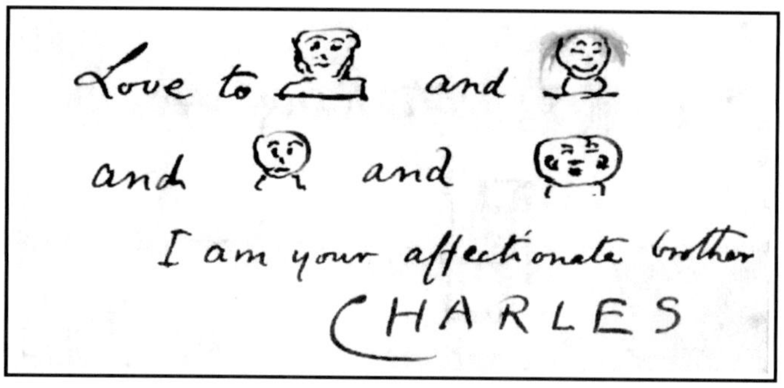

Love to ☺ and ☺ and ☺ and ☺

I am your affectionate brother
CHARLES

WELCOME HOME, SOLDIER! THE VYNE RECEPTION PARTY IN 1918 FOR CHARLES CHUTE, RETURNING WITH A MILITARY CROSS

CRICKET TEAM AT THE VYNE IN THE 19TH CENTURY
from there, Theo Chute (*right*) went on to play for Essex County

ETON 1899:
COLLEGE WALL TEAM
Jack Chute is one from left in back row. He and his brothers all won scholarships to Eton or Winchester & to Oxford; Jack (after an injury) returned to Eton as a house tutor

Jack aged three

SUMMARY: THE WIGGETT CHUTE FAMILY
(Names underlined were owners of the Vyne)

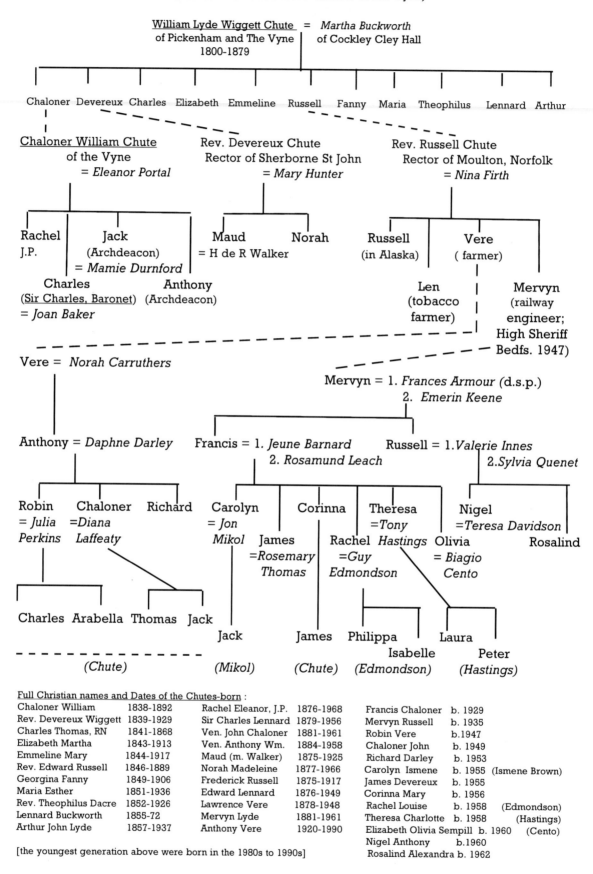

Full Christian names and Dates of the Chutes-born :

Chaloner William	1838-1892	Rachel Eleanor, J.P.	1876-1968	Francis Chaloner	b. 1929	
Rev. Devereux Wiggett	1839-1929	Sir Charles Lennard	1879-1956	Mervyn Russell	b. 1935	
Charles Thomas, RN	1841-1868	Ven. John Chaloner	1881-1961	Robin Vere	b.1947	
Elizabeth Martha	1843-1913	Ven. Anthony Wm.	1884-1958	Chaloner John	b. 1949	
Emmeline Mary	1844-1917	Maud (m. Walker)	1875-1925	Richard Darley	b. 1953	
Rev. Edward Russell	1846-1889	Norah Madeleine	1877-1966	Carolyn Ismene	b. 1955	(Ismene Brown)
Georgina Fanny	1849-1906	Frederick Russell	1875-1917	James Devereux	b. 1955	
Maria Esther	1851-1936	Edward Lennard	1876-1949	Corinna Mary	b. 1956	
Rev. Theophilus Dacre	1852-1926	Lawrence Vere	1878-1948	Rachel Louise	b. 1958	(Edmondson)
Lennard Buckworth	1855-72	Mervyn Lyde	1881-1961	Theresa Charlotte	b. 1958	(Hastings)
Arthur John Lyde	1857-1937	Anthony Vere	1920-1990	Elizabeth Olivia Sempill	b. 1960	(Cento)
				Nigel Anthony	b.1960	
				Rosalind Alexandra	b. 1962	

[the youngest generation above were born in the 1980s to 1990s]

APPENDICES TO PART ONE

*19th century
book-plate*

NOTES TO FIRST PART

Sources
"History of the Vyne" (1882) by Chaloner William Chute, for background, source references other than those given below; quotations from letters of Chutes and some from Gray and Walpole. (Copy at Hampshire Records Office (`HRO`) Winchester.)

Chute Collection, series ref. 31M/57, in HRO.

On Chaloner Chute I: Manning's `Lives of the Speakers` (1851)
> Diaries of Bulstrode Whitelocke 1605-1675, ed. Ruth Spalding
> Parliamentary Reports 1659
> Lives of the Norths, by Roger North
> Dictionary of National Biography (which quotes further sources)
> Records of St. Nicholas Church, Chiswick.

Re Lady Dacre, House of Lords Reports (see our p.77ff) and Roger North *op. cit.*

Historical Manuscripts Commission Reports, especially Downshire and Rutland/Belvoir Collections, for letters from or concerning Chaloner Chutes II and III and Edward.

"Originals Abroad" (New York 1952) by Warren H Smith, re John Chute & Grand Tour.

Letters of Horace Walpole (several editions available) re John, Anthony & Francis Chute.

Eliza's diaries; Memoirs of Wm. Wiggett Chute and of Caroline Wiggett; all in HRO.

Letters of Jane Austen, ed. Deirdre le Faye, with data on Lobb Chutes & Caroline Wiggett.

Jane Austen: A Life, by Claire Tomalin (good on relationships with the Chutes)

Reminiscences of Caroline Austen (The Jane Austen Society). Re: Mrs Wheeler p.31ff.

"Sherborne St. John & The Vyne in the Time of Jane Austen" (2003) by Rupert Willoughby

also, on the Vyne as a house, and its contents:

National Trust guidebook; numerous articles in Apollo, Country Life, etc. and large hardbacks on great country houses.

Treasures on view elsewhere
<u>Victoria and Albert Museum, London</u>:
- Edward Chute's "Basingstoke Monteith" in Silver Gallery;
- Terracotta maquette by Thos. Carter as trial model for Speaker's effigy in Tomb Chamber, in V&A Sculpture Gallery;
- Silver Communion Set presented by Eleanor Jane Chute to Girls Friendly Society for chapel use.

<u>Speaker's House, Palace of Westminster</u>: Tankard presented to Chaloner Chute for defending the bishops against Parliamentarian impeachment.

<u>Hermitage Museum, St Petersburg</u>, in the Walpole Collection: Van Dyck portrait of CCI's cousin Thomas Chaloner (a Regicide)

Tombs and Memorials
Parish churches of Sherborne St. John (Hants): tombs of WLWC and descendants.
> (Mystery re earlier Chute memorials; see p.61 above, last para.)
> Inscription on tower re Elizabeth Chute's donation.
> South Pickenham (Norfolk): Thos Chute/Eliz. Rivett; Devereux Chute; Lobb Chutes and Mayor Wiggett & his wife, and others.
> Moulton St. Michael (Norfolk): records of Rivetts, of Revs. Russell & Theo Chute, and the J S Wiggett-design rectory.
> Chiswick (London): Chaloners and CC I.
> Crudwell (Wilts): WLWC's father & siblings

Further Biographical Detail:
For the Chutes mentioned in First Part, more detail can be found after p.194 in "Leaves on the Family Tree" (research notes on wider Chute history).

DOROTHY, LADY DACRE

There are so many portraits of this lady that one might imagine she had virtues or achievements to be celebrated. Two genuine Van Dycks of her were recently sold in London, the first in 1986, the second (which had languished in a theatre props warehouse) in 1998. The two at the Vyne are copies, but their prominence, together with the three other portraits of her own family which she brought there, might lead us to suppose that she was responsible for her husband Chaloner Chute buying the Vyne.

There is no evidence at all for this, and up to now the Chutes have kept tactfully silent about her character. Not so her own family, one of whom (the historian Roger North) said she treated people "*scurvily*", "*accusing and railing at him* [her nephew] *all the town over*" when she had misinterpreted a good turn he had done her in court. "*She carried the quarrel so high as to get one of no small account to let [the Attorney General] know what a snake ... he had in his bosom. In short she intended his ruin if possible*".

The nephew in question rose to become Lord Guilford, Keeper of the Great Seal, yet Dorothy "*defamed [him] in this manner... for several years ... she never failing to make use of him when she found it might be of profit to her; and yet she never could afford him a good word to his and her dying days*"*.

This was the woman, foolish but remorselessly spiteful, whom Chaloner Chute chose for his second wife in 1649. To us, his choice is incomprehensible. He already knew the North family well, and they must have derided or pitied Dorothy's character; yet for reasons unknown Chute married her and promised her enormous wealth. It was an aberration by the great lawyer for which the Chute descendants paid dear. To them she was the worst of all ancestors by far; a cuckoo who barged in during her husband's declining years, and after his death used her family's legal clout to asset-strip the Vyne without mercy.

It is historical fact but rarely mentioned in the history of the house that, after 10 years' marriage to the Speaker, she mounted a colossal financial claim, persecuted his heirs and drove them out of the Vyne for some 25 years. That explains the odd gap in 'Vyne history' between the Speaker and his grandson Edward. It is a strange story which deserves recording.

Dorothy, Lady Dacre (1605-1698) was an aristocrat by birth and by her first marriage. As the eldest daughter of Dudley, 3rd Lord North she grew up in a literary/intellectual atmosphere at Kirtling, Cambridgeshire. Her father was a statesman, musician, poet and French scholar, and he happened to 'discover' the spa of Tunbridge Wells. Three of her nephews were national figures in the Law. By legal eminence and clever footwork the Norths managed not to fall out with either Royalists or Parliament. (It was a

---

*Roger North, *Lives of the Norths*, 1972 re-print, vol.1 pp 60-61)

later Lord North whose subservience to King George III led to the American War of Independence.) They were not wealthy but achieved a series of profitable marriages; Dorothy grew up knowing the importance of money.

In 1625 she married Richard Lennard, 13th Baron **Dacre** of Herstmonceux, Sussex. His mother was Chrysogona Baker, whose child-portrait hangs at the Vyne, and one of his forbears was hanged in 1543 for killing a gamekeeper. Dorothy North was his second wife and became stepmother to his son and heir. When she was only 29 her husband died; her stepson inherited Herstmonceux Castle, and she went sadly home to Kirtling with her daughter Catherine.

Sutton Court, Chiswick.

To understand the role of bad luck in what followed, we must mention the house where Chaloner Chute lived when he married Lady Dacre. Chiswick was a fashionable riverside village outside the built-up area of 17th century London. It became widely known after 1725 when Lord Burlington built Chiswick House, but in the 1640s its notable residents included:

> the Chaloner family, cousins of Chute's mother,
> the Barkers at Grove Park (one of whom has his portrait at the Vyne),
> Lord Paulet (whose main seat was Hackwood Park, Basingstoke, and who may
>   well have encouraged Chute, his neighbour, to buy the Vyne),
> Chute himself at Sutton Court.

The Manor of Sutton had belonged to the Dean and Chapter of St Paul's Cathedral since before the Conquest. They leased it out, and in 1639 one Thomas Edgar took a 21 year lease but shortly afterwards sold it to Chaloner Chute. Now came the Civil War, and on 12 March 1643 this manor, together with all the cathedral's property, was sequestered to the Lord Mayor and Citizens of London. Chute promptly purchased the lease from the trustees of Parliament and spent £5,500 on a new house (say £300,000 in today's terms); there he brought up his children after his first wife Ann Skory's death.

By 1649 he had lived at Chiswick for 6 years, was lay rector, had presented bells to its church and made a vault there for the body of his first wife. His son Chaloner (we will call him "CC II") was 19 and unmarried. His daughters were aged 21 and 18; Ann was engaged to their neighbour Henry Barker.

Marriage to Lady Dacre

In 1649 Chaloner Chute re-marries, at the age of 54. Dorothy is a forceful lady of 44 with a young daughter. He has no noble blood, but she has been 15 years a widow (which implies she was not rich) and at her advanced age she can do no better. Chute is a 'stately figure' at the top of his profession who offers to settle a huge cash sum on her; and now that the King is under sentence of death, she sees advantage in marrying a man who has friends in Cromwell's Parliament. She finds Chute even more attractive on learning his plan to acquire a huge Tudor palace built by a Royalist family who are now impoverished in the King's cause. (The Vyne, before he reduced it, was on similar scale to Herstmonceux Castle, where she had lived with her first husband.)

As the year closes and the King's head falls, Dorothy is safely married to one of the new men of power, with their Chiswick and Vyne residences both held under the laws of the new régime; he also has a business address near the Law Courts. She no doubt cooperates in his plan to alter the Vyne to more manageable size, and perhaps we should give her credit for having the idea to add a Classical Portico. Around 1655 they moved into the Vyne and all seemed set for a prosperous old age. As Dorothy may have planned, CC II conveniently married her gawky daughter and a baby came in 1656. Then Chute senior was elected Speaker, and unlimited social prospects opened before her - if Parliament agreed a republican constitution and had Chute to thank for his diplomacy in bringing the arguments to an end.

But, as we have read earlier, Parliament did not agree, and everyone's dreams fell apart. By April 1659 Dorothy's husband was dead of overwork, CC II inherited the Vyne, Parliament was in terminal chaos, the Army revolted, and everyone talked of bringing back the King.

The Disaster of his Death

Dorothy was in despair. She had twice been widowed, twice seen a stepson take over her matrimonial home; her prospects were in ruins. At the least she could have expected to stay at Sutton Court, but at the 1660 Restoration, England tried to put the clock back. The Dean & Chapter of St Paul's sent bailiffs to the manors which were now reinstated as Cathedral property. Sutton Court (land and house) were taken over by the Dean of St Paul's - and, of all insults, leased to his own brother. She petitioned the Church, but they retorted that the old 21-year lease (1639-1660) had expired, and they saw no reason to make concessions for the widow of one of Cromwell's grandees.

Surely, we ask ourselves, the late Speaker had made proper provision for her? Indeed he had, but there was now a new régime, and he was no longer there to fight for the best deal possible. Before the Restoration she had been legally secure; he could have easily renewed the 1639 lease he had bought from Cromwell's commissioners.

His Will was correct and conscientious, leaving the Vyne to his son CC II and making Lady Dacre trustee for the maintenance of the younger grandchildren, who were not in line to inherit the estate. His Will drew attention to a Deed he had already made, under which his widow would have lifetime enjoyment of Sutton Court, and he expressed the wish that his son and wife would ultimately give the manor for the building and endowment of a hospital *"as I have always purposed to myself since I was necessitated to take a conveyance of that estate"*
and he also directed *"that this hospitall shall be continued as long as the land shall continue out of the church's possession, to whom I could heartily wish the inheritance restored, and a lease for three lives, warranted by law, accepted in lieu thereof".*

Having previously guaranteed her a huge jointure (see below), he had done all he could for his widow and children. But there is a legal maxim that `death always comes at an inconvenient time`; and how true in this case. The Speaker died in 1659, a year before the Sutton lease was due for renewal; without it, he had no tenure to grant her under the Deed. In his lifetime, nobody could have foreseen the Restoration; but, if he had lived, he might well been able to make a deal with the new régime.

As it was, we can imagine the Church commissioners throwing back at Lady Dacre the words in his Will about wishing the manor returned to them and/or used for a hospital. "My Lady, those were your late husband's sentiments - good Christian ones, indeed. We are astonished at your plea that you need Sutton for your home. Did not your late husband buy a great house at the Vyne, profiting from the poverty of his late Majesty's friends. No, my Lady; the Chutes have done well enough during the recent troubles."

Dacre vs Chute

The Lord Norths rode smoothly across the transition back to monarchy, and Dorothy probably felt cheated that she could not do the same. Chute had promised the North family, probably before their marriage, that he would either give her £500 a year or, failing that, a sum of £5,000 (around £250,000 today).

CC II now fought on her behalf to keep the house and lease of Sutton Court, assuming that, being worth more than £500 p.a., it would discharge this particular duty to her. She also received a £900 legacy under the Speaker's will. CC II was horrified when, on failing to get instant renewal of the Sutton Court lease, she haled him, her stepson/ son-in-law, to court claiming £5000 plus damages. In this suit she was backed by the North family, and she won her claim.

CC II eventually succeeded on appeal in getting a new lease at Chiswick. She took the house, saying she needed it and her other bequests from the Speaker in order to meet her obligations to the younger grandchildren. But with this done, *she still demanded the full £5000 in cash* (telling the court that there were "abundant assets at her husband's death") and obtained a Chancery decree that CC II must pay £5000. He was outraged. Being a lawyer himself, he would hardly have let it go to court unless he had a good case. The precise legal arguments are now lost, but we can see conflicting views as to the relation between the various documents under which the Speaker had provided for his family - i.e. whether they were cumulative or mutually consolidating. The Court favoured the case of the noble Lady as against the Parliamentarian gentleman.

Chutes - Out !

From 1664, the Vyne was placed under sequestration, so that a bailiff administered the estate and gave Lady Dacre its proceeds. This meant that for the last 2 years of his life (1664-66) CC II was barred from living there. (We assume it was at his father's old business address at St. Martin in the Fields that he and Catherine brought up their four children - Chaloner, Edward, Elizabeth and Thomas.) At the Vyne, the bailiff cut huge quantities of timber - on one account, £6000 worth - and sold it for Lady Dacre's benefit. She refused to credit a penny of this income against the £5000 !

"Exit, Pursued by a Bear"

CC II died young, with the debt unpaid. Lady Dacre at once revived the claim and sequestration order against his eldest son Chaloner ("CC III") who was then a boy of only 10. And when <u>he</u> died, she again revived the orders against his brother and heir Edward.

Lady Dacre, with Chute money, did give her younger grandchildren Edward and Thomas a good education, thus complying with the Speaker's request in his Will. As at May 1685 she said she had spent £1232 on them. Moreover her North relations did what they could to further Edward's and Thomas's careers.

But she would have nothing to do with the eldest sons. CC II never lived to build up much income from the Bar, so some Chute money must have descended directly from the Speaker to his son and eldest grandson; they had something to live on, even with Lady Dacre milking the Vyne estate. But the early deaths of these two men at 36 and 29 were surely connected with the severe strain caused by Lady Dacre's persecution. Other Chutes, before and after them, lived to normal ripe age.

Chaloner III

He was only 10 when he inherited the Vyne in 1666. At the age of 23, while perhaps still living with his mother in London (imagine how she must have felt about *her* mother's behaviour), he began a series of appeals in the House of Lords against Lady Dacre's demands; these, the entry for 13 Nov.1680 shows, had somehow risen to £12,000, and included her costs of bringing the legal suit against his father! He alleged

Catherine, dau. of Lady Dacre and wife of Chaloner Chute II

that,while a minor, he had been induced by her to agree concessions which were unreasonable, and claimed she had received £8000 but given the family no credit. She counter-petitioned, and eventually (1685) the Lords shut them both up by refusing further discussion and confirming the original £5000 order plus damages. (*See H. of L. MSS for 1679, pages 152-4, item 209 with notes.*)

CC III paid £2000 on account, and Lady Dacre, for the first time, let him go and live at the Vyne; but within months he was dead, leaving £3667.12s.5d debt still outstanding.

Chaloner Chute III, son of CC II and Catherine

Sir Anthony to the Rescue

After suffering so much from the aftermath of one marriage, the Chutes struck gold in the next two - those of Edward and his brother Thomas. Edward became engaged to Katharine, daughter of Sir Anthony Keck, a rich lawyer. Thomas married an East Anglian heiress, bought a Norfolk estate, and was no longer concerned with the Vyne.

Sir Anthony saw how his daughter's social position would leap if she moved into the Vyne. He decided to use his wealth to pay off the final debt to Lady Dacre and get from the Chutes, in exchange, a mortgage in the Kecks' favour on the Vyne estate. This settlement got Lady Dacre off their backs and insured Katharine against Edward's future behaviour as her husband. In 1685/6 the legalities were set up*, after which the young couple were married. Her family became long-term benefactors to the Vyne

---

* In Hampshire Records Office, docs. ref. 31M57/109 -115

and she bore Edward 10 children, rounding off a fruitful life by bearing John Chute, the Vyne's classical architect.

Lady Dacre finally died at the age of 93, having worn down the Chutes for two generations. We can never know if CC II had first made her 'flip' with some tactless remark, or if she decided that if she, the aristocrat, could not have the Vyne then neither should the common Chutes. (It is amusing to find that on 4 July 1661 she claimed to the House of Lords a Privilege of Peerage which she had lost on marrying a commoner, but lost her claim!) In all the 17th C. documents from which we gather this story, one looks in vain for any redeeming feature in her character or behaviour. Her own cousin Roger North, as we saw, regarded her as either bad or mad. So it remains a mystery why the Speaker married her. She treated that marriage, or at least its aftermath, as a business challenge, and to hell with human feelings!

But on a positive note, let us try to feel sympathy for a lady of no great beauty or brain in a generally brilliant family, who lost two valuable husbands and two stately homes, was expropriated from Sutton Court for years at the Restoration, spent most of her life in widowhood and only got her pay-off when she was too old to make much use of it.

Notes:

Main sources, as indicated, are the House of Lords Journal and MSS, Roger North's History, and the sequence of Deeds c.1685 in HRO between Dacre/Keck/Chute. Her claim in 1661: Portland Papers at Longleat. PO/ Vol. XXI, folio 183. Re Sutton Court and detail of CC I's Will, see Daily Graphic for March 23,1899 and Chiswick Times of about the same date (HRO doc. 31M59/1194)
In 1664 CC II succeeded in obtaining a lease of Sutton in trust for Lady Dacre.
CC's Sutton Court house no longer stands, but the name persists in several Chiswick streets today, as does Grove Park where the Barkers lived. It appears that a single road separated the Chute & Barker properties. Henry Barker, whose family were Royalist fighters, became CC II's trustee and (under his Will) residuary guardian of his children.

Bulstrode Whitelock's Diary gives Lord Paulet as Chute's friendly neighbour at Chiswick. It is guesswork that Paulet, knowing Sandys needed to sell the Vyne, approached Chute as being likely to prove an acceptable neighbour in Hampshire, rather than some wilder Parliamentarian.

Pictures. That on page 77 above is the author's photo of a Vyne portrait 'after Van Dyck'. There are two supposedly genuine Van Dycks of Lady Dacre, ref: the 'Observer' for 22 June 1986 and the 'Times' for June 8, 1998.

VanDyck portrait used as Theatre prop!
The latter source, displayed under "Lady Dacre" on Internet, contains an article revealing that the portrait was used for a long time as a theatre prop before its painter was recognised by a Sotheby's expert. That one appears to have gone to Toulouse Museum.

Money values. Above we have used the index which gives £1 in 1650 = £50 now, but there can be no proper equivalence, as at that date people lived far more hand-to-mouth. Only the rich could afford the high borrowing rates of the 17th C which were well into double figures, and there was none of today's land scarcity which inflates house prices, nor our global market which enables finance houses to pay their boards and employees huge salaries and bonuses. The Vyne, remember, cost Chaloner Chute just over £30,000.

Dusty old master unearthed

HORACE WALPOLE'S GOTHICK PLANS FOR THE VYNE

(a talk given by Francis Chute to the Friends of Strawberry Hill in 2002/03)

Here at Strawberry Hill we are enveloped in Walpole's Gothick vision - as executed for him by his chosen architects, prominent among them his close friend John Chute. And at Chute's own home 'The Vyne', which was originally a Tudor palace, his ceremonial portrait holds in its hand a parchment showing an elevation of his house reshaped into Gothick style. The question behind my talk is this: why is there no sign of that Gothick exterior when you look at The Vyne today? It is a fair question, because (a) the gothic revival was a growing force when Chute inherited the house in 1754, and (b) though Walpole won the greater fame on account of his writings, "Chute was the greater innovator. Walpole himself admitted it".*

Walpole was only 22 when they first met. He had left England on his Grand Tour, taking his spaniel and the poet Thomas Gray for companions. While their sedan chairs were being carried across the Alps, the spaniel went off on its own business and was grabbed by a wolf. The men however reached Italy safely, and ended up in Florence at the house of Horace Mann, the British Resident. It was there in late 1739 that they met John Chute and his cousin, who were likewise on the Grand Tour. Chute had been a solitary boy with a passion for the arts, but (so far as known) no formal training. Studying architecture in Italy he was making up for time lost. They all seem to have hit it off at once, and became the firmest friends for life.

Walpole's personality was so singular that his friendships suffer by association. One historian**, for whom Walpole was "arrogant, tetchy, snobbish, malicious, jealous and small-minded", describes his "passion for the handsome bisexual Henry Fiennes Clinton", who (he claims) introduced Walpole in Italy to "a dubious loose-living circle which included the homosexual John Chute, theatrical and flaunting, but someone who was to stay the course as the one constant member of what Walpole called his Committee of Taste". This is standard knock-about journalism today, but (so far as Chute is concerned) is questionable as history.

John Chute was indeed accompanied in Florence by a young man, Francis Whithed, whose portrait hangs at the Vyne. Whithed was a cousin of his mother's and John had taken him to Italy after the young man had been ill-treated by his elder brother. The two were so inseparable there that they became known as the "Chuteheds". What lies behind that? Well, nothing of a homosexual nature can be proved either way, but I am struck by the tone of one of Chute's letters to Walpole. Let me try this idea on you.

Chute had made a rather dim joke about an Italian cardinal "dying of the smallest pox he had yet encountered", and Walpole wrote back in ecstasies about the joke. Chute was rather surprised, and in an attempt at wit, wrote a tedious caricature of himself as destined to be Walpole's royal jester. It struck me that that sort of laboured self-caricature is what you expect from a lonely personality, someone perhaps who feels that his true self finds no correspondence in another. Would it really square with Chute having the kind of inner completeness which springs from a loving relationship - with someone of either sex?

The explanation of the so-called "Chuteheds" is really much simpler, if less 'newsworthy', as was pointed out in a book entitled "Originals Abroad" (publ. 1952) by Warren H Smith, one of W S Lewis's research assistants in the Walpole museum at Farmington. In effect he says this. Chute was much older than the rest of the dilettanti who gathered in Florence, and was a warm-hearted and serious man, with no son and no close family. He virtually adopted Whithed as a son, and their relationship had a certain symmetry. Whithed was far richer than Chute, but Whithed was very deaf and shy in company. So Chute provided the conversation and the contacts, and young Whithed paid more than half of the bills. Apart from this,

---

* Nigel Nicolson in 'Great Houses of England'.
** Sir Roy Strong in 'The Spirit of Britain'

Whithed had a perfectly normal private life in Italy - normal by 18th century standards - as he kept an Italian mistress who bore him a daughter. Years later, after Whithed died, John Chute took on responsibility for educating the little girl in England. So the question of homosexuality is at least unproven and in any case irrelevant.

If John Chute was theatrical, it was perhaps a defence mechanism in one who was born the youngest of 10 children. His mother died when he was a child, and he was disliked by his elder brother Anthony who succeeded their father at the Vyne. The only mystery is what John had done between the ages of 16 and 38, and whether he had any architectural apprenticeship. By 1739 when he arrived in Florence, he was deep into architecture, drawing assiduously, and he spoke French and Italian. So when Walpole, Gray and Whithed assembled at Horace Mann's house in Florence, John Chute was maturer in age and experience. But we guess he had never had the privilege of a carefree student life, since he was happy to enter into their spirit, to behave like an undergraduate, and enjoy their flippant and supercilious humour.

He had a lot of background in common with Walpole and Whithed; like them, he was the youngest child of his parents; like them, he got on badly with elder brothers; and all of them had come to Italy, like a cultural blood-bank, to get their transfusion of renaissance art and sunshine. Florence is one of many cities described as a sunny place for shady people; in fact, Chute disliked most of the stereotyped Englishmen doing the Grand Tour, who pretended they wanted education but spent their time seeking Roman statuary at a bargain price. John, by contrast, was there for serious study, and he deliberately scandalised them by talking Italian, carrying a fan and dressing Whithed in "a coat all over spangles".

Unlike most visitors, Chute stayed on in Italy for 7 years after Walpole and Gray left, and Walpole found him surprisingly sharp at bargaining for genuine antiquities and getting them shipped to England. One example was the famous Boccapaduglia Eagle, recently unearthed in Rome, which John skilfully secured for Houghton in 1745.

This helped to seal a friendship which lasted a lifetime. On Chute's death in 1776 Walpole wrote that over many years it was a surprise if three days passed without them seeing each other, and that they would often sit quietly reading for hours in each other's company, enjoying a kind of telepathic communion. It was in the confidence of this friendship that Walpole conceived the idea of giving the Vyne a Gothick make-over. When John inherited in 1754 Walpole rushed to the Vyne with a gleam in his eye, saw that it looked run-down, and drew up an `Inventionary` of changes to give it a `truly Gothick air` and cosy it up for the Committee of Taste. As if this was not enough, Walpole kept returning to the Vyne with Bentley, another `Strawberry architect`, to dream up further projects for John to get on with.

Now we come to our point. When art historians call the Vyne the "epitome of changing fashions in architecture" why do we see so little of Horace Walpole's plans to gothicise it? In his life-size portrait, John's parchment shows the Vyne with pinnacles, battlements and a loftier elevation, plus flanking colonnades and so on. But you would never guess it today.

In principle the idea was not unique, as the gothic revival was firmly in fashion. Another 18th century portrait, strikingly resembling John Chute's, is that of Sir Roger Newdigate of Arbury Hall in Warwickshire. In his portrait he reclines languidly in an armchair, holding a plan of his ancestral home remodelled into Gothick style. The parallel stops there, because Sir Roger got on and did it. Arbury Hall, after treatment by Sanderson Millar, became a Gothic Revival showpiece. But in John Chute's hands, the Vyne stayed as it was. Why so?

Chute after all was one of the Committee of Taste; he was a Gothick enthusiast and toured the countryside with Walpole studying and making notes on gothic designs. To Walpole, Chute was "the genius behind my poor Strawberry", where the great Gallery, at least, is agreed to be wholly Chute's design. He had the capability; plans displayed in the Vyne show that he worked as a gentleman-architect on other neo-gothic houses. So what was the problem over the Vyne?

The expert who wrote the NT guide-book airily concludes "Chute was never to resolve the conflicting instincts he had about the exterior" as witness the hundreds of drawings he made in both gothic and classical styles. I am no expert, but this verdict has never satisfied me. Chute was 75 when he died, surely old enough to make up his mind. The possibilities must have been argued hour after hour by the two men, and Walpole never gave up; we have his letters to Mann and others despairing of Mr Chute ever getting on with the job.

This historical question mark brings us together here this evening.

We all know the dangers of trying to reconstruct the past. Malcolm Bradbury declared that "history is the lies told by the present to make sense of the past". So how are we to understand the human motives of 250 years ago? Let us fall back on what a teacher told me at school: "my boy, you will never understand any historical event if you cannot explain it from outside time, i.e. from past, present and future". This is a difficult test; but let me try it out on you in this context. I will welcome your comments.

First, is there an argument from the past? Well, I see Walpole and Chute as escaping their pasts in different directions. The Walpoles owned Houghton Hall in Norfolk, a massive neo-classical "statement" of Sir Robert's arrival at the very top. Much of Norfolk vulgarity horrified Horace, like the county squires who gorged on beefsteak and had to be levered into their coaches. But Horace inherited, from somewhere, a butterfly mind. He was bored with the daily grind, with all the constructive part of life that did not yield a clever epigram or a sneering jest. To escape that reality he took a dream from the Middle Ages; you can romance there at will.

Chute stood in quite a different scenario: his family home was already an ivy-mantled relic, as inaccessible as the Sleeping Beauty's castle. It had ghosts enough, down to John's own brothers and the mother who died in his childhood. The last thing he wanted was to increase the "gloomth" of the Vyne. He had been domineered there by his brother Anthony, whom Walpole described as a "capricious monster" of "vinegary temper". It was to escape from all that, from an England which was still burning witches at the stake, that John had joyfully gone south, to the warmth, light and liberation of the Renaissance, and had for seven years revelled in its architecture, the purity of the Classics, the exuberance of Counter-Reformation Baroque, and the endless originality of Italian design and decoration.

Their personalities were chalk and cheese. Horace gathered architectural ideas as he gathered gossip, but John had the single-mindedness needed for bringing an individual work of art to fruition. It is laughable even to imagine Horace disciplining himself for the months or years it took John to work out the exact proportions for the Staircase at the Vyne. In that time, Horace would have been round and round the salons, boudoirs and coffeehouses, and produced a volume of brilliant and gossipy letters. With the Prime Minister for father, he had total security. He was confident, his personality was darting, malicious, fanciful; what caught his eye were oddities which he could turn into a witticism, or silly details that he could inflate beyond all proportion. Chute had no such confidence; he was careful, as Horace noted, to think two or three steps ahead. He may once have carried a fan but he was never (as Macaulay described Horace's affectations) "a face covered by mask within mask". As an architect he saw a project whole, from foundations upwards. The comfort he sought was in completeness.

You find that completeness in Classicism. The architecture of a masculine culture under-pinned by mathematics and reason. Looking at its grandeur and balance, you can find (if that is what you want) art at arms length, and a refuge from fears and self-questionings, from all the capricious emotions latent in the human mind - indeed from everything that the gothic and romantic movements looked for. By 1745, Chute was talking of settling permanently in

Florence. Unhappily, just then a favourite brother died, back in England, so that John was next in succession to inherit the Vyne - that "mouldering estate" - on Anthony's death.

Consider now the argument from the present-day, John's present-day. Forget art for a moment; what about money? Could John actually <u>afford</u> a major reconstruction of the Vyne? Well, a notice appeared in two London papers on 28 May 1754 saying "Last week died at his seat in Hampshire Anthony Chute, Esq of the Vyne. By his death an estate of £4000 a year and a very considerable personal fortune devolves to his brother John Chute, Esq. of Argyle Buildings". At the same time, Horace Walpole wrote him a mocking letter expecting him to be "courted by chancellors of the Exchequer for your interest in Hampshire, by a thousand nephews for your estate, and by my Lady Brown for her daughter... you will have strong port of a thousand years old got on purpose for you at Hackwood House because you will have lent the Duke £30,000..."

How wonderful if a word of it was true! If you look in the Hampshire Records Office, there are three cold and unromantic documents in the Chute collection:
1. His brother Anthony, lately deceased, left some melancholy accounts in MS, financial accounts which include a list of what he calls 'avoidable' and 'unavoidable' expenses. Avoidables range from "going to Town by self" (he was, after all, an MP!) down to clipping hedges. He wryly commented "£450 in the whole yeare will be the Expence in Town or out of it, and I think verily will be with management sufficient. Though ye yeare 1742 I spent above a hundred more, though £150 less than I had done ye yeare before that."
2. A note that the year's profit on the whole Vyne estate in 1760 was less than £400.
3. A Deed taken out by John Chute in 1762, mortgaging the Vyne house and estate, to raise the sum of £6,500. This is flabbergasting. With little other income of his own, having cashed in his mother's bequests, and at the age of 61, he borrowed 15 times the estate's gross yield.

The first of these documents shows us the truth. The "vinegary temper" of Anthony may have been partly due to to gout, but mostly to the knowledge that he could not afford to live in the style of his forbears. Unlike them, he had not married money, and his parents had spread their wealth over 12 children (including his two step-brothers) plus a handicapped sister-in-law. We are driven to conclude that in the early years of the 18th century, a period when English farmers had never had it so good, the Chutes were crassly incompetent at running their 4000-acre estate. They were after all, lawyers and politicians who had just wanted a stately home within reach of London. Evidently nobody, in four generations, had learned the rudiments of estate management.

But wait. What about those London newspapers saying the Vyne was worth £4000 a year and a great fortune? The farcical truth is that Horace Walpole had dreamed up this fantasy and had it put as a joke into the fashionable Press. A great joke, and Walpole admitted as much, but imagine the effect on poor John Chute. The reason Anthony had made no will, and had not disinherited the brother he disliked, was that he had nothing but the house itself to bequeath. So the Chute who in 1754 had just become a major public figure in Hampshire was actually impoverished, but obviously could not rush into print to deny having this great fortune. From now on he would have to live with the consequences. So when John sat alone in the Vyne at dinner and re-read the offending newspaper, he must have realised that from now on he had to be careful of young Horace. Undergraduate humour was all very well in Florence; but not for someone who was soon to be High Sheriff of the County of Southampton.

There remain for us the third set of reasons, those working back from the future. John was the last of the male Chute line, and he greatly respected his ancestry. What was to become of the estate when he died? If he flew in the face of tradition and blew the whole £6,500 he had borrowed on creating a gothick fantasy, who would end up owning the house? Creditors would move in, and the achievements of Chaloner Chute the Speaker would be forgotten, for lack of a worthy monument.

John must have had two objectives here. As an architect he wanted to make his mark on the Vyne; as a Chute, he wanted to secure its future. We have talked about art; we have talked about money; now we are into planning and diplomacy. John had cousins in Norfolk, named Lobb but of Chute blood. They happened to be rich and they had always been friendly with him; but how could he bring them into the solution of his twofold objective?

He had to plan a delicate negotiation, starting from a position of weakness. Weakness, because he needed to get at the Lobb cousins' money. But they were jolly extroverts, perfectly happy in Norfolk with their fox-hunting neighbours, and with no reason whatever to be interested in the Vyne. What he actually achieved was an astounding success. We don't know the details of how he crept up to the finished deal, but somehow, in exchange for promising him the succession to the Vyne, he induced his young cousin Thomas Lobb, living miles away in Norfolk, to guarantee the £6,500 mortgage on the Vyne and give John a free hand to spend it on major innovations. Perhaps he threw in the argument that a house so near London would help the Lobbs to a place in Parliament and a social leg-up.

But if the Lobbs were tempted in this way, they were still Norfolk men, and in Norfolk the correct style of home for an M.P. was a house like Houghton or Holkham. No way would they pay for John to build them a gothick fantasy. This is the great irony, that only by bowing to the Norfolk taste which had repelled Horace Walpole, could John Chute get both finance and a future for his own ancestral home. John's extra success was to have young Lobb's agreement to change his name to Chute.

So there you have it. John built the Classic Staircase and the Tomb Chamber, leaving space for Thomas Lobb to add his own shield on the plinth below the Chaloner Chute effigy. Lobb became Lobb Chute and paid the bills for John's work, and his son William John Chute did indeed become an M.P. and owned the Vyne after him into the 19th century. As Master of the Vine Hunt, young William was even able to lead the great Duke of Wellington a chase.

And if you wonder why the columns round the Classic Staircase are of wood and plaster, it is because the Vyne's foundations would never have borne the weight of marble - even if John could afford it; nor could marble have been carted there until miles of roadway, far beyond the Vyne's boundaries, had been totally reconstructed. That expense was beyond his means. The same is true of the additional third floor which is shown in the drawing on the parchment. So when the guide book says that John's hundreds of drawings of the Vyne, with elevations variously remodelled in gothic and classic styles, reveal an uncertainty of mind, do not be misled. Once John had looked facts in the face, done his deal with the Lobbs, and explained it to Walpole, the die was cast; and the drawings may have been mental exercises, a diversion to keep their imaginations active.

Those drawings (sometimes criticised for their over-mathematical style) may have been no more than diversions; but I prefer to think they were a tactful way of making an aesthetic argument. You see, as a respected father-figure he could never accuse Walpole of bad taste, and say that there is no way that an architect of integrity can dress up a genuine low-lying Tudor house into a mock mediaeval castle; nor that if you want a genuine Gothick feeling with soaring columns and secret romantic chambers, it is a bad idea to start with a house which - assuming you need to keep the few bedrooms - has only 13 feet head-room. But you *can* draw elevations which, without comment, drive that point home. And you can have your portrait painted, life-size, with your hand holding a grand gothic exterior plan, which everyone will see in centuries to come. I can imagine no more graceful tribute from the owner of the Vyne to the owner of Strawberry Hill.

So there we are. There will be other explanations of how John and Horace resolved their different aspirations for the Vyne, but this is the version on offer to you this evening. Ladies and gentlemen, thank you for your kind attention.

JOHN CHUTE - COMMEMORATIONS

left: pen-portrait by the fashionable artist Rosalba, Florence 1741.

below: the concluding paragraphs of Horace Walpole's brief "history of The Vine", in which - after snide comment on Anthony Chute's "alterations rather than improvements" - he listed the "Beauties" of John's work, whom he praised as "an able geometrician ... an Exquisite Architect of the purest taste both in the Grecian and Gothic Styles"

(Since John had not done all that much to implement the gothicising `Inventionary`, Horace could not resist inserting here something wholly irrelevant to The Vyne, viz. that John had produced a chaste Gothic design at Donnington!)

> ...a type of Inigo Jones.
>
> Anthony Chute Esq. the last Descendent but One from the Speaker's eldest Son, sashed the garden-front, & made many alterations rather than improvements.
>
> But the principal additional Beauties to the Vine were the Works of his younger Brother John Chute, who was an able Geometrician; & was an Exquisite Architect, & of the purest taste both in the Grecian & Gothic Styles. He erected from his own designs the beautifull Scenery of the Staircase with its two Vestibules, tho' unfortunately cramped by want of larger Space. He improved the front of the House, enlarged the stoned Hall, decorated the Antichapel, & the Chapel itself, the sides of which above the Stalls were painted by Signor Roma from one of the Greek Isles; & built the pretty Chapel on the right hand, to receive the fine tomb & cumbent figure in his robes of his ancestor the Speaker.
>
> Mr John Chute enlarged the water, built the bridge, cut the Walks in Morgueson & erected there the Statue of the Druid, & he too made and planted the noble Terrace that parts the road from his own grounds.
>
> Mr John Chute gave the Designs for the Seat of Mr Andrews under Donnington Castle in Berkshire near Spinhamland; as chaste a Specimen of Gothic Architecture as exists any where.
>
> Orford
> March 18th 1793.

PRIVATE LIVES AT THE VYNE AROUND 1800

TWO ARTICLES BY RACHEL CHUTE (1876-1968)

---

1. COURTSHIP AND MARRIAGE

Towards the close of the 18th Century there were living at Oakley Hall a Mr and Mrs Bramston. Mrs Bramston before her marriage had been Miss Mary Chute of the Vine (so spelt for a short period) .

She was a great letter writer, and one of her chief correspondents was her husband's cousin, Mrs. Hicks Beach. Most of the letters consist of friendly, rambling small talk; but they contain in places, delightful glimpses of life in the past. Especially vivid are those which concern the courtship and marriage of Mrs. Bramston's sister, Ann Rachel Chute.

Feelers

The first of of these is dated February, 1793. It is evidently written in reply to a letter from Mrs. Hicks Beach, saying that her brother-in-law, William Hicks, would like to pay his attentions to Miss Chute. She wishes to know whether Mrs. Bramston thinks that these would be acceptable. Mrs. Bramston writes back:

"Your intelligence has not surprised me tho it has rather puzzled me ... I have some old fashioned notions of Delecacy that perhaps are now Obsolete. I do not think I should act a sister's part to endeavour to find out her Sentiments and send them to you unknown to her. But as you ask me for my own opinion, I shall give it. I have not the least reason to think that should a proposal be made, it would be rejected. The Senior part of the family I know she much admires, and I never heard her speak otherwise than well of the Gentleman in Question.

Difficulties

Evidently Mr. Hicks was encouraged, and the wooing goes forward. There were, however, difficulties. Mr.Hicks lived in Gloucestershire and Miss Chute lived at the Vyne, with an unmarried brother and sister. And her brother was a Member of Parliament, and often away in London.

"Therefore," writes Mrs. Bramston, "as Mr. C. is now in town, a vis at the V would, I think, lay both parties under very disagreeable circumstances, and I think at all times a personal declaration is very awkward on both sides. It appears to me that a letter from the Gent to Mr. C . . . or from Lady H. (Mr. Hicks' mother) to the lady, would be the most desirable manner, and I think in the Circumstances, the latter to be preferred."

Terrible Faces

Perhaps Mrs. Bramston was wise in recommending that this particular proposal should not be made in person; for we are told that William Hicks had a very bad stammer, and made terrible faces when he spoke.

The next letter expresses a doubt whether Lady Hicks will approve of a proposal being made by letter. Mrs Bramston is worried. She would like to ask William to come and stay at Oakley Hall; but great alterations to the house are going on.

"We have no other Bed up but what we sleep in; our kitchen is not finished, our servants are not in; we have only one room below and one above furnished."

She suggests that Mrs. Hicks Beach might go and stay at the Vyne.

"You could send a letter by a servant the day before, to say you would call at the Vine for a day or two, and then you might stay for as long as you like ... 1 can meet you at the Vine, so that I think this affair would be arranged without the formality that generally attends these matters."

Etiquettes
Mrs. Bramston is well aware that things may still be difficult.
" I often say I wonder there are any Weddings, for there are so many etiquettes that it requires as much deliberation as settling the affairs of a Nation."
However all went well. We do not know how the final result was reached, but the last letter gives a full account of the wedding in Sherborne St. John Church, on October 8th, 1793.

Intimate Wedding
We note that the wedding guests were very few in number. Only those relations who lived near to the Vyne and the friends who lived at Beaurepaire a mile away seem to have been there. Neither the bridegroom's parents nor the sister-in-law, who had been so intimately concerned, were present. This was quite correct according to the custom of the time, when weddings were thought of as intimate occasions, and large gatherings of relations and friends were not expected.

In this last letter, Mrs. Bramston is staying with her brother at the Vyne. She takes advantage of his privilege as a Member of Parliament to "frank" her letter, by putting his signature on its outside cover. This will mean that it will travel free of postage charges, which would otherwise have had to be paid by the recipient. The ink of Mr. Chute's signature is still as black as on the day when it was written.

What the Ladies were wearing
Here is the account:
"I know you will have a curiosity to hear all about our proceedings yesterday; and will give you a slight sketch. To begin with the Bride, who was arrayed in a Clear Book Muslin Jacket and Coat which was very full and very long, and bound with white satten ribband which looked very Handsome over a white silk petticoat, a white satten Bonnet; with a band of Gouffred white Feathers and one white (long?)

feather; a lawn Cloak bound with Valencienne Lace, and I assure you she looked very Elegantly Dressed.

Mrs. Bramston "(herself)" in a Muslin petticoat with a Quilling at bottom, a clear work'd Muslin robe Pink satten Hat, a Bouffant round the Crown and white feather pink sash and shoes, very smart and looked like a Paisanne on the stage. Mrs Brocas (of Beaurepaire) in a beautiful clear Muslin worked in small sprays of Lilac and Green, new. Miss Chute in a white Persian robe, Green Cloud, muslin petticoat, Yellow Hat, Lilac ribbands."

A cloud was probably a long scarf. The name survived into the late 19th century as a name for a very soft black woollen tubular scarf, worn by old ladies.

The universal wearing of muslin must have been very chilly in an unheated church at this time of year. It was, however, in great favour at this period, its introduction from India having given ladies for the first time the possibility of wearing a more delicate material than the stiff brocades hitherto in general use for ceremonial occasions.

Finally we hear of Miss Augusta Bramston. She was Mr Bramston's unmarried sister, and lived at Oakley Hall. She was always given the courtesy title of "Mrs." according to the custom of the time for ladies who had attained a certain age. We note that she wore her hair powdered in the fashion of the previous generation as might have been expected in the case of a somewhat older woman.

"Mrs A. B. , new muslen gown, lilac ribbands, Her Hair powdered and Black Satten Shoes. All the Gentlemen in New Habitiments. We had 3 carriages to Church where we all behaved very well... We spent the day very pleasantly, and it went off much better than those days generally do."
A very satisfactory end to the story.

2. CAROLINE'S LIFE AT THE VYNE

BY RACHEL CHUTE (1876-1968)

William John Chute, owner of the Vyne from 1790 to 1824, had no children. He had a second cousin, James Wiggett, with whom he had been at college, and to whom he was much attached.

James Wiggett was rector of Crudwell in Wiltshire. He had been left a widower with a young family of two boys and five girls. Mr. and Mrs. Chute were fond of children and they offered to take one of the little girls, to bring up as their own. So in the year 1803, Caroline Wiggett, aged three-and-a-half, came to the Vyne to live there as an adopted niece. Later Mr. Chute and his brother Thomas decided to choose Caroline's brother William to be their heir.

Memoirs
Both brother and sister have left notes of their early memories about the house and the village, and some of these notes are of considerable interest. The first public event of which Caroline tells is the jubilee of George III in 1810 and the way in which it was locally kept. She says:

"We gave a dinner to all the poor, and placed two old villagers who had served their masters 50 years top and bottom of the table, with crowns on their heads. Old Bush, the butler, was also one of the half-century employees. He let off some fireworks in the evening, made by himself, which delighted me.

Waterloo Night
The next public celebration took place in honour of the battle of Waterloo; Caroline says: "We gave a dinner to all the poor on a grander scale than at the jubilee, adding a band and dancing, and illuminated the house, having a most brilliant effect from the road. I prepared it all myself, by making clay candlesticks with so many candles in each window, all over the front; and they were all to be lighted at a moment's notice, just before the people left. It was such a surprise, and there was such a hurrahing. There must have been about 30 windows on the front of the house, so that the making of the candlesticks must have been quite a big business.

Sunday School and the Church
Another kind of activity is then reported: "Next year, my aunt opened a Sunday-school, then almost an unheard of thing. We attended the whole day, in two cottages, one for boys, the other for girls; but in a year we had so many scholars that we adjourned to the present Rectory. [This was then unoccupied]

"Sherborne St. John church in those days had only one aisle, and there were high pews on each side, and a large square one opposite the pulpit called the Squire's Pew. This was a large room with a ceiling over it, and the only opening for air or light was given by some twisted rails just below the ceiling; the Brocas pew was over it, but was used as a Gallery for the barrel organ and children who sang there. It seems likely as the Chutes and the Brocases (who lived at Beaurepaire) were frequently quarrelling in former days, that they had quarrelled about the site of their pews, and that the dispute had been settled by one being placed over the other.

"The pulpit was covered with red cloth; but many years after, it was discovered that the pulpit itself was made of oak, and beautifully carved, so the drapery was taken off.

"In the lower part of the Church sat all the poor women, on not much better than benches with backs. In the gallery the singers and other men sat; not called a choir in those days.

."Smallbones was clerk for many years, and sat under the clergyman's desk. As he played the bassoon at the last Amen, he had to walk up to the gallery.

"Mr. Austen was the vicar. He used to ride over from Steventon where he lived. In Lent all the young people of the parish stood before him in the Church before the first singing, to say the Catechism.

"When I was old enough I was one of them, and trembled when Smallbones in a most sonorous voice cried out, 'Children come and say your catechism!' Then the pews opened to let out the various children. I was so glad when my turn was over.

"Edward Austen used sometimes to accompany his father: and when he did so, he said it with us. The school children consisted of Aunt Chute's dozen, who she clothed alike. They used formerly to sit round the communion rails: but when the Sunday School was set up, they were obliged to sit in the middle of the Church.

Clothes

"The women mostly wore nice Bath cloaking, which every winter was given to them in turn with blankets, rugs, and swansdown waistcoats for the men.

"When I was able to buy and give away on my own account, having a large Sunday School, each year a dinner was given to the children, up the avenue, of roast beef, and plum pudding and gooseberry pies. They wore white tippets and aprons, and straw bonnets trimmed with pink, as a uniform.

"I could not entirely clothe so many, though I had had before six little children who I did clothe, and made the frocks myself. They used to come down to me on a Sunday for me to teach, which I began at 12 years old; but when the larger school was formed, of course there was no necessity for the smaller one.

"I gave the hand organ to the church,

which was put up over our pew in one called the Brocas pew. It was not a good situation for it, but there was no other. I took a great deal of trouble in teaching the girls to sing, which they did very nicely. Once a week they came to the Vyne to practise. Once I went to the organ; but it was hard work.

The Dorcas Shop

"At Michaelmas we held the Dorcas shop in the chapel parlour which lasted a week; having all sorts of materials etc., from Basingstoke. I was shop keeper; Aunt Chute, secretary or bill-maker. Calico, prints, stockings, sheeting etc. were sold, the people having contributed half the price. They were delighted, thinking the materials very good; but some of them were tiresome and particular in choosing. I have stood for seven hours yarding off calico, it was very fatiguing, and nearly knocked me up; but we led a quiet life, and it was a change.

Caroline's 21st Birthday

"The great era of my life was the celebration of my 21st birthday. Not one of my happiest days, but the happiest day of my life.

"I determined to give a dinner to all the poor of the parish; knowing that more good and real pleasure to myself and others could be given by that means than by a foolish ball to the rich.

"I had a glorious day - July, 7,1820. Long tables were placed up the avenue with green arches top and bottom. The school children's table was placed across one end of the large one. The bit of green lawn in front was well mowed; a beautiful platform covered with evergreens and flags was erected for the band and dancing.

"Each family had a ticket given them by my aunt according to their numbers, for beer, which they presented to the butler, so that all had enough and not too much. An ox was killed for the purpose and roast beef, veal, plenty of vegetables, gooseberry pies and plum pudding was the dinner.

"They all came down in procession headed by the band, and school children dressed in white tippets and aprons; the boys, pinafores with pink rosettes on each; banners in pink and white; and the villagers had made me a beautiful flag in white silk and gold letters, with 'Caroline for ever' on it.

"A poor woman having heard that I wished as many as possible to wear a pink rosette, brought up old ribbon, dyed it, made rosettes and sold them; so that when the procession came down the gravel walk, they all marched round me making their obeisance, as they took their seats at the tables. The children sang the grace made for the occasion. I was almost overcome, and I heard that Uncle Chute's tears even were seen. A tea was given from six to eight to the tenants' wives and daughters, with large iced plum cakes. They came in and out as they liked. The tenants had their punch and smoking in the steward's room. By 11 o'clock all was as quiet as if nothing had happened, and I went to my bed tired, but much gratified with the day's proceedings, for all went off so well.

Vaccinations in the Kitchen
Mrs. Chute (usually called in the village "Lady Chute" though she had no claim to the title), was a woman with many interests. Mr. William Clift, a member of a much respected farmer family, once told the present writer that he well remembered coming up to the Vyne with a party of other children about the year 1838, to be vaccinated by Mrs. Chute in the big stone floored kitchen. He especially remembered the plate of raisins placed on the long kitchen table to be given to the children as a reward for submitting to the vaccination, and to keep them from crying.

Painting and Reading
Mrs. Chute was fond of painting, and many oil paintings formerly hung on the walls at the Vyne copied by her from paintings mostly by masters of the 17th century. These copies probably had been made when she and Mr. Chute were staying in London on account of his duties as a member of Parliament. She was a reader, and entered in her little red diaries the name of the books she was reading; she always had on hand a volume of sermons, and a volume of history, chosen from among the many leather-bound volumes still on the shelves of the library at the Vyne.

Music for Visitors
Mrs. Chute had a sister who was married to Mr. Charles Smith of Suttons Park [in Essex]. The Smiths had a large family, and nephews and nieces from Sutton were frequent visitors at the Vyne. Caroline writes:

"One of our amusements was, before the gentlemen joined us after dinner, to stand behind the pillars in the hall and sing trios, and suddenly the dining room door would open, and we received such applause and encores. Ours was real music."

Young William Wiggett Makes A Mark
The way in which William Wiggett became well known to Mr. and Mrs. Chute is delightfully told by his sister:
"About the year 1819 or 1820 my dear brother William was asked by my uncle to spend part of his long vacation with us; you can imagine the pleasure it was to me. He slept in Uncle Thomas' room, and we used to chat between the doors." (William was slightly younger than Caroline.)
"He was a great favourite with all the household; so sweet in his manner, gentle, good tempered, and unobtrusive. He contented himself with reading and walking, playing the flute and singing with me.

"Now and then Uncle Chute would say 'Wiggett, will you like a ride?' or 'will you go out shooting?' which of course William was glad enough to do for a change, though quite satisfied without these. By that time we had a billiard table, and many games we had together.
"These visits made my uncle well acquainted with William's character, and they soon saw how fitted he was to be the future owner of the house."

Mr. Chute died in 1824 and his brother Thomas in 1827, but the arrangement was that Mrs. Chute should continue in possession of the Vyne during her lifetime. So she and Caroline went on living there together. Neither of them were strong; and frequent visits from the local doctor (called "the surgeon") were necessary.

Enter Dr Workman
The consideration and status given to "the surgeon" in those days were very poor. It is amusing to read in Mrs. Chute's little red diaries "Workman came today" (many times repeated). After a while, however, more respect was shown and the notes say "Dr. Workman came today." Later on came a still further change: "Tom Workman came today." After this we are not so much surprised to hear that Tom Workman and Caroline have become engaged.

It was a happy marriage. Dr. and Mrs. Workman lived at Brambleys, a nice old house with a charming garden, which was then on the outskirts of Basingstoke. It is now well known to most residents as the home of the many clinics which are held in its spacious rooms.

Caroline writes, "When Tom went out in his carriage, I enjoyed going round with him. I often took the reins, and we used to sing duets as we went along."

Wiggett Chute
William Wiggett succeeded to the estate when Mr. Thomas Chute died in 1827, and he then, as directed by his cousin's will, took the name of Chute in addition to his own. His recollections begin with a description of his father:
"My Father was a great Beau in his younger days, and like Mr. William Chute was very deferential to Ladies, and would never bear the familiarity with them of later days.

Deference to Ladies
" In my Boyish days it was the custom for the Ladies to walk down to dinner first, the Gentlemen following them, and when a little later the distance between them was diminished by their walking down together, the Gentlemen only touched the Lady's hand with the tips of his fingers. I can well remember my Father's horror at being desired to give his arm to his dinner Partner."
William Wiggett Chute came to live at the Vyne when Mrs. Chute died in 1842. He found that the estate needed much attention.

Estate in Decline
"All the upper lands were unenclosed and held on half yearly tenures, and were divided into numerous small plots, divided by grassy banks or balks and occupied by different tenants in indiscriminate confusion. The whole of the fields were open to all the various occupiers in common, so that the growing of turnips or any kind of roots or winter crop was impossible, whereas thistles and weeds of all kinds abounded.
"The woodlands were divided into small enclosures, bounded on all sides by wide oak and hazel rows, or rather little coppices, and being undrained and excluded from the sun, consequently very wet, were of little value.
"The property was divided into small occupations, rented in some cases by tenants who lived at Basingstoke or elsewhere, there being no house on their farms; a very few of the Tenants had any Capital, or were able to pay their rents with any regularity, and they were always in arrears with their payments.
"The roads - if roads they could be called, for they were little better than driftways, and generally impassable by anything but carts or wagons - were very bad, and I have seen Mrs. William Chute's carriage stuck in the mud on the hill in the middle of the village.

Last Place on Earth
"It was possible to drive from the village to the Vyne; but impossible to go beyond the Vyne stables on wheels, giving rise to the old saying that the Vyne was the last place made on earth, and that Beaurepaire was made after it."

(printed in *Hampshire*, May 1966)

MARRIAGE AND CLASS IN THE 19TH CENTURY

For readers who would like to meet the Vyne's inhabitants more closely, there are more than 200 pages of surviving 19th C. letters and memoirs to bring them to life: The letters of Eliza Chute, wife of William John, and those of Jane Austen; the reminiscences of Jane's niece Caroline, of Caroline Wiggett and of her brother Wm. Wiggett Chute. And Eliza's diaries 1792-1820 survive in Hants archives.

Here we offer just one example. Since Caroline Wiggett is the most `human` of our family sources, we copy the letter she wrote to her brother William congratulating him on his engagement to Martha Buckworth and, with anxiety and shame, admitting her own engagement to the family doctor, Thomas Workman. The problem which rends her conscience is that the good doctor is not officially of her social class, she being the Chutes` adopted niece. (Eliza seems to damn the betrothal with faint praise, but we wonder how much effort *she* had made to find Caroline a more `suitable` husband.)

From the Vyne
9th Jan 1837

To W L Wiggett-Chute, Esqre, at Pickenham

Congratulate you my own dearest brother that I will and do with all the heart & soul of an affectionate sister. You seem indeed to have made a most excellent choice, & only may your dear Martha make you as good a wife as you deserve to possess, I remember Mr Buckworth the father I conclude but you do not mention her age, think not to tire me with any particulars of a future sister who I shall love, if not for herself for her husband's sake, never mind, in _____ if she is the person you love. I have so often heard you really were going to be married that I begin to believe it, I suppose people soon see into hearts, & that one person`s idea is soon turned into many. I shall long to hear all about it which I shall soon do as you are so soon coming, I quite agree it will not do to tell Aunt A. by letter as she is more absent than ever but she will be delighted ever taking an interest in you but do not put off your marriage too long... your wife takes you for better for worse & it is only fancy you are not rich enough for you need not launch out with splendour, you will let your best days pass otherwise; you speak as all lovers do lover like. Spencer was thought so <u>cool</u> till he was in love, then that somehow vanishes.
How delighted poor Papsy will be! his little eyes will twinkle more than ever, you may depend on my keeping the secret.

Now dear as you have told yours, & that you are <u>in love</u>, and can have therefore a fellow feeling for a fellow creature, & that creature a sister, who except one, loves you better than any earthly being,

I must open my heart and come out at once with what half <u>kills</u> me, till you say you will not reject, & despise, your poor sister Caroline, who has taken a step for her own happiness, but with the chance of losing the affection of some part of her family, & perhaps her own beloved William;

I know you now guess what I am going to say, I am engaged, & to the only Being who could ever make me happy, to my own Dr. Mr. Workman; if I were young and healthy it would be different, but soon likely to be left alone in the world, even now obliged to fly from it, do not blame me for having chosen a <u>gentleman</u>, well educated, much beloved, highly respected, & who has proved himself the kindest of the kind husbands, who has always liked me, who is now so attached to me, who I know so well, whose profession <u>I like</u> but at the same time is the only thing against it, & after all, what is it? That he is a surgeon, who Mrs J. Portal has every day for 2 hours at a time, & in God's eyes, what are any of us?

Now dear I have said this much, I must say how it stands. Except to one or two it is a profound secret, not for my sake but for his, he could not resist telling me his mind so soon, not for want of affection to his late wife, but because he knew I fear my feelings & thought suspense hurt my health then the last words of his poor wife were, to <u>love me</u>. But as he can visit me as the M.D. no one thinks of it, & the truth as I believe will be a surprise to few, & then it will be a 9 days wonder.

Aunt C. [Eliza Chute] I told it to directly and she told me, she had said she always thought it would be; & she really seems quite happy, for tho' she says it is not brilliant, she likes him, & I am not so young, & she is glad I should have a Protector. Frances I mentioned it to & told her to find out any of your feelings but not to tell, so pray do not appear to know it, unless you choose to ask Aunt C what she thinks as if by chance, then perhaps she may say. We cannot be married till the twelvemonth is over, so best not known.

Maria Smith knows it, I told her, to have someone to whom I could talk of it; for really I did not know how I adored him, & only pray I may not too much, & that I may make him as good a wife as he deserves to have; anxiety I shall have plenty of, but the dispositions of his children are sweet, & in a short time we shall make over 2000 per annum, plenty, & I have my own fortune at all costs, oh! if it pleases the Almighty to spare him to me!
[He was a widower in poor health and had several sickly children]

I have no doubt of my happiness, but I tremble at that, he has had so much anxiety, & is so harassed about, that a constitution cannot last for ever, poor man! I seem his only comfort, & he does not marry me from any ideas of station, but from pure love; for his family are very independent, & would not like it, thinking me sickly & ___ but Mr W. is doing all he can to correct my temper, & Aunt C told him she thought he would improve me; he is so like you in many things.

We are to live at present in Mr _____ 's house. It is singular the thing Aunt C wished settled before she died should be so in prospect at the same time. She has been more than usually kind of late, so that it has been a pleasure to live here, except that her health is not nearly so good, she owns it now the keeping up too; some how I cannot but think she feels a something that tells her time will not be long here, so surely noone ought to regret my choice. She is today gone to Glanville, for a few days, I have often been backwards & forwards, but perhaps my attraction is here & she does not mind that

I am exceedingly comfortable, & if it were not for my blisters, & my hand are better, but I had a bad spasm at my heart a day ago, poor Mr W. had never before been with me in a bad one, & he was quite alarmed indeed they are awful, & when one hears of the numbers going off poor Mr Ponsonby died at M_____ Green, just as he was sitting down to dinner with his family, of a heart complaint I believe.

I trust your Martha has some health, we are such poor things. I shall long to see her. I wrote to Anna I should go to Bath when you did, that is if you acknowledge me as a sister, which indeed I trust you will as we do not alas often meet. & I can bear little anxiety of mind; it will be such a relief to me to know that in gaining the affections of a beloved husband, I lose not those of a darling brother; for there is no disgrace in the match, many have done the like, my family are not necessary to me, still I should not like to give them up.

Our two letters are mutually interesting to each other, mine seems only filled up with what will not be so to you, but I have no news to tell, but to say I shall ever be

Your attachd affec sister
-    C Wiggett

WHAT`S IN A NAME ?

CHUTE

The earliest-dated interpretation of the name comes, on the authority of Manning`s "Lives of the Speakers" (publ.1851), from Silas Taylor, a 17th C. antiquarian in correspondence with CC I, who considered that the name *"carries the memorial of the almost forgotten third nation of the Germans that conquered the Britons..."* (i.e. the Jutes). This is consistent with a tradition that Chute was one of the earliest surnames to be used in Norman England, since it would be a natural identification for people of an unusual racial origin or language. The question, <u>which</u> set of Jutes the name might mean, is something we will consider on p.111.

The French word *chute* is shunned as a surname because of its shameful connotations, e.g. bankruptcy, hair-loss, offcuts, and waste disposal. For pleasant things like waterfalls their normal word is *cascade*. In Wiltshire there is Chute Forest and its group of villages named from *chute*, the old Saxon word for forest (written `cetum` in Domesday Book). But we have no known connection there. To have named a family "Wood" would have been pointless as an identification in the early Middle Ages when so much of the island was covered in trees. Later on we do find the name "de Chut" in MSS for people unrelated to us; they perhaps, and the families named Chuter, could have been the ones associated with forests or wood-working. On p.107 we enlarge on this question and deal with a red herring in the Somerset river Chew, on which lie Chuton (Chewton) villages.

PS. Chute is preserved as a `middle name` in the Cottrell and Ellis families, of original Chute blood; also, strangely, in Marden, Herefordshire, where George Chute (p.145) married the local heiress.

CHALONER

The name is of great age, meaning a weaver or seller of bed-coverings. It comes from the Middle English word *"chaloun"*- a blanket of the type made at Chalons-sur-Marne, the old centre of the Gaulish tribe known in Latin as Catalauni.

Speaker Chute`s mother was Ursula Chaloner, and in his honour the Chute family have a habit of naming sons "Chaloner", whether related to him by blood or not. There are "Chaloner Chutes" from Ireland and America and in the Lobb Chute and Wiggett Chute lineages. However, in the period and area covered by this book, the name seems not to have brought much luck.

<u>Having earned high honour by 1600, the Chaloner family then lost it with a vengeance</u>: -

In 1643   Richard Chaloner, eminent citizen & linen draper of London, was condemned for trying to bring King and Parliament to a negotiated settlement without bloodshed. Cromwell called this treason, and Chaloner was hanged in front of his house.

In 1649   Thomas and James Chaloner were Regicides, members of the court which condemned Charles I to death; both brothers met violent deaths in 1660/1.

In 1692   William Chaloner "the notorious coyner" was hanged at Tyburn.

<u>For 300 years the name scarcely helped the Chutes</u>: -

Chaloner Chute I died from frustration and overwork 3 months after becoming Speaker.
Chaloner Chute II had a miserable life at Lady Dacre`s hands and died at 36.
Chaloner Chute III suffered likewise from the Lady and only survived to 29.
Chaloner Chute IV (Edward`s 2nd son) died in Holland aged only 16.
The very next Chaloner C (son of Thos. Lobb Chute) died when he was 31 as a result of bathing in the early morning after a Ball and catching fever.
Chaloner William C (19th C. historian) had chronic bad health and succumbed at 54.
Challoner Francis C, soldier from Ireland, was killed shortly after reaching France in 1914.

NAMES IN THE SERVANTS' HALL

Using Internet, everyone can now research their ancestry. Having looked at the Chutes of the Vyne we must ask: `what of the Servants of the Vyne?` In its old sense they were very much part of the `family`. Their labours and loyalty preserved the house, cushioned the Chutes and looked after their young children. We cannot pretend to re-create here the range of their tasks or the conditions they endured in that cold, clammy house and its stables. From 5 a.m., fires were lit, livestock needed attention, and servants who `lived out` were walking to work in all weathers. However sympathetic the Chutes were as employers, the long day's work of a servant battling against dirt, damp and disorder, was primitive, exhausting and unhealthy. At day's end, by lamplight, overalls and aprons must be ironed and spotless, ready for the morning inspection by the Housekeeper when (after 1842 at least) the staff lined up in the Ante-Chapel, ready for the Chutes to lead them into Chapel.

> *(The writer remembers this routine in the 1930's, punctually at 8.20 a.m. Prayers were read by Charles Chute (later Sir Charles) as Head of the Family; we then waited in the Chapel Parlour and discussed the day's plans, so as to give the staff time to set out hot breakfast in chafing dishes on the sideboard in the Saloon - which was then used as dining room.)*

Most of those servants have, alas, no memorial. But as a late gesture of appreciation, we can repeat here the surnames of a few who, according to Census records, worked at the Vyne about a century ago. This may encourage others to trace their families and history.

In 1871: Allam, Carter, Caulcotte, Coling, Coskeran, Darvis, Elcox, Lewis, Newby, Park, Souch, Sparshett, Wright, Wynn.

In 1881: Binbridge, Gillingham, Gosling, Pearse.

In 1891: Dunn, Holloway, Kennard, Kneller, Miles, Smart, Stevens, Tigwell.

In 1901: Hobson, Best, Duffin, Durbridge, Hillier, Ilsley.

For 1871-1891 the names are of of female indoors staff; for 1901 when no Chutes were in residence, we name the men who maintained the stables and gardens. The Census (every 10 years) gives Christian names, ages and birthplaces. It is surprising how few were born near the Vyne, since in the 19th C., to help feed her family, many a girl began her working life by `going into service` near home. But we find these women born as far away as Shropshire, Norfolk, Worcestershire, Dorset. Mr and Mrs Hobson were Irish. Only some 15 families in our sample were even from Hampshire. Is there an interesting explanation?

Unfortunately we cannot bring this list more up to date, because 1901 is the last year for which Census date are released to the public. In the 1930's, the writer remembers, there were about five female staff in the house led by "Wellman", the friendly and efficient lady Housekeeper. After 1939, people dispersed into war-work, Charles Chute became totally occupied serving the county, and Joan Chute somehow maintained The Vyne with Mr and Mrs Gibbs and part-time cleaners.

To all of those, named and unnamed, who served The Vyne through thick and thin, we surely owe an immeasurable debt.

CONTINUITY

Wars and changes of ownership are nothing new to The Vyne - as our story shows. The estate lives on happily today in the hands of the National Trust, and by their courtesy the old family has kept a connection through occasional weddings (*see opposite*) and reunions at a concert or play. Recently an added dimension has sprung from the Trust's "Visitors Book for Chutes", which records the `homecoming` of distant Chutes from Ireland, America and continental Europe. For them, and us, The Vyne supports any amount of ancestral pride.

Which brings us appropriately into our Part Two - the broad, deep stream of family history. Overleaf, we will introduce it with a fanfare of heraldry going back to 1268 !

"The most heavenly Chapel in the world" - as Horace Walpole called it - continues to draw Chutes to The Vyne for their weddings. When James and Rosemary were married here in 1994, they continued a tradition dating back to the time of Henry II, when a Chantry Chapel was licensed at the Vyne. It was consecrated by the Bishop of Winchester in 1202 and rebuilt on the present site in about 1520, with its famous stained glass and carved oak stalls. After 1750 John Chute gave the Chapel gothick wall-hangings, to please Walpole, and the Tomb Chamber to commemorate his ancestor, The Speaker.

In the main house, John's Classical Staircase provides a magnificent stage-set for a Chute bride of our time.

SECOND PART: 900 YEARS OF THE CHUTE FAMILY

THE BETHERSDEN CHUTES' HERALDIC ROLL 1268-1698*

Compiled by George Chute of Bethersden in 1698, to glorify his ancestors on his elevation to the baronetcy. Shields show Chute arms and those of wives/husbands.

Panels 1 to 4: 1268 - 1500

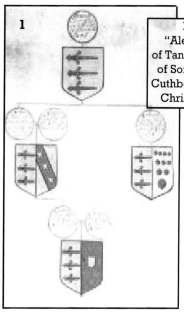

1. *left:* from "Alexander Chute of Tanton in the county of Somerset 1268" to Cuthbert Chute 1308 = Christian Chideake

2. *right:* through Phillipp 1332 and George 1344 to Ambrose = Anabell Chichester.

3 (*above right*): from Edmond = Dyonice Stourton 1379 to the brothers William, Henry, Anthony & Robert

4 (*near right*):
left: Anne Chute
centre: Robert Chute = Alice Barkley
right: Christopher Chute = Ammerika Wellgrove.
below centre: Charles Chute 1480 = daughter of Sir John Cheney, Kt.
(*this last marriage was key to the Chutes' later fortunes*)

(Edmond; cont/ opposite)

* See Family Trees 1 & 2 printed on pages 104 & 127

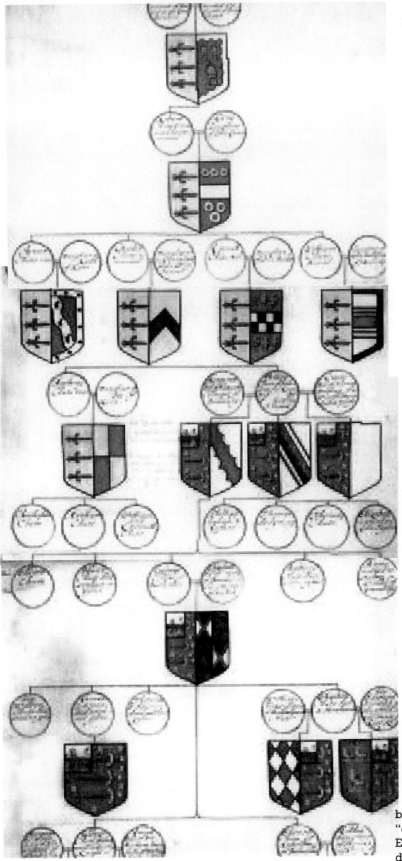

Edmond Chute with the claim that he "sould the mannor of Tanton to the Lord Denham" *(no mention of Edmond`s wife)*

Robert Chute "sonne and heire maried Jane daughter of John Lucas"

left to right: brothers Olyver, Charles, Lyonell and William *(only Charles`s descent is shown)*

left: Anthony C = "See of Kent" right: Philip`s 3 marriages, to Culpeper, Gyrling and "Dussing" *(actually Ensing);* the Canton first appears, top left corner of shield

above left: 4 sons of Anthony shown, but no descent, *(though Arthur was ancestor of the Vyne Chutes, and Lyonell of the huge American branch)* centre: George of Bethersden = Eliz. Gage

left: Sir Walter, James & Thomas, all unmarried. right: Elizabeth Chute`s marriages, to Fitzwilliam & Tirwhit.

bottom: Sir Geo. "of Stockwell", & Edward "of Appledore & Bethersden"

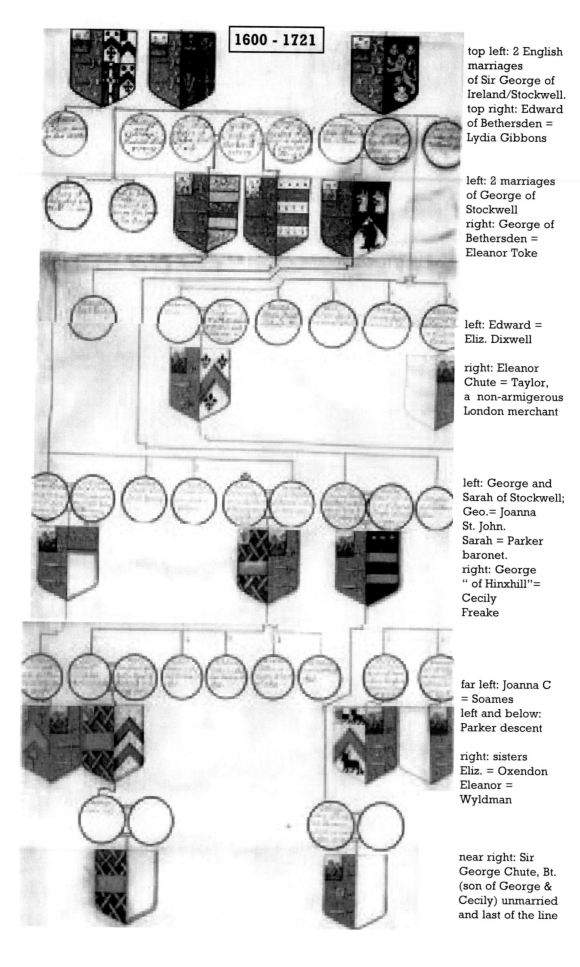

1600 - 1721

top left: 2 English marriages of Sir George of Ireland/Stockwell.
top right: Edward of Bethersden = Lydia Gibbons

left: 2 marriages of George of Stockwell
right: George of Bethersden = Eleanor Toke

left: Edward = Eliz. Dixwell

right: Eleanor Chute = Taylor, a non-armigerous London merchant

left: George and Sarah of Stockwell; Geo.= Joanna St. John.
Sarah = Parker baronet.
right: George " of Hinxhill"= Cecily Freake

far left: Joanna C = Soames
left and below: Parker descent

right: sisters Eliz. = Oxendon Eleanor = Wyldman

near right: Sir George Chute, Bt. (son of George & Cecily) unmarried and last of the line

SECOND PART
NINE CENTURIES OF THE CHUTE FAMILY

These "nine centuries" of Chute tradition stretch from **1066** when their reputed ancestor, perhaps a mercenary seaman of Jutish blood, served Count Robert de Mortain, the half-brother of William the Conqueror; through **1268** when the family tree begins with Alexander Chute of Taunton; and on to **1956** when the family resigned its symbolic centre at The Vyne. Within those time-limits, our book will focus on the family in England and Ireland, since the flourishing Chutes in America (founded 1634) have already published histories of their lineage.

Most 'gentry' families in England lack satisfactory mediaeval records to prove their private traditions, often because they came late to land-ownership or political power. The Chutes share this problem before 1500, though from then on, historical MSS fully confirm the family's tradition. And for the earlier centuries one need only reject a few odd claims which seem to have crept in (as was the fashion in the 16th century) with a view to 'dignifying' their ancestry.

One can therefore trace the family's long march up to national status, and give a full account of their tribulations in the religious turmoil from Reformation to Commonwealth, and their maturity into "county families" in Kent, Hampshire and in Irish Kerry.

For easy reading, however, we will leave such detail for an Appendix, and select for our narrative a few figures from different periods who strike us by their characters or events in their lives. These include men of the theatre and artist's studio, soldiers, politicians, a tobacco-ridden poet and (why not?) a black sheep, because the lawyer-Chutes who held The Vyne for 300 years are not typical of this many-sided family.

Their friendships add to the general interest. At The Vyne we saw the Chutes' relations with Thomas Gray, Horace Walpole, Jane Austen and the Duke of Wellington. Other famous names will follow, including the courtier/adventurer Walter Ralegh (*we will keep to his spelling*), the poets Donne and Lovelace, the actors Henry Irving and Ellen Terry and, in the 20th C., the artists Stanley Spencer and Eric Gill.

Those who seek ancestral Romance can of course hunt for clues in the misty Middle Ages and, if they hanker for a Norman connection, can embroider the legend of our Jutish forbear. But there is adventure enough in the historic period 1500-1660, when the family name was alternately blessed and reviled in the royal Court. Philip Chute saved the honour of Henry VIII; Sir George joined the queen's force against a Catholic invasion of Ireland; but the royal courtier Sir Walter Chute, who had fought alongside Ralegh against Spain for Elizabeth I, was thrown into the Tower of London by her successor James I.

Walter Chute struggled with the onset of the 17th C. scientific revolution, when sons first learned to reject their fathers' beliefs. But it was the more mundane threat of economic recession and civil war which induced Lionel and Rose Chute in 1634 to brave months in a small boat and face the monsters and demons shown on contemporary maps of America. Twenty-five years later, Chaloner Chute was to die in the attempt to formulate a democratic republic for England (which might have changed the whole course of American Independence). Happily Lionel and Rose survived and founded a dynasty in the New World, which forms the great majority of the Chute family today.

But to begin at the beginning, we pick up the family tree with the 13th century Alexander Chute, and then examine how a rude Jutish sailor's blood-line might become English gentry, make their money, and rise to the inner circle of the Tudor court. With Philip Chute to act as our 'mole' inside 16th C. government, the proven biographies will begin.

CHUTE FAMILY TREE - 1. FROM 1268 TO 1550

[it is not claimed to know names of Alexander's ancestors]

ALEXANDER CHUTE 1268, of Taunton, Somerset, England

JOHN = Jane Brumfield 1274   **RICHARD**

CUTHBERT = Christian Chideake 1308

JAMES = Miss Greenfield   **PHILIP** = Miss Britton 1322   **ANTHONY** = Anne Treforth

GEORGE = Miss Tirrell 1344   **JOANE** = Sir John Carminow Kt.

AMBROSE = Annabell Chichester *[sole recorded survivors of the Black Death]*

EDMOND = Dyonice Stourton 1379   **CHRISTIAN** = Ralph Menell

WILLIAM = dau. of
Archdeckne   **HENRY** = Joane Baskerville c.1420

ANTHONY = Miss Clifton

ROBERT, d. 1435
[marriage/issue not recorded]

ROBERT 1438 = Alice Berkeley   **ANNE** = Sir John
Ilsley St Maur

CHRISTOPHER =
Ammerica Waldegrave
[issue not recorded]

CHARLES = Miss Cheney

EDMOND "who in 1502 sold the Taunton lands and moved to Sussex"*(near the Kent border)*

ROBERT = Jane Lucas

OLIVER
=Miss Redd   **CHARLES**
= Miss Cripps, of Kent   **LYONELL**
= Miss Butler   **WILLIAM** = Miss
Badlesmere, of Tonbridge

ANTHONY
= Miss Gee of Kent   **(?) ARTHUR** =
Margaret Playters
of Ellough, Suffolk   **PHILIP, Standard-Bearer to King Henry VIII**
at the Siege of Boulogne 1544; Captain of Camber Castle;
for his valour, was awarded heraldic honours and
granted lands and monastic spoils in.Kent; d. 1566
3 times married:

= (1) Joan née Ensing, of
Winchelsea, widow
with son Thomas.   = (2) Margaret Culpeper
of Bedgebury, who bore
to Philip the children who
survived them   = (3) Eliz. Girling, of
Wrentham, Suffolk;
their 1 son d. infant.

ANTHONY`S DESCENT (Tree 4, p.160)          PHILIP`S DESCENT (Tree 2, p.127)

ALEXANDER - THE ARMIGER?

England has many levels of antiquity and legend. Glastonbury, in Somerset, in the south west of England, is one of those semi-magical places which draw people from afar to share a sense of mystery deeper than human memory.

We can picture **Alexander Chute**, one day around 1265, riding over from Taunton to Glastonbury with his sons John and Richard; they wanted to see the inauguration of a new Abbey, on a site that was already sacred. There had been an old pagan temple there, and then a 7th century Saxon church where kings were buried. Now came the 13th century Abbey (*below*). This building has long since been ruined, but the great new Kitchen which the Chutes also saw is wonderfully preserved (*next page*). Today his boys would most likely be coming for the pop music festival. Many other visitors are drawn here by the legends of Camelot - of King Arthur and the Round Table; or by a belief that Joseph of Arimathea visited the place and planted the famous Thorn which blooms at Christmas.

The Chutes of Somerset

`Alexander` is the name whom the Chutes give to the first in their family tree. He himself is a shadowy figure, but Somerset is where Chutes are first recorded. Documents from 1206 to 1775 show Chutes (variously spelt) at Taunton, Bridgwater, Wells and Combe St. Nicholas; they could well have been established in the county before these records began.

Somerset was a favoured place to live. This seems surprising since its centre used to be under water every winter, and it got its name from the summer pasture to which shepherds brought down their flocks when the flood receded. But it was warm, with oblique benefit from the Gulf Stream, and after land drainage it even produced wine from vines in the Glastonbury levels. The countryside was lush and easily navigable; a thriving economy developed, based on apples, corn and wool. Being near the coast, the county was strategically important. All this made it prime land for the Norman invaders.

Ousting the Anglo-Saxon landowners, King William seized for himself and his kin a large proportion of the productive land, leaving a few manors to his bishops. The bishopric of far-away Winchester had long since owned the manors of Taunton, and in 1066 a Norman ecclesiastic took it over. He became the richest bishop in England, and Taunton - where `Alexander Chute` held office - was one of his most lucrative estates.

The Abbot's Kitchen at Glastonbury, built in the time of Alexander Chute

Truth and Legend

For centuries the family named `Alexander Chute` as their first historical ancestor, and in this book we will treat him as historic, but of lower status than usually claimed. The ancestral parchment taken by Lionel Chute to America in 1634 (and recently rediscovered), and the monumental heraldic roll (pp.100-102) drawn for Sir George Chute of Bethersden in 1698, which John Chute inherited and brought to the Vyne, agree on the specific date, 1268, for Alexander; perhaps that of his death. Thus at some previous period, persuasive evidence of that ancestor may have survived. John was a stickler for accurate heraldry, and he copied the Alexander tradition on to his design for the Memorial Tomb at the Vyne.

The loss of that evidence, at least for now, leaves us with a critical choice: we can dismiss all `unproved tradition` as worthless, and remark that if Alexander was so important, why was no descendant given his name for 300 years? Or we can wait and see, discreetly suspending judgment in case modern scholarship and/or retrieval techniques bring corroboration or correction to light*. Your editor sees less harm in taking the latter course.

In this book, therefore, we will no longer put quote-marks round the name of `Alexander`, because Chutes (however named) <u>did</u> live in Somerset, they <u>did</u> develop within the grain of England's rise to nationhood, and they <u>were</u> undoubtedly gentry in the mid-1400s. At some stage their traditional pedigree mattered to them. Legend need not be `true` to be effective; a family which believes it has dignified ancestry behaves appropriately, and ends up *being* different to one which, for example, thinks itself `untouchable` or born to slavery.

If a reader feels it a waste of time to hold a candle to this doubtful parchment, he can turn directly to the historical Philip (p.122). Our next few pages will simply use traditional Chute names to reconstruct how an immigrant family might have risen through the dirt, plagues and obstacles of mediaeval Somerset into gentility, wealth and ultimate honour at Court.

---

* And we may remark that though the16th C. Philip was highly prestigious, very few Chutes bear his name.

Humble Beginnings

Written evidence of the family in Somerset begins with "Adam Chut", a tenant farmer at Taunton in 1206-9; the same name is shown in a list of Taunton farmers around 1245, and "Philip Choette" is given lands *in servicio regis* at Winford, north of Wells, in 1234. The will of "Margaret Chyte" in 1378 is the first surviving for a succession of Chutes at Bridgwater; these are named in land and taxation documents, as were their descendants at Shepton Mallet (1575), Wells (1634 on) and Combe St. Nicholas Manor (1650-1720). *(See p.203 ff for possibly longer tenure).* An Adam Chut and his son Richard, landholders in Madresfield, Worcestershire c. 1280, might have been early emigrants from Somerset.

These variations in spelling, quite normal for the period, can be further explained by the derivation of the family name from "Jute" - a foreign tribal name. It is noteworthy that, in researching historic MSS, almost* every Chewt, Chawte, Choute, and suchlike beginning with "Ch-" is found (where proof is feasible) to be a member of the same family. By contrast, those spelt "Shute" or "de Chute", e.g. in Hampshire and Dorset, are unconnected, being derived perhaps from the Saxon word *"chute"* for forest (*"cetum"* in Domesday).

> One should not read too much into English place-names, since Chuteley Hundred in Hampshire, Chute Forest in Wiltshire, and Chuton (originally Chewton) on the Somerset river Chew, all pre-Conquest names, have suffered numerous corruptions over time, and no connection has ever been found or reliably claimed between them and the family under discussion.

Nothing survives to connect these early Chute names. Unlike the nobility, they held no estate for which land-deeds might have been kept; systematic parish records for commoners only began after 1500. Therefore we may never know if Adam, the yeoman farmer, was a mainstream ancestor, or owed his surname to service under a Chut. But at least the surname is proved at Taunton, which is a first step to tracing the original Alexander.

The Chute Coat of Arms

"Gules three swords barways the points towards the dexter ppr. pomels and hilts Or" is the resounding heraldic blazon of the family arms which we see in brass on a tomb in Suffolk dated 1607, in stone on the Vyne's Classical Portico (c.1655), and in

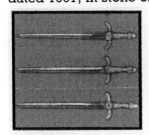

colour on John Chute's design for the Memorial Tomb. This version (*left*), its red field and its placement of swords, became 'traditional'. It suited the Chutes to imply that it went back to Alexander. But there is some confusion because in 1698 the Bethersden Chutes had a different armorial painted (*right & p.100*) for Alexander. Whichever was the initial form, it is evocative and uncomplicated. The number 3, of primitive magic overtones and recalling the Holy Trinity, was a natural talisman for any family, as were the uncompromising swords of the Norman overlords. Other families have based their arms on a 3-sword motif, but ours appears to be the simplest version. This suggests antiquity; indeed the historian of Kent, writing in 1798, described Philip Chute's inherited coat of arms as "antient". However, we have no evidence to suggest that they date back to Alexander.

---

* The alleged early "Chutes" in Kent have almost always proved to have been of the Chicche family.

The Bishop and his Bailiff

The first Chute to become an *armiger* displaying 'arms' had attained the rank of a 'gentleman', a member of the ruling military caste in Norman society.

A reason to doubt that this was Alexander is that he was <u>not</u>, as legend claims, "Lord of the Manor of Taunton". There were several manors in and around Taunton, and their legal lordship was continuously in possession of the Bishops of Winchester since before the Norman Conquest and into the 19th Century.

How could this material error have crept into the Chute tradition? There are more or less pardonable explanations. Consider first the practical situation in the 1200s.

The bishops were absentee landlords with busy lives based on palaces in Winchester, the first Norman capital of England, and then at Southwark in London. Their property was of huge geographical extent (*diagram opposite*) and they were important politicians and ecclesiastics. In an era of horse transport and indifferent roads, how often could they spare time to visit a distant place like Taunton?

Sheer remoteness from Court meant that the bishop's deputy at Taunton, be he Bailiff or Steward, was *de facto* Lord of the Manors in the eyes of the neighbourhood. He ran the estate; he stood in as chief of defence when the constable of Taunton Castle (*above and left*) was in process of change-over (the post being held by senior gentry in rotation); he dispensed civil justice at the manor courts, received rents and fines, and each year he went to the bishop's palace to render the manor's financial accounts to his Chief Steward at a ceremonial audit.

This, we surmise, was Alexander's actual position; as an "office of dignity" it might have entitled the holder to assume heraldic arms. But in any case, if he gave satisfaction the bishop might let him pass on the position to his son, and so on. This could reputably explain how the Chutes came to be recorded as "Lords of the Manor".

Nothing remains of a former manor-house, but Taunton Castle, built by bishops of Winchester between the 12th-15th centuries, much slighted in later wars and recently restored, is now a museum and a fine hotel. The first castle on this site was built in about 700 A.D. by a powerful King Ina of Wessex, the founder of Glastonbury

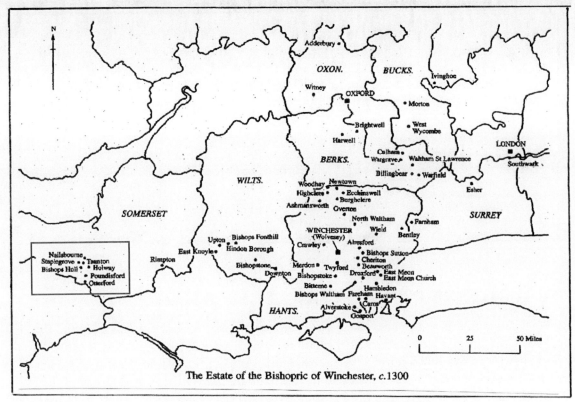

The Estate of the Bishopric of Winchester, c.1300

(Taunton and neighbouring manors are at far left)

Dignification

Another explanation, of course, is that the Chutes fell into the unscrupulous practice of deliberate family `dignification` after 1500.

England`s famous class system dates back to the 11th C. racial division of society into Normans (victors) and Everyone Else (vanquished natives). Before long most people`s origins were mixed beyond trace, but the lingering magic of class and birth drove the *nouveaux riches* to invent for themselves Norman ancestries. (Even today in republican America, babies are baptised Norman, Herbert (of lordly birth), Eugene, etc.)

Ironically, while Henry VIII was downgrading the job prospects of the old nobility, families of the new rich jumped in to claim arms from the mediaeval period. So when Philip Chute, on rising in honour in the 1540s, added crest and motto to his family arms, we wonder if perhaps he also invented the two legends:

that Alexander Chute had been Lord of Taunton Manor, and that in 1502 the Chutes had sold *that* Manor (there were in fact several) to one "Lord Denham, from whom descend the Earls of Bridgwater".

The "Denham" legend is pure fiction; none of it fits the facts. We have now jumped ahead, far beyond Alexander, but an innocent explanation of the 1502 story is that a Chute of Taunton, wanting to move away, sold-up to his cousin from Bridgwater who had prospered in trade (which the snobby Tauntonian did not want to admit). Was this deal accidentally garbled in the record, or did some later Chute hope to win points at Court by inventing an ancestor who traded property with the nobility?

Whatever the explanation, both these modest, though untrue, dignifications won their way into`history`, and are still re-printed in the pages of Burke`s.

A few pages on, we will return to *terra firma* and re-create a Bailiff's daily work, and that of his wife. We can do this because the whole economic life of the Taunton Manors was summed up in Winchester Pipe Rolls - accounts and statistics - and some still survive from the 1200s. One good reason for reserving judgment on Alexander's status is that only two of these Pipe Rolls, for the years 1301 and 1410, have as yet been deciphered and published in English. We may yet be told more on Adam and Alexander.

But before reading the prosaic detail of crossbows, swans and the cost of clearing dung, we have to venture into mistier landscape, because for many Chutes the key question is - where did we come from? **What was Alexander's ancestry**?

Faced with the fantasies proclaimed on one Chute website, your editor felt obliged to re-examine history and traditions, and deduce a more likely tale. Yes, we have a quite romantic ancestor; but we need not dream of Crusades (too costly for Chutes) or unicorns (visible only to virgins), since he displays an even older myth, that of the Quest.

ANCESTRY BEFORE ALEXANDER

A thousand years in the past, there was a boy born in a settlement by the shore of the North Sea. Much later, a city called Hamburg would be built nearby, but in Viking days it was a flat agricultural plain, the diminished homeland of the old race of **Jutes**. In their folk-memory - the stories told round the fires on cold winter nights - one heroic saga was of the mighty ancestors Hengist and Horsa who had mounted an expedition to the isle of Britain, outwitted its king Vortigern, captured horses, women and treasure and with wonderful slaughter had created the great Kingdom of Kent. Exquisite Kentish jewellery was now among the artefacts traded daily at the great entrepot of Hedeby, not a day's ride from the boy's village. Some Jutes in England had taken over the Isle of Wight, and others (says the historian Bede) established distinct

Jutish enclaves within the Saxon-dominated counties of southern England. Yes, a tribal culture to be proud of.

But now, after the year 1000, Jutish survivors in their old homeland were being squeezed between aggressive kingdoms, Sweyn's Denmark to the north, Flemings and Franks to the south.

Jute ancestors from Hengist & Horsa's force in 449 A.D. Boars on the helmets advertise their ferocious courage. The Romans called them Gutae, from their Gothic origins

The boy left no records; it was left to one 12th century historian to report in a Latin manuscript that a man with a name like `Edvard le Choute` had once represented a Norman Count at a meeting at Dives during preparations for the 1066 conquest of England. There is no evidence that this man was our ancestor, but since that same Count, Robert of Mortain, took over much of Somerset - where Alexander Chute was to live - there is the possibility of a link.

Chute Traditions. For our own quest we inherit two generalities. One, the tradition that Chute (however spelt) was one of the earliest surnames used in England.

Two, the statement of the 17th century antiquarian Silas Domville Taylor, with whom Chaloner Chute the Speaker corresponded, that his surname "carries the memorial" of the Jutes.

Now if Alexander Chute was a dignitary in about 1260, we can be certain that the Jutes from whom he descended were not Hengist & Horsa`s men, who had long ago merged into Anglo-Saxon England. The Normans so heartily despised the `natives` as a race, that only an exceptional few were let into the social class of local government; we cannot see `native` Chutes as having had any claim to such privileged treatment. What other traditions exist?

"Baron Edouard"

The first `red herring` on our trail is a supposed ancestor "Baron" Edouard le Choute. Contemporary documents show that no Baron of that name had a command at the Battle of Hastings. All the Norman heroes of 1066 are listed on the roll of honour which one can see at Battle, Sussex; there is no such name on it. (In any case, England`s baronial families are thoroughly documented, and we are not among them.) Again, there is no mention of "le Choute", or any recognisable variant of the name, in Domesday Book, that exhaustive inventory of land-ownerships in England made for the Norman kings in 1087.

So the real Edvard was not noble or rich, and he lived among Normans who despised every other race. Yet after 8 generations his descendant appears as a man of dignity under a Norman bishop, a man proud to bear a name advertising his Jutish descent. To try and explain this paradox we must look into history books.

Finding Ships and Mariners for the 1066 Invasion

Duke William had an army, they say, of 25,000 knights and foot soldiers, plus four horses per knight. To get them across the Channel he suddenly needed thousands of ships. The main Norman fleet had gone to colonise Sicily, and William had not replaced the ships. His dukedom was now a successful land empire, marketing goods south and east into the Continent; the borders he defended were now inland.

So, as the Bayeux Tapestry graphically depicts, there was a burst of shipbuilding in Normandy, but local resources fell short of his demands. The Duke sent out for help.

Count Robert of Mortain (William`s half-brother) supplied nearly a fifth of all the 696 ships listed as being personal contributions of nobles and prelates. But where could the Count find 120 ships, after using every carpenter in his own forests? Brittany in the west and Flanders in the east were already providing their national fleets to help William, so Robert must have sent agents beyond Flanders and into Jutish homelands. It is probable that among the Jutes whom they bribed to join them were ship-owners whose ambition vaulted beyond their family farms. If one was named Edvard, he could have gone on to be Robert`s man at Dives.

ASSEMBLING A FLEET FOR THE NORMAN CONQUEST

The Bayeux Tapestry shows frenzied activity among Norman foresters, carpenters and ship-builders to prepare for the 1066 invasion of England.

But, as scholars have pointed out, even had there been enough manpower, and enough food for them on site, to build a large fleet within Normandy in so short a time (which is questionable), there were (a) problems of river access into inland forests for floating out tree-trunks and ships, and (b) few estuaries within each Count's domain, suitable for final ship construction and proving for seaworthiness. This would have created an intolerable bottleneck. Therefore William's Counts, especially Mortain whose domain was deep inland, were forced to seek additional ships from outside Normandy.

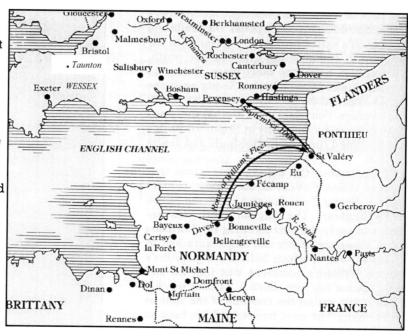

William assembled his fleet at Dives in May/June 1066, but was delayed there for months by unfavourable winds. His soldiers grew restless and food ran low. At this stage he would have sought all available advice from expert seamen. This is when an `Edouard` is said to have been called in by Count Robert of Mortain. Only after the fleet moved NE to St Valéry, and the local saint's image was paraded round the town, did the wind start to blow from the south and the ships at last sail to England.

Apart from the main flotilla to Pevensey, William sent detachments further west to head off any English reinforcements. We cannot know which route was taken by Edvard. After victory at Hastings, William swung his main force west and north via Winchester to Berkhamsted, where he received the royal family's surrender.

As for Edvard, he may have been a fisherman or coastal trader with just one boat. We cannot know his skills, but if indeed he once stood-in for Count Robert at an operational meeting, he may have shown some special maritime expertise which the Normans needed.

The Bayeux tapestry shows some ships carrying horses, others carrying armed men

William's army included a host of mercenaries and adventurers. But if Edvard, on landing, was noticed killing enough Englishmen, he could have risen in Count Robert's service. He is likely to have brought friends with him in 1066; speaking their own dialect together, they would naturally be known in England as "the Jutes".

The Conquest was not completed at once. There were so many local uprisings that William gave up his initial policy of conciliation and resorted to massacres up and down the country. Edvard the Jute had bloody work for years. Count Robert, as the new King's half-brother, took most of Somerset, and may have given Edvard a job in the county, or recommended him to the Norman bishop who received the lands of Taunton. Edvard could now take a wife and have a son. Among the racist Normans, the label "Jute" would stick to his family; but it would now be a label of affection, not contempt, since Edvard had won his spurs and proved his loyalty to the new ruling class. He was, however, too junior to receive land, so we do not find his name in Domesday Book.

> **Nobody will ever trace the exact origin of the Chutes in England, but this hypothesis matches known history, fits the awkward facts and would explain the tradition that our surname was one of the earliest.**

After 1066 it took at least seven generations for Edvard's descendants to make good in Norman society. But they had latched their fortunes to the ruling class, so it was just a question of which Jute, Chowte or Chewte would first have the extra ability and/or the right contacts to achieve a position of dignity. This man, if we accept tradition, seems to have been Alexander.

ALEXANDER, HIS LADY AND HIS MANOR

(Not strictly Chute history, but portraying something of a 13th C. Steward`s Life)

Managing the Taunton Estate

It will help to bring Master and Mistress Chute to life if we consider the running of their estate. We know enough of his times to be sure that Alexander was an educated and efficient manager as well as sharing the common skills in agriculture.

In the era before hotels existed, every decent manor house acted as **lodging** for passing nobles or dignitaries. Master Chute had to be ready to entertain the Bishop`s friends, and please his superior by giving them due ceremony; thus he probably spoke **languages**, Latin as well as Norman French. We might also credit his descendants with some knowledge of Flemish and/or Italian, since Somerset`s ports of Bristol and Bridgwater attracted foreign merchants buying English wool.

There was also a **military** dimension. Taunton was a short ride from the sea, and Wales was across the water. Alexander was born under bad King John whose war with France kept England at risk of invasion. There was also risk of rebellion in Wales. Even after John died, coastal areas had to keep a state of military readiness since, with few intervals, England remained at war with France until 1450. At **castles** like Taunton`s, the post of Constable was often held in rotation by nobles or gentlemen for temporary periods; so the manorial Steward was needed to manage hand-overs and fill gaps of tenure himself, in time of peace or war. No Chute was official Constable, but the family always had to be efficient soldiers.

Population

At this point, we must remind ourselves how tiny England`s population was then. Today we have over 60 million in the U.K.; in 1300 there were barely two million. Taunton, now a solid county-town, had then only 500 registered adult males, plus monks at the old abbey, a few houses and a castle clustered round the river bridge. Bear this small scale in mind when you read the economic inventory of Alexander`s manor. And, London being 2 or even 3 days` ride away, you realise how much real authority rested on the man on the spot.

Annual inventories and audit details

of the Bishop`s properties survive from this period, written in Latin on parchment `pipe-rolls`, headed, in Taunton`s case, with the name of the Constable and clerk who presented them. *(All can be seen on microfiche in H.R.O.)* From the extract shown below, you will share your editor`s relief that some have been translated.

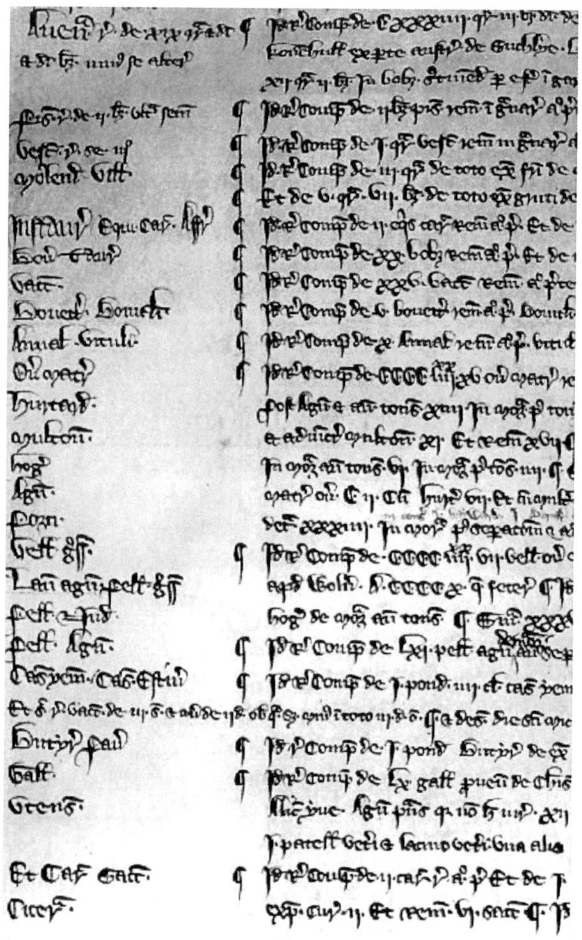

~ 114 ~

One of the translations, entitled *"The Pipe-Roll of the Bishopric of Winchester 1301-2"* by M. Page (Hampshire Record Series Vol XIV, 1996), by courtesy of whose editor we also copy the map on our p.109 above, tells us, for example, that in a financial year when Alexander's son or grandson was responsible:

Taunton Castle held 990 crossbow bolts; 2 hauberks; 1 roll for burnishing arms; 10 iron helmets; 10 padded tunics; 10 painted shields; 12 crossbows of which 2 have two-feet: & "5 crossbow bolts and 34 lances remain from previous year".

The Manor:
Livestock was 3 plough-horses, 29 old oxen of which 6 died in murrain, 9 swans remaining which had 14 offspring this year (2 of them sold, 21 remain).
Salt in store recorded: 7 quarters, 5 bushels. (Salt was the main preservative in the days before refrigeration .)
We can read the numbers/disposals of such humble domestic items as chests, brass pots, brass posnets, a tripod, copper pans, a great lead vessel, a gridiron, casks, tuns, tubs, barrels, axes, carts, wagons, a ewer and a basin, plus "1 coffer bound with iron to put treasure in".

We are not told how many men - whether `free` tenants or `unfree` *villeins* or slaves - worked under the Chutes to feed the manor and make its profit for the Lord Bishop.
But **income and outgoings** of the manor were reported to the tiniest detail, so we can read the annual cost of items ranging from:
- Clearing Dung from castle and sheepcote, and "Liveries" (corn paid to servants in lieu of wages), down to
- Buying Summer Robes for the Constable and Castle Clerk, paying Expenses of Justices and for "holding the hunt" (perhaps several gallons of ale?).

The 10 Mills of the manor earned in the year a total of £79. 4 shillings. 5 pence & three-farthings for wheatmeal, maslin, oatmeal and malt. Unit netbacks (in our parlance) varied during the year from 1s 8d per quarter of 2nd grade malt up to 6s 8d per quarter of wheat flour or 1st grade malt. (A Quarter was 8 bushels, approx. equiv. 290 litres.)

Calculating the Bishop's Income
These details were minutely reported on parchment each year for each manor of the Bishop's estate. **Annual audits** took place at his palaces at Wolvesey in Winchester or Southwark, near London. Human nature being what it is, the pipe-rolls show frequent corrections and crossings-out where keen-eyed auditors refused to accept an account or suspected cheating.

In that year 1301/2, net income from episcopal properties was the huge sum of **£4,121.** Together with all his other perquisites, the Right Reverend Lord Bishop earned as much as a high-ranking earl.

Keeping yeomen & yokels in order

Before the invention of police, the Lord of the Manor, or Master Chute in his absence, 'maintained the peace'. The earliest system of community policing was **frankpledge**, whereby the men in each parish were banded into tens, and each ten men became mutually responsible for their band's behaviour. When the Steward or Sheriff investigated a crime or a person's whereabouts, the other nine in his band had to tell the whole truth or all face the consequences.

Common Law, enforced at a Manor Court, was based on "custom", which partly dated back to Saxon times. In land which was controlled by a secular baron, he might re-write the custom of the manor to suit himself - the barons' ideas of justice being notoriously rough and ready. However, where the law was enforced by king or bishop (as at Taunton) it followed traditions going back to the old Saxon parish meeting under the oak tree, where a local jury, who all "knew the form", decided if a person's behaviour accorded with custom or not.

To complicate life, the modern world had brought in the **feudal system**, a Norman invention which tied everyone into a network of mutual obligations as "lord" or "vassal". The precise degree of obligations could vary in practice, and was often a matter of hard bargaining,

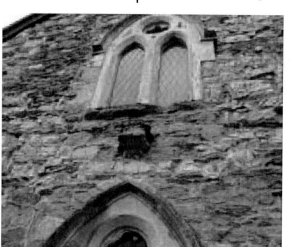

settled by the relative clout of each of the parties. This led to endless disputes over theory and performance, and these were judged under **King's Law** by the visiting Sheriff. He was another dignitary whom the Chutes had periodically to feed and entertain.

Getting Educated

To cope with these varied responsibilities, how did the Chutes of that remote area gain the necessary education? Typically, the son of a gentleman was placed, as a sort of apprentice, in the 'family' - in its original sense of the whole household - of a noble or a high ecclesiastic. There, a chaplain, one of the few who were literate, taught the boys how to read and write and say their catechism. The women of the family and the servants showed how the work of the household was done, and the boys learned skills on the job. At the same time they learned good manners, social behaviour, how to treat people of different classes. Growing up, they could rise on merit, in theory even to the senior positions in the household such as Steward of the Kitchen. From that lucrative post, various low-born men entered the gentry.

For example the poet Chaucer, the son of a tradesman, began his education in a Countess's entourage.

A vanished Chute emblem? The Priory Barn is one of few surviving buildings in Taunton of early mediaeval origin (now much restored). On the stone boss below the upper windows, a 3-sword emblem was clearly visible up to 1940 when it was mentioned in a guide-book.. It is now eroded beyond recognition.

But, first of all, a boy must learn how to fight. This part of his education was given him by the soldiers of the family. The lord employed them as bodyguard, to clear the road during his travels, intimidate the neighbourhood and generally demonstrate his `state`.

Since the immediate descendants of Edvard the Jute were not yet gentlemen, we must assume that for some years after 1066 the Chute ancestors served as simple soldiers in a lord`s entourage, picking up Norman customs as they went along.

Manorial bailiff supervising harvesters

Mistress Chute at the Manor

Though the mediaeval Chutes left no writings, other families did; and from one series (the Paston Letters - records of a yeoman farming family in East Anglia from the 1300`s on) we can get a good feel for the life of a wife. These describe several generations of matrons who are by no means slaves to their husbands, but rather their advisers and trusted lieutenants.

In one sense, they had no choice, being usually married off by parents, for economic or social gain, to men they hardly knew, living miles from their own families. Therefter they were locked into a degree of isolated intimacy which we - with our easy transport and ceaseless communication - can hardly visualise. No more can we enter into those centuries of loveless marriages where the wife lost all personal freedom and forfeited her property to a possibly repellent husband. But as in some Asian households today, a wife might find relief by matching her intelligence or patience against her husband`s and quietly proving herself superior.

Let us always guard against the fallacy of thinking our early ancestors inferior to us

in intellect or imagination. To survive their insanitary and violent world without today`s medicines or technology, and keep up their Christian faith and standards of decency, called for far more courage, patience and inventiveness than most of us need today.

Devotion?

Men, not women, determined what was kept on record; but, allowing for this, we see in the Paston series a picture of matrons who are so devoted to their lord`s interests that their many children take second place; indeed better wives/ housekeepers than mothers. Their surviving letters show them taking part in the legal and business interests of the family, as well as in the domestic sphere where naturally they ruled supreme.

To organise the feeding and clothing of the inhabitants of one or more manor houses was in itself a task for a life, requiring a high level of administrative abilities. In this task Mistress Chute could count on an ample supply of servants, though perhaps not on their intelligence or speed of response.

Household needs

These, of course, could not be met by 'impulse shopping' at Taunton. Everything that the estate could not supply must be ordered in the necessary quantities months beforehand - wines from France, sugar grown in the Mediterranean, spices, pepper, oranges, dates, and the better kinds of cloth.

As to **home produce**: the preparation, curing and storing of the meal, meat and game off the estate and the fish from the ponds, besides the command of the dairy, the brewhouse, and of the kitchen (often a separate building with its log-fire roaring up the great chimney) were all under the supervision of the lady of the house. Add to this the problems of **cleaning the house,** where the main hall was as busy as our railway termini. Men, dogs, servants in and out carrying loads, attending to guests, or simply coming to warm themselves at the central fire, from which the smoke made your eyes smart and blackened the beams until it escaped through open windows or a hole in the roof. (Glass was too expensive a luxury for anywhere but the best bedrooms.) Since church dignitaries might arrive with their retinues at any time, waving a letter of introduction from the Lord Bishop and expecting comfort and entertainment for a day or more, Mistress Chute could never let domestic standards slip.

Much of the **clothing** of the manor-house inmates was spun and woven, cut out and made up in the house or in the neighbour-

spinning and carding, in a 14th century scene

hood under the lady's orders. Her daughters did not go to town to buy their dresses, but one might hope to have the stuff for her best dress fetched from Bristol or (for a very demanding girl) from London.

In this hard-working family life, there was not much welcome for a superfluity of maiden aunts or elderly spinsters. There was a recognised way to deal with that problem...

Get Thee to a Nunnery

If a girl were not married off, she must if possible be placed in a convent. To be well rid of her, money was piously paid, and there was the girl respectably settled for life. In effect you paid a dowry to get her accepted as a bride of the Church.

But that did *not* mean she had a call to the religious life. The records of frequent bishops` visitations show that there was "a good deal of female human nature in the nunneries" and that "in vain the bishops attempted to dislodge the regiments of hunting dogs and hounds, even of monkeys (imported via Italy) with which, contrary to rule, the poor ladies solaced their long leisure".

No doubt some unwanted Miss Chutes disappeared from history into such sanctified oubliettes. We certainly do not find many of them recorded in the family tree.

We will now leave Alexander`s scene and move quickly on through the Middle Ages towards actual Chute biographies.

THE BLACK DEATH

From Alexander to Edmond lie 250 years of the Middle Ages, during which the Chutes of Taunton and Bridgwater had no importance outside the West Country, and left minimal record because they did not own significant land. For this period we offer one vignette.

In the winter evenings of 1348, Ambrose Chute and his wife Anabel sat in their hall at Taunton looking at each other with desperation, as rain came down day after day and the Black Death raged through the West Country. The household were all huddled in there for comfort. But whatever the disaster, there is always someone who makes it worse, so let us picture a blind man crouching in a corner, moaning in a cracked voice:

> " *This ae night, this ae nighte*
>   *- Every nighte and alle,*
> " *Fire and sleet and candle-lighte,*
> " *And Christe receive thy saule...*
>
> " *From Brig o` Dread when thou may`st pass,*
>   *- Every nighte and alle,*
> " *To Purgatory fire thou com`st at last;*
> " *And Christe receive thy saule...."*

Bubonic plague (brought in by rats on a ship) struck people without warning; perhaps our two were tough, or just lucky. "So vast a multitude was carried off", wrote the monk William de Dene, "that nobody could be found who would bear the corpses to the grave. Men and women carried their own children on their shoulders to the church and threw them into the pit." How many Chutes perished we shall never know; only Ambrose and Anabel`s names survive on our family tree.

> *"The whinnes sall prick thee to the bare bane,*
> *"And Christe receive thy saule..."*

This ghastly epidemic was regarded as God`s punishment for a sinful people. It erased whole communities and village-names from the map but, ironically, it may have helped both England and the Chutes in the long term. The immediate consequence was that land fell waste all over the country. Manpower was so scarce that, for the first time in our history, farm labourers were able to bargain for a better wage. But as a result farm incomes plummeted and, where manpower was short, arable land became destitute . The best way to exploit this surplus acreage was to convert it from arable into pasture; to sheep.

This revolution hugely enriched England, and wool (previously a small-scale and high-quality trade) became the major bulk export industry over several hundred years. At Taunton, it seems, the Bishops found they could no longer rely on steady income from arable farming of manorial land by direct labour under the Steward's supervision; it was now more profitable to receive cash as capital or rental, i.e. to sell parcels of land or rent it out on long lease and leave the risks to someone else.

But who, at Taunton, were in the best position to organise the bishop's land disposals and acquire the best of this newly available land for themselves? Who else but the Chutes, who had been and might still be Stewards. This could explain the tradition that Edmond Chute 'sold the manor'.

Anyway, whoever bought it from them in 1502, the Taunton Chutes must have accumulated valuable lands, enough to qualify Charles for a knighthood and raise the family into the 'county' league, so that they could now attract wives - as the family tradition asserts - from prestigious clans such as Baskerville, Berkeley and Cheney.

Upwardly Mobile Marriages
It was surely to glorify his ancestry that Sir George Chute, baronet, commissioned a scribe in 1698 to draw the Bethersden Chute Heraldic Roll. (Sir George came from the family branch shown on p.127.)

There are some errors in the 'BCHR' (as we shall call it), but it provides a colourful record of our early genealogy, and we can presumably take it as broadly accurate. This section for the 15th century shows the three prestigious marriages we have just mentioned. The **Baskervilles**, Sheriffs of Hereford, claimed Plantagenet blood and were hereditary Champions of the King. The **Berkeleys** lorded it over the West Country from Berkeley Castle, where King Edward II had been foully murdered.

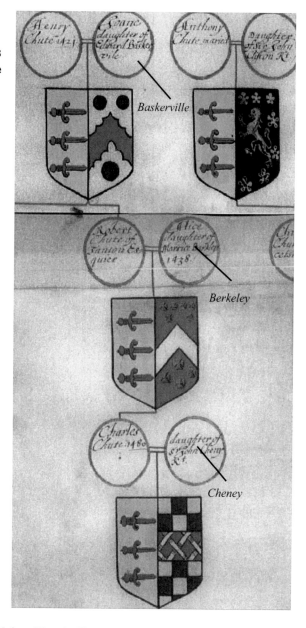

Baskerville

Berkeley

Cheney

The **Cheneys** were among the most powerful families in Kent and Sussex. One of them fought for the Tudors at Bosworth, and they rose in royal favour in the next century.

To have married into such company, the Chutes had evidently become men of substance by 1450. Most probably they had made money from **wool** - initially perhaps from Ambrose buying up land in a rock-bottom 14th c. market and breeding sheep for all he was worth. *"Our island"* wrote a social historian *"produced the best wool in Europe, and had for centuries supplied the Flemish and Italian looms with material with which they could not dispense for luxury production, and which they could get nowhere else. The Woolsack, the symbolic seat of England's Chancellor in the House of Lords, was the true wealth of the King & of his subjects."* By 1400, Lombard Street in the City of London had been named after Italian wool merchants from Lombardy. It is to wool exports that southern England owes the towering churches in villages from Somerset to East Anglia.

Early Capitalism

The Chutes must have joined in when England began to export wool-cloth. This process needed many crafts - carding, spinning, weaving, fulling, dyeing and cloth-finishing - all different and specialised. The only way that all the processes could be carried out without crowding people into factories in towns, was to have an organiser who employed the various crafts-men and -women in their homes. This early `capitalist` was essential to the whole chain. He had to collect the raw, the part-processed and the finished material at each stage, physically check it and transport it from craftsman to craftsman, from village to town and from town to wharf. He had to have capital so that cottagers could be paid on the spot and the whole sequence for a given amount of wool could proceed smoothly. In this way a standard product could be marketed and new cash brought into the system, so that the whole cycle could be kept in operation.

So important did this manufacture become for England, that out of 97 Lords Mayor of London from 1509-1607, seventy-two had made their fortunes by dealing in wool-cloth.

Another Chute `Baron` who Wasn't

Their 15th century leap up the social ladder must have become legendary in the family. Why else would Sir George Chute, 250 years on, invent the fiction that an ancestor had a Government post in 1435? The BCHR clearly shows Robert Chute (in the family tree at the 8th generation from Alexander) as "Sergeant at the Lawe & Baron of Exchequer" in the 13th year of Henry VI.

This claim is wholly untrue. The man who held those positions was a **Robert Shute** from a different family, who lived in the 1500s! It is an extraordinary example of what a 17th C. baronet would stoop to, to glorify his pedigree. (The Shute family could so easily have shot him down.) Even so, for the idea to take root, it must have echoed some Chute memory of a glorious 15th C. ancestor - or one whose marriage was a cause for perpetual celebration.

The Cheney marriage in about 1470 was the catalyst for the Chutes of Taunton to seek a `seat` nearer Westminster and London, where positions of power were opening up for the gentry. The Cheneys had land to offer their relatives, and the Chutes settled on the Sussex/Kent border. Later, under Henry VIII, Sir Thomas Cheney became Court Treasurer and Warden of the Cinque Ports, in charge of naval defence of the south-east English coastline. It was his patronage which gave Philip Chute a start in public life.

This concludes our sketch of how a family like the Chutes might have risen in education, efficiency and wealth to the status of higher gentry between 1066 and 1500.

PHILIP CHOWTE, THE KING`S STANDARD BEARER AND HIS LINEAGE IN SUSSEX AND KENT

HENRY VIII`s ENGLAND

Philip Chowte (as the name was spelt in his day) was born into an island which had at last found nationhood. In the 450 years since the Norman Conquest, grammar schools had been founded to spread learning and the English language; scientists like Roger Bacon and reformers like Wyclif had challenged the authority and dogma of the Roman Church; Chaucer the poet had fashioned English into a language of great literature; exports had brought wealth. England was tough and independent, no longer a mere outpost of Europe.

The Chutes in the Middle Ages, growing within the grain of society, had been part of this progress. From rude soldiers they became estate-managers and protégés of a great bishop; they acquired literacy and social polish; surviving the plague, they became traders, landowners and wealth-creators. By their wits and industry they climbed into the social class which owned great estates, and from whose ranks men could attract patronage at Court and exercise power under the king. At some date they acquired a coat of arms.

If, therefore, it turns out that - in the fashion of his age - Philip deliberately inflated the dignity of his ancestry, he did have a background that was well worth celebrating.

PHILIP CHOWTE, STANDARD BEARER TO HENRY VIII

**CAMBER CASTLE,
SUSSEX, BUILT 1540**

of which Philip was
governor from its
first construction until
his death. Erected by
Henry VIII as coastal
defence with a garrison
of gunners, it is now a
sombre ruin, isolated,
through silting,
a mile from the sea

HORNE`S PLACE, APPLEDORE
with a 15th C. chapel to the rear

OLD SURRENDEN MANOR,
Bethersden
parish

Both houses have been heavily restored in the intervening centuries. Horne`s Place can be visited by arrangement.

WHERE ON THE MAP? - CHUTES OF KENT 1560-1721

It took 500 years from their Jutish ancestor setting foot in this island, for the Chutes (to use their final spelling) to achieve the coveted social status of a 'county family'.

Philip Chowte the Standard Bearer acquired lands across Kent, the garden of England, and his descendants centred themselves in Bethersden parish, living at Surrenden Manor (soon to be known as Surrenden Choute). The **Choutes of Bethersden (1560-1721)** were the first of three family dynasties to have a stately home and rolling acres. Next came the Irish **Chutes of Tullygaron (1600-1900)** and the **Chutes of the Vyne (1653-1956)**. All of them supplied High Sheriffs to their counties and Members to national Parliaments.

Kentish Properties. Philip must have wanted his sons to form a network of local squires in Sussex and Kent, as he carefully allocated groups of landholdings between them. But his son George was sharp and ruthless, and within a few years had taken over Surrenden Manor, which had been left, with its farmlands, to his brother Anthony, a poet. Anthony was reduced to advertising himself as "a poore Gent", seeking literary patronage in London and scraping a living as a ship's purser. George may have gone on to antagonise his own sons as well, since both Walter and George jr. sought their fortunes as soldiers far afield, and neither received bequests in his Will.

The youngest brother Edward inherited the lot, and he added another manor at Hinxhill, E. of Ashford. Most of the Choute properties are shown below; it proved to be a mistake to bring them all under one master since many were neglected, especially those on marshy land round Appledore. When in 1721 Sir George, baronet and MP, died childless, he left no property to Chutes of his own blood; by his Will all the surviving family estates went to a cousin by marriage - Edward Austen, a distant relative of Jane, the novelist.

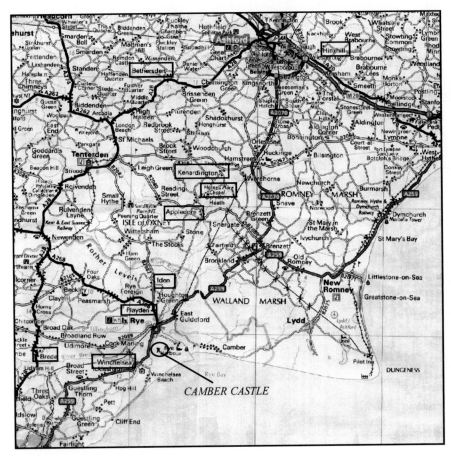

CAMBER CASTLE

Places of Chute connection marked to left

Hinxhill

*Bethersden/
Surrenden Manor*

Kenardington

*Appledore and
Horne's Place*

*Iden
Playden
Brede
Winchelsea (Philip's
constituency)
Camber Castle*

*[Outside this map,
Philip's lands at
Godmersham, Herst
& Chilham lay NE of
Ashford, and at Sedlescombe, W of Brede]*

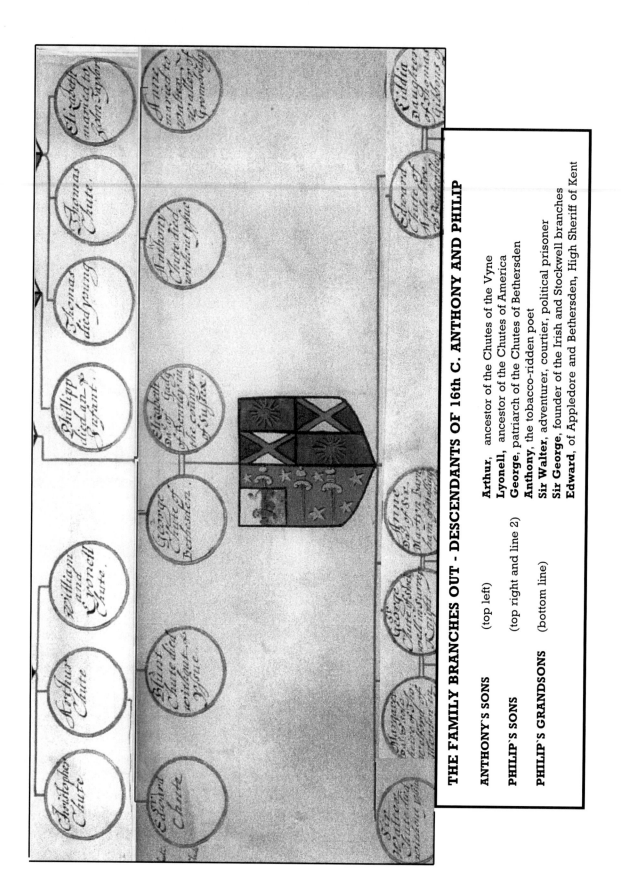

THE FAMILY BRANCHES OUT - DESCENDANTS OF 16th C. ANTHONY AND PHILIP

ANTHONY'S SONS	(top left)	**Arthur,** ancestor of the Chutes of the Vyne
		Lyonell, ancestor of the Chutes of America
PHILIP'S SONS	(top right and line 2)	**George,** patriarch of the Chutes of Bethersden
		Anthony, the tobacco-ridden poet
PHILIP'S GRANDSONS	(bottom line)	**Sir Walter,** adventurer, courtier, political prisoner
		Sir George, founder of the Irish and Stockwell branches
		Edward, of Appledore and Bethersden, High Sheriff of Kent

CHUTE FAMILY TREE - 2. DESCENT FROM PHILIP

brought forward from p. 104

THE CHUTES OF BETHERSDEN, 1550-1721 & OF STOCKWELL 1610-1700

from the 5 children of Philip Chute and Margaret Culpeper

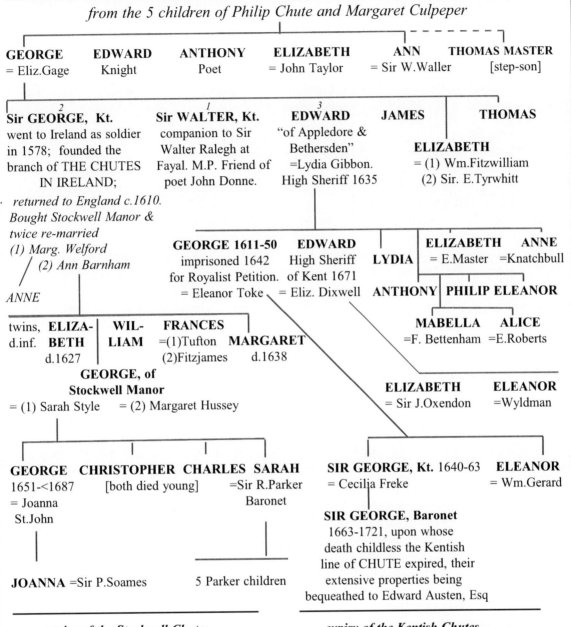

GEORGE = Eliz.Gage   **EDWARD** Knight   **ANTHONY** Poet   **ELIZABETH** = John Taylor   **ANN** = Sir W.Waller   **THOMAS MASTER** [step-son]

Sir GEORGE, Kt. [2]
went to Ireland as soldier
in 1578; founded the
branch of THE CHUTES
IN IRELAND;
*returned to England c.1610.
Bought Stockwell Manor &
twice re-married
(1) Marg. Welford
(2) Ann Barnham*

ANNE

Sir WALTER, Kt. [1]
companion to Sir
Walter Ralegh at
Fayal. M.P. Friend of
poet John Donne.

EDWARD [3]
"of Appledore &
Bethersden"
=Lydia Gibbon.
High Sheriff 1635

JAMES

THOMAS

ELIZABETH
= (1) Wm.Fitzwilliam
(2) Sir. E.Tyrwhitt

GEORGE 1611-50
imprisoned 1642
for Royalist Petition.
= Eleanor Toke

EDWARD
High Sheriff
of Kent 1671
= Eliz. Dixwell

LYDIA

ELIZABETH
= E.Master

ANNE
=Knatchbull

ANTHONY   **PHILIP** **ELEANOR**

twins, d.inf.   **ELIZA-BETH** d.1627   **WIL-LIAM**   **FRANCES** =(1)Tufton (2)Fitzjames   **MARGARET** d.1638

MABELLA =F. Bettenham   **ALICE** =E.Roberts

**GEORGE, of
Stockwell Manor**
= (1) Sarah Style   = (2) Margaret Hussey

ELIZABETH
= Sir J.Oxendon

ELEANOR
=Wyldman

GEORGE
1651-<1687
= Joanna
St.John

CHRISTOPHER **CHARLES**
[both died young]

SARAH
=Sir R.Parker
Baronet

SIR GEORGE, Kt. 1640-63
= Cecilia Freke

ELEANOR
= Wm.Gerard

SIR GEORGE, Baronet
1663-1721, upon whose
death childless the Kentish
line of CHUTE expired, their
extensive properties being
bequeathed to Edward Austen, Esq

JOANNA =Sir P.Soames   5 Parker children

expiry of the Stockwell Chutes   *expiry of the Kentish Chutes*

The blood of Philip will have survived through
descent in the female line. His remains lie in the
Horne Chapel at Appledore Church, Kent where
his shield (*right*) is still displayed. The last two
Sir Georges are buried at Bethersden Church.
The only surviving memorial to the Chutes of
Stockwell is a brass tablet in Lambeth Parish
Ch: to little Margaret who died in 1638, aged 6.

"OUR BELOVED SERVANT PHILIP CHOWTE"

Philip's is the one unforgettable portrait at the Vyne. Though burdened with robes, gloves and a puppy-dog, and framed with emblems, he glares from the shadows like a Chinese ascetic - giving nothing away. He is in fact the centre of a curious mystery. **Philip (c. 1506-1566)** never lived at the Vyne, but hangs there because he was the Speaker's great-uncle. In family history, he was the first to enter Court circles and one of few to gain wealth by his own efforts. His military valour added a canton to the Chute heraldic arms, the broken-dagger crest and the motto *"fortune de guer"*.

Standard-Bearer

The mystery concerns something he did while serving Henry VIII as his Standard-Bearer. That may sound to us an empty ceremonial office; not so, when you served a Tudor monarch. Henry was never more conscious of his image than in dealings with France, and when he besieged Boulogne in 1544 the Royal Standard* flew proudly at the centre of his Court. Its heraldry included the *fleur-de-lys*, which Plantagenet kings had adopted in order to flaunt England's claim to the French Throne.

King Henry was always a dangerous and suspicious man. Now aged 53 he suffered chronic pain from swollen legs, which made him a bad-tempered employer, one whom you must not fail at any cost, whether in action or ceremony. But Philip, though not even of knightly rank, won the king's gratitude and a royal jewel for his valour at Boulogne. He was publicly rewarded with the heraldic honour, the captaincy for life of a coastal castle and also, for a while, with property confiscated from monasteries.

The Chowtes' Rise in Dignity

But first, how did he reach this position? In 1502 Edmond Chute - at that date written Chowte or Chawte - moved his family from Taunton to Sussex, perhaps to be nearer the royal Court, seat of political power. Edmond's mother was born a Cheney, from an influential family of Norman descent, which enjoyed favour at Court after one of them fought for the Tudors at Bosworth. They owned many manors in southern England and it seems likely that they sub-leased one near the Sussex/Kent border to the Chowtes in 1502.

Sir Thomas Cheney, King's Treasurer and Lord Warden of the Cinque Ports, had a great house in Kent with a retinue of 400 young gentlemen in readiness to repel invasion. To young Philip he gave the patronage needed to step on to the ladder of public service. His career began as Jurat, local government officer, at Winchelsea in Sussex. He gained power in the area, making his seat at the then strategic river-port of Appledore, just into Kent. There he acquired from a Catholic family the house which is still called 'Horne's Place' with a (?)haunted

> * For any army at war, the **Standard** had held a mystical significance since time immemorial. In the Old Testament a tribe pitched its tents round its standard; in war the men gathered round it (Book of Numbers, ch.2.)
>
> In victory, you planted your standard on the hill you had stormed. At the Battle of Hastings in 1066, it was not the death of King Harold which made the English give up hope, but the loss of their standard to the Normans.
>
> To lose it was tribal disgrace. The prophet declared that when the Assyrians are scorched by the fire of the Lord
> "THEY SHALL BE AS WHEN A STANDARD-BEARER FAINTETH" (Isaiah 10.18)

14th century chapel which you can see today. (Appledore lies inland from the delightful old seaport of Rye.) This is a brief outline of Philip`s public career.

1527 Jurat, Winchelsea. 1536-1545 Yeoman of the Guard. 1539 captain of Camber Castle, then under construction near Winchelsea, Sussex. At the Dissolution, given custody of confiscated monasteries at Winchelsea and Faversham (later conveyed to Cheney.) 1541 returned to Parliament as a Burgess for Winchelsea.	1544 Standard-Bearer in royal bodyguard on campaign to France and at Siege of Boulogne. July 1545, his Captaincy of Camber Castle was extended for life, with a pension. From 4 March 1550 (if not earlier) lifetime Bailiff of the Manor of Frostenden, Suffolk for Queen Anne of Cleves. 1555 Searcher at Chichester, Sussex. 1557-1564 Comptroller of Customs.

Royal Bailiff to the "Flanders Mare"

Henry VIII`s fourth wife Anne of Cleves suffers in history from his spiteful rejection of her as a "Flanders mare", and his beheading of the minister who arranged the marriage. For political reasons it went ahead, but was soon annulled. The king consoled Anne by giving her properties in England, and Philip Chawte was the man he appointed as her Bailiff in Suffolk.

(In Suffolk Philip met Elizabeth Girling of Wrentham who became his third wife.)

The Siege of Boulogne, 1544

Background.
Henry VIII`s break with the Church of Rome added fuel to a long-standing vendetta between England, Scotland and France. Scotland was then an independent kingdom, and as Catholic as France. In 1544, Henry had set up a dynastic agreement designed to unite Scotland with England by marrying Mary, the future Queen of Scots, to his son Edward. He thought the deal was sealed and safe; however, the Scottish Queen, Princess Mary of Guise, was furious at this agreement made by male politicians, which would have subjected her Catholic daughter to a Protestant prince. She "scotched" the deal, a promise was broken, and French troops were invited into Scotland to forestall any English punitive aggression.

Attack!
Henry, outraged, organised a two-pronged attack in 1544, on Scotland in May and on France in June. He led the latter campaign in person, having won a pledge from the Holy Roman Emperor, Charles V, that they would quickly join forces and march on Paris. At the last minute the shifty Emperor backed out, leaving Henry to fight on alone. The English force never got beyond Boulogne, but the town did fall to them, and the French had to pay a huge ransom for its return.

An account of the "Siege of Bullen" is preserved in the National Army Museum. It is full of the doings of noble lords (being the ones who supplied the soldiers) and of "His Majestie`s" leadership which was crowned with victory. Nowhere does it mention Philip Chawte - the soldier who was neither noble nor knight, but whose valour won extraordinary commendation and rewards from the King. Why not? - we may ask.

What we know of Philip is that he was brave and in royal favour. But if we peer into the mist to try and understand his place in history, we stumble into the world of Tudor control freakery, with the same unscrupulous "spin doctoring" and "economy with the truth" as we suffer from our rulers today.

Spin-Doctoring for the King

Henry VIII's was surely the archetypal Cult of Personality - promoting England through his own "Majesty", the title he himself invented. Especially on French soil, whether in 1520 at the "Field of the Cloth of Gold" (an extravagant display to show that England had arrived on the world stage) or in his 1544 invasion of France, he required his courtiers to maintain a propaganda screen in which he was always the hero. After Boulogne was captured in September 1544, a war-artist painted a scene of the siege *(opposite)* and there in the centre is King Henry standing in full armour and directing operations. That was the good news - for public consumption.

The bad news - for our consumption - is that the ageing king's legs were now so swollen with dropsy that for much of the time he was carried on a litter. Occasionally, for show, he donned a breastplate and was hoisted astride his horse, but by no means could he have remained standing in heavy armour for any length of time.

Philip's `deed of valour`

This was never recorded, though it was of such striking importance that the King:
- gave to this ordinary soldier (not even a knight) a sapphire from his own royal ring;
- awarded him a Lion of England to be added as a Canton to his family coat of arms;
- enriched him with spoils from monasteries;
- further, confirmed for life his command of Camber Castle with a garrison and a personal pension. And astonishingly, after Henry died, Bloody Mary and Elizabeth I each endorsed Philip's governorship.

This last fact may give us a clue, because from religious antagonism each of those queens routinely dismissed all the public figures appointed by her predecessor. One must deduce that Philip had done such a favour to royalty, as such, that in his case they each confirmed the reward given him by Henry VIII. So what had Philip done?

State Secret !

In vain will you search for clues in contemporary records of the siege. The story is always that "His Majestie" moved around with calm and stateliness, in command of operations until victory was won. Of course it is.

Who, if he valued his life, would dare to write down what we guess to be somewhere nearer the truth: that at a moment when least expected (say, at night or during a ceremonial parade or during a thunderstorm), an élite band of French, perhaps sent directly by Francois I in Paris, made a desperate sally to kill or capture King Henry, helpless in his litter ? And that **the duty officer of the guard on our glorious monarch, who fought tooth and nail to save him from utter humiliation, was none other than Philip Chawte**. It would have bankrupted England to pay a "king's ransom" for Henry's safe return, and even a hint that the king had been in such danger would have shattered the Tudor `image`. We cannot be sure, but it would all add up.

Philip wisely agreed to adopt a low profile in public, and conspired with the Court and the few men who knew the truth to keep the episode out of public knowledge. He held on to King Henry's sapphire - that most personal token of thanks - for 20 years, but after Bloody Mary died, he tactfully returned it to Queen Elizabeth's Chancellor.

In that steely-eyed portrait you see a man who could keep a secret.

SIEGE OF BOULOGNE - DETAIL FROM THE CONTEMPORARY OFFICIAL PICTURE

The King is shown standing, wearing armour and holding a marshal's baton as he commands the artillery from what appears to be a small enclosure.

The engraving in question is a copy of the 16th century original painting made for Sir Anthony Browne, Master of the King's Horse, and kept at Cowdray House, Sussex until it was destroyed by fire in 1793. A few years earlier this engraving (now in the British Museum) had been copied from the painting.

There is no doubt of the propaganda intent of the original painting, because in 1772 it was described in detail by the Vice-President of the Society of Antiquaries when he and other experts inspected it; see the final two lines of this paragraph:

Description (abridged) of the painting of the Siege of Boulogne, by Sir John Ayloffe.

On the left hand is a view of the upper town, defended by a strong wall, with ramparts, bastions, etc. On the east side of the town is the citadel. Beneath these is a view of the lower town, river and harbour, with part of sea between the jettee heads and the harbour. In the foreground is the main English camp, from whence the approaches are being carried on for attacking that part of the high town which faces the sea. Over it is written "THE KING'S CAMP." At the eastern corner of this camp is a battery of some thirty guns, commanded by the King in person. He is dressed in compleat armour standing within a busque of high trees. In his right hand he holds a battoon of command, as directing the operations....

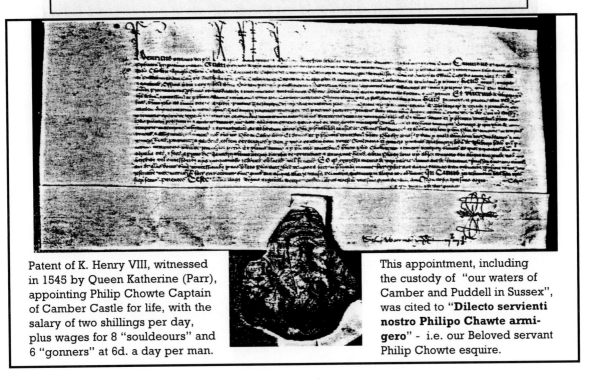

Patent of K. Henry VIII, witnessed in 1545 by Queen Katherine (Parr), appointing Philip Chowte Captain of Camber Castle for life, with the salary of two shillings per day, plus wages for 8 "souldeours" and 6 "gonners" at 6d. a day per man.

This appointment, including the custody of "our waters of Camber and Puddell in Sussex", was cited to **"Dilecto servienti nostro Philipo Chawte armigero"** - i.e. our Beloved servant Philip Chowte esquire.

Cinque Ports United vs. Yarmouth

Philip acquired properties all round Appledore, to the N & NE - at Kenardington, Bethersden, Godmersham, Chilham & temporarily Faversham; and to the west - at Iden, Brede, Sedlescumbe, etc. As this map shows, much of what is now land between Appledore and Winchelsea was then navigable water, and Philip's properties (ringed on the map) put him in local control. One official responsibility was the Camber salt-pans (now pasture land), but his authority over local fishermen involved him in a most curious bit of ancient history, which incidentally seems to have caused him to settle his brothers in East Anglia and brought him the job as Anne of Cleves's bailiff in that same area.

Winchelsea and neighbouring ports form the 'Cinque Ports and Two Ancient Towns', which were, from olden times, responsible to the king for protecting this corner of England from foreign attack. In return they enjoyed unusual privileges, and in a Charter of 1278 Edward I gave them the extra right to sell fish and dry nets at Yarmouth in Norfolk and for their bailiffs to control its annual herring fair. This put the Cinque Portsmen and Yarmouth fishermen at loggerheads, and they came to loathe each other. So much so that in 1297 when K. Edward's navy was gathering against the French, the Portsmen turned from the enemy to destroy 32 Yarmouth ships, killing 200 of their men. For 250 years this bloody feud went on, until Henry VIII stopped the Portsmen sending bailiffs to Yarmouth. He needed tough men to suppress the Portsmen's resentment of this 'insult'; Philip had a dangerous job in laying down the law. We deduce that he paid his brothers to remove to East Anglia to police the Portsmens' compliance, but that, to avoid being ill-treated by the folk of Yarmouth as 'stinking sussexmen', they made their homes a safe distance to its south.

A Very Slow-Acting Curse?

Philip continued to watch the horizon into Elizabeth's reign and one of his letters survives (Jan. 1559/60), passing intelligence to Government on French shipping. The war against France never ceased; when not raiding the English coast, the French had ships ready to help Catholic Scotland in case it made any attack against England's "heretical queen".

This sectarian hatred touched Philip personally. A Curse was reputedly set on him by the Hornes, the Catholic family from whom he took over his house. The text of the Curse, as it comes down to us (*right*), contains an error of fact and is suspected to be a 19th century pastiche. But it is in tune with the deep hatreds that resulted from the attainder of Catholics and their deprivation of civil rights under Elizabeth.

"Hea be accursed in hys slepying evere night.
hea wil be dreamd of devils, awoked with fright,
na place to reste hys bonnes at Hornes be set.
One year, not more hys lyffe be best,
Deepe neathe stone hys bonnes to dust
An beit so, hys kin fa evere cussed.

Fowle Queene Bess did steale owr place
An give to Shutte of Camber fa grace*,
Na man of Appuldre werked hys soil
Hea looked afar for men to toil.
Shutte wil go an tyme wil tel
How short hys travel ta hys hell".

---

*This is incorrect, as Philip stated that he bought the house from Henry Horne (probably c. 1560). Henry himself was never attainted, and his heiress daughter Benedicta was only declared Recusant in 1570, long after Philip's death. But read on...

This Curse, even if historic, did him no harm in his lifetime, since Philip lived beyond 60 and had three wives, a flock of children and a reputation of lasting honour. But as the following story shows, it could just have disturbed him 250 years after his death!

He had desired in his Will to be buried in *"my chapel in Appledore Church"*, i.e. the Horne Chapel. This was done, but in the 19th century two coffins were dug into his remains, and part of his broken skeleton came to light a century later.

A local antiquarian describes how he found it during restoration work c. 1925:

"We found the original floor under a wooden one. It was a mass of brickbats and broken flagstones extremely decayed. On levelling this we came on a small barrel vault with a shaped uninscribed tombstone lying loosely over it. This vault ran west from about 9 feet from the east wall of the chapel. It evidently had displaced Phillip Chute from his grave as, beyond a few fragments of the skeleton, nothing remained of his interment. These were re-buried under the floor of the sacrarium.

The vault contained two coffins, those of Jeffrey Munk, ob. 1817, and his third wife..."

The floor was repaired, levelled and "tiled, largely with the 14th century tiles found in the church, with modern pantiles to fill the gaps. I have had cut in the stone the inscription he desired to have placed on it: **Phillip Chute, bur'd 7 April 1566**.

I have been unable to find the exact date of his death". (Dr F W Cock, in Archaeologia Cantiana Vol XLIX; 1935)

Conclusion

This adds up to a remarkable personal story. Philip may have owed his first advancement to Cheney patronage, but he succeeded in public life (as reported in dozens of MSS and later records), earned great rewards and a royal jewel, and evidently never put a foot wrong in his relations with a fractious and bloody-minded king. This silver coin *(right)* was struck in 1544, the year of the Siege of Boulogne, and gives a chillingly candid portrait of Henry VIII, the master whom you must never fail but who might change the rules without warning, as Cardinal Wolsey (among many) knew to his cost*:

"O! how wretched is that poor man that hangs on princes` favours. There is, betwixt that smile we would aspire to, That sweet aspect of princes, and their ruin, More pangs and fears than wars or women have; And when he falls, he falls like Lucifer, Never to hope again."

There was little easing of the pangs and fears under succeeding Tudor monarchs, which makes Philip Chowte`s unbroken royal favour all the more extraordinary. But it had a human cost; when you look at his steely portrait you can see the strain that Philip endured, of watching, calculating and surviving in those tumultuous years.

[*Shakespeare; King Henry VIII, Act 3, Scene 2]

FLOGGING THE DEAD POET

As a contrast to our great achievers it is a real pleasure to introduce someone whose life of well-meaning failures, and being usually in the wrong place at the wrong time, qualifies him for membership of the Not Very Good At Anything Club.

Philip's son Anthony (c.1535-1595) has, nonetheless, earned lasting fame by appearing in the prestigious Dictionary of National Biography, ranked as Poet on the strength of his epic "Beawtie Dishonour'd". He is the only other Chute beside Chaloner, the Speaker, to be in the DNB, so we must respect him, even if that poem of 197 stanzas was far too long for most people to read at the time, when its subject, Edward IV's mistress, was scarcely news, having died 100 years earlier.

However, the memory of his life is surely poetic, being condemned to survive only through the slanderous abuse of a hostile journalist. When we have filtered out the slanders, Anthony comes across as endearingly human; he does seem to have had the habit of getting things wrong.

The journalist was Thomas Nashe, a popular social satirist and poet, whose libellous epitaph in 1596 on the lately deceased Anthony begins as follows:-

"Chewte, that was the bawlingest of them all, & that bobd me with nothing but *Rhenish furie, Stilliard clyme, oyster whore phrase, claret spirit* and *ale-house passions,* with talking so much of drinke within a yere and an halfe after died of the dropsie, as divers Printers that were at his buriall certefide mee. He beeing dead, I would not have reviv'd him, but that the Doctor (whose Patron he was) is alive to answere for him."

What *is* all this about? Well, in choosing a patron to advance his career as poet, Anthony had innocently stumbled into one of the literary feuds which delighted the chattering classes of Elizabethan London. The patron he chose was a Cambridge scholar named Gabriel Harvey. Unfortunately for Anthony, his patron had fallen foul of Nashe, and for years Nashe and Harvey traded insults in print. The public loved it; and the exercise became so important to Nashe that, when one day Harvey tried to make peace, Nashe refused to see him - having just finished writing his most vicious squib*, which he didn't intend to waste!

In it, Nashe side-swiped at the dead Chewte, whom Harvey had called an "orient wit", for attaching a sonnet of his own to Harvey's latest outburst. "But this was [Harvey's] tricke of Wily Beguily herein, that whereas he could get no man of worth to crie *Placet* [sign of approval] to his works ... these worthlesse Whippets and Iack Strawes [i.e. Chewte & others] he could get..."

Having sampled the abuse which blighted Anthony's memory as poet, let us try and distil some of his earlier misfortunes from the following tirades of Nashe:

"Chewte, is hee such a high Clearke in hys Bookes? I knew when hee was but a low Clarke, and carried an Atturnies bookes after him. But this I will say for him, though hee be dead and rotten, and by his obsequies hath prevented the vengeaunce I meant to have executed upon him: of a youth that could not understand a word of Latine, hee lov'd lycoras [licorice], and drunk posset-curd, the best that ever put cuppe to mouth; and for his Oratorship, it was such that I have seen him *non plus* in giving the charge at the creating of a new Knight of *Tobacco;* though, to make amends since, he hath kneaded and daub'd up a Commedie, called "The Transformation of the King of Trinidadoes two Daughters, Madame *Panachaea* and the Nymphe *Tobacco*" and, to approve his Heraldrie, scutchend out the honorable Armes of the smoakie Societie."

* called, rather improbably, *"Have With You To Saffron Walden" (the market town where Harvey lived)*

1. If indeed Anthony, as a boy, was so un-teachable that he knew no word of Latin, and went on to devil for an attorney like any humble student, his father had obviously put him into a dead-end profession. In any case he could not be trusted to speak in public, because, even among friends, he froze when proposing a toast.

2. This sense of inadequacy drove him to tobacco for solace and it is fair to assume it gave him lung cancer, since he died 20 years before his elder brother George.

3. By middle age, out of the Law and writing poetry, Anthony tried to make ends meet by serving in a naval expedition. But (?of course) the one he joined was a national disaster and he was lucky to get home alive*. *"His voiage under Don Anthonio was nothing so great credit to him as a French Varlet of the chamber is; nor did he follow Anthonio neither, but was a Captaines Boye that scorned writing and reading, and helpt him to set down his accounts and score up dead payes"* [i.e. take credit for pay saved by men's deaths].

Given the disgrace in which the ships came home it is a fair guess that Anthony himself never got his due pay.

4. But give him credit for effort. In 1594, now nearly 60, Chewte tried Heraldry for a source of income. Describing himself "a poore Gent and a Scollar without friends", he claimed a competent knowledge of Latin, French and Italian and, being willing to offer himself for examination in all parts "belonging to blazon", applied for the post of Pursuivant at Arms. (No luck there)

5. By now you are wondering why the rich Philip Chawte's son, who was left a clutch of fertile Kent properties by his father in 1566, including those at Bethersden, was "poore and without friends" 28 years later, and struggling for a living.

One cannot avoid the conclusion that his eldest brother George of Bethersden was a stinker. As mentioned above, we find George in possession of virtually all his father's properties, in direct contravention of Philip's careful allocation of lands between his five heirs.

However it came about, this was the cruellest of Anthony's mishaps in life.

6. To conclude; what did he achieve? Nashe records these of Chewte's poems: **"Beawtie Dishonour'd, written under the title of Shore's Wife"** (the 197-stanza poem on Edward IV's mistress); **"Procris and Cephalus"**; but Nashe says of these 2 poems that *"it would rust and yron [iron] spot paper to have but one syllable of their names breathed over it"*; **"King of Trinidado's Two Daughters"**; **"Tabacco"**.

7. In the end he smoked himself to death, having heraldically designed *"the honorable Armes of the Smoakie Societie"* viz a shield bearing *"a pipe between two daggers per pale, in chief a crowned head between two sprigs of tobacco"*. But even this conceit fell flat, as the next crowned head, James I, loathed tobacco and led a campaign to stop his subjects smoking**.

Alas, poor Anthony. Things went wrong for you so often, but we are on your side.

---

* This was a less than glorious Elizabethan exploit. In 1579/80 the last member of Portugal's ruling dynasty was dying, and our Queen wanted to prevent Spain seizing Portugal with its American and Eastern dependencies, its navy and its material possessions, which would dangerously upset the international balance of power. There were 6 claimants to that throne; Don Antonio, a bastard nephew of the late Portuguese king, was the one who won Elizabeth's approval. If Nashe can be relied on, Chewte was purser to an illiterate ship's captain on this ill-fated venture. Don Antonio's expedition, including some English soldiers, sailed in 1580 but was overwhelmed on landing by the Spanish army of Philip II. Don Antonio fled to the Azores; the English ships limped home in disgrace.

** Later, James I lost his battle against tobacco, but decreed that it must not be grown in England and could only be imported from Virginia and Bermuda. This clever device looked vaguely moral and/or hygienic in England and was popular with colonial growers, but its real merit was in simplifying the task of collecting customs duty. To make sure, Charles II sent sheriffs around to uproot all the illicit tobacco still being grown in England. By 1688 an excise collector could report that: "the custom of tobacco is the greatest of all others, and doth amount now to 400,000 pounds per annum".

PHILIP'S WARRIOR GRANDSONS

The westward view from Surrenden Manor is timeless. Past its great log-store and pond, the rich flat fields stretch towards Bethersden under skies so wide that one feels poised to be swept off into travel and adventure. We can so easily picture a peaceful scene in 1570 - two boys at the pond, 'Watt' and 'young George' aged either side of 10, watching the ducks, sailing their boats and boasting of what each would do when he grew up. Their famous grandfather Philip has died, and they vow to be as brave and honoured as he was.

They knew about English merchants who sailed to romantic shores - Africa, India and the Levant, and they had dreamed of sailing the seas and coming back with treasure. But now, said their father, the Pope had excommunicated our new Queen Elizabeth, and this boded trouble ahead from the French or Spanish. The boys had a nasty feeling that their mean old father would slide out of anything dangerous; but they themselves would certainly be ready, like proper Chutes *[also spelt Chowte, Chewte or Choute]*, to fight for our queen.

And indeed after 8 years young **George Chute** did leave home, joined the queen's colours for a military mission to Ireland, and was horrified to be involved there in a bloodthirsty massacre of Catholic 'rebels'.

Walter Chute was not allowed to go with him, being the eldest son of a big land-owner. George Chute senior had steadily manoeuvred the family estates into his own hands; this had caused serious ill-feeling, but it put Walter in line to inherit a huge acreage of farm and forest; he had to stay at home and learn how to run it.

But as time went on and Walter matured, it seems that his father became impossible to live with. So, leaving estate management to his slower-moving brother Edward, Walter also left home to fight for the Crown. As we find in the next chapter, his first blooding was in a daredevil mission headed by Sir Walter Ralegh (under whom his brother George had also served in Ireland). During this expedition the two Walters came to know Jack Donne, then a 'gallant', a man-about-town, but destined to be one of England's greatest poets and preachers.

Young George meanwhile had settled in Ireland, made money, married and had a family. But after his wife died, either the life bored him or he, like his own father, got on badly with his sons. In 1608 he left them in Ireland and moved near London, where he started a whole new life as lord of Stockwell manor. Having won wealth and land, he re-married in old age and produced a son - yet another George - to carry on this family branch. It lasted in Stockwell up to 1700.

In 1603 Walter Chute entered Court, serving the incoming King James I; but, imbued with new ideas from Ralegh and Donne, he grew to loathe the king's behaviour and publicly protested. Walter was thrown into the Tower; his father promptly disinherited him and left everything to Edward.

Edward, as youngest surviving grandson, was astonished to inherit virtually all the lands Philip had amassed in Kent & Sussex. Walter had been 'cut off' by their father and George was settled independently at Stockwell. Edward fathered a huge family and bought yet another manor at Hinxhill; he moved there himself and left Surrenden (by now known as Surrenden Choute) to his children. Some of their descendants must surely be alive somewhere today, though the male line, badly hit by smallpox, died out in the 18th century.

We will see Edward's lineage remaining fiercely Royalist in the long struggle between King and Parliament. Walter's 'treason' was forgotten, and after the Restoration, Choutes became county Sheriffs. But, first, we look closer at the adventures of Walter and George

THE 1614 WILL OF GEORGE CHUTE OF SURRENDEN, KENT, SON OF PHILIP, THE STANDARD - BEARER

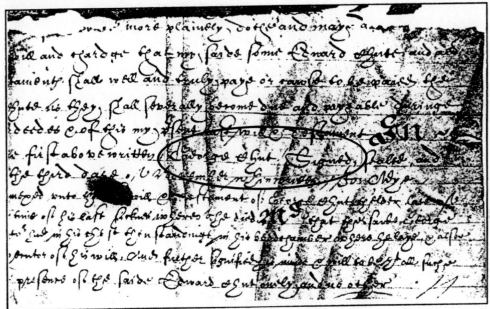

One of the earliest surviving family documents, written in 1614 and proved in 1618; it remains almost intact, a sheet of some 2 ft. 6 inches square, in Lambeth Borough Archives, Camberwell, London *(reproduced by permission)*.

In the upper extract above, "**George Chute**" shows his choice of spelling (his father Philip had signed himself "Chowte"), though the ringed words in the lower extract read "**George Chut signed**".

Testator was father of Sir Walter, Sir George, Edward and of others who did not reach adulthood.

This Will effectively cuts out the older two, though there had been a protest at a father being so "unnatural" as to disinherit an eldest son. This document established Edward`s lineage at Bethersden.

SWASHBUCKLING AGAINST SPAIN

Now, dear reader, your life is in your hands; with Walter Chute you have joined Sir Walter Ralegh's landing-party to attack Spanish-held Fayal in the Azores in 1597*.

    (Note: The Azores were vital to Spanish shipping. Ships in the 16th-18th C. had to follow the wind. Spaniards going to America used the `trade winds` blowing to south-west, taking them between the Azores and Canaries. Returning with gold, they started north from the Caribbean to catch the `westerlies` blowing from Florida to Europe; English ships caught them in the Florida Strait or, nearer home, at the Azores.)

    "As we made onwards with our boats, the shot played so thick upon us that in truth the mariners would scarce come forward ... and in like sort did I see some there stagger, and stand blank, that before made great shows and would gladly be taken for valiant leaders; and some of these our Rear Admiral [Ralegh] did not spare to call upon openly, and rebuke aloud with disgraceful words, seeing their baseness. And withal finding a general amazement amongst the mariners .. with a loud voice he commmanded his watermen to row in full upon the rocks, and bade as many as were not afraid to follow him."

As the bows crashed on the reefs, Ralegh jumped from his boat and, limping and cursing in the surf as the bullets strafed about him, ordered his men onwards. It was a superbly courageous moment, and the abashed Spaniards "began to shrink, and then seeing us come faster upon them, suddenly retiring, cast away their weapons, turned their backs, and fled".

The writer of this story, Sir Arthur Gorges, was a privateer like Ralegh and the Earl of Essex, who were commanders of the expedition under Admiral Howard. Whenever storms separated the English fleet, Ralegh and Essex took their ships off on rival missions against enemy vessels. Once, when Essex was away, Ralegh resolved to attack Fayal. After securing the beachhead, Ralegh made for the town to re-provision, and led the vanguard in person.

"Our Rear-Admiral, accompanied with divers other gentlemen of the best sort to the number of forty, in the head of all the troops ... with no other armour than his collar (a bravery in a chief commander not to be commended) led on the company with soft march, full in face of the fort ... whilst with great ordnance and musketry were we very shrewdly pelted."

They fought into the bastion, "in which doing, we were shrewdly troubled with the great artillery which did beat upon the old walls alongst the which we were to pass ... two of our train had their heads stricken clean from their shoulders, myself was then shot through the left leg with a musket bullet, but missed the bone being but a flesh wound, but the bullet did burn both my silk stockings and buskin as if it has been singed with an hot iron ... the Rear-Admiral also was shot through the breeches and doublet sleeves in two or three places.

"And still they plied us so fast with small shot as that (I well remember) he wished me to put off a large red scarf which I then wore, being (as he said) a very fair mark for them. But I was not willing to do the Spaniards so much honour at that time

---

* For a fuller account see, for example, Stephen Coote's Life of Ralegh

... and therefore told the rear-Admiral again that his white scarf was as eminent as my red, and therefore I now would follow his example".

The town fell before such ostentatious bravado.

Who were those "gentlemen of the best sort" who in their silk stockings emulated Ralegh's death-defying heroism? A critic calls them "the band of reckless and raffish young men who sailed with Essex to Cadiz and the islands". One was Walter Chute. Another, surprisingly, was John Donne, the poet, who was to be Dean of St. Paul's and first great preacher of the Anglo-Catholic church (*"never seek to know for whom the bell tolls..."*) At that stage Jack Donne, man about town "was not dissolute but very neat, a great visitor of ladies, a great frequenter of plays, a great writer of conceited verses".

In these alarming surroundings, Chute and Donne began a friendship which led to them sharing a year of travel together on the Continent in 1606. But first they had to get away from Fayal alive. The attack had been victorious, but the next day it nearly turned to disaster. Behind the mask of comradeship, Ralegh and Essex were at daggers drawn. Ralegh was one of the Queen's favoured courtiers, but Essex had wilder ambitions. Handsome and talented, he was too young to think of marrying the ageing and childless queen but was high among those who intrigued to succeed her on the Throne. He later over-reached himself, and she sent him to the block. But in 1597 he was in full cry, and bitterly jealous of Ralegh's glamour and achievements.

Ark Royal, flagship of Lord Howard as Admiral of the Fleet

When Essex reappeared off Fayal from a less successful venture of his own, Ralegh's brilliant capture and sack of the town seemed like a personal insult. Essex angrily demanded a court martial and Ralegh's death. When Ralegh coolly defended himself, Essex cashiered all the officers who had taken part in the victory. At this, Ralegh shouted that he and his men would stand and fight rather than be so humiliated. A desperate incident was boiling up, and only Admiral Howard's personal diplomacy saved the honour of the expedition. But from then on, Essex was Ralegh's open enemy at Court. When we read that Walter Chute was imprisoned after this venture, it seems that he may have been one of the heroes whom Essex was hell-bent to humiliate.

SIR WALTER BREAKS RANKS
WARRIOR/PHILOSOPHER/POLITICAL PRISONER

Sir Walter Ralegh, the most glamorous courtier of Elizabethan England - soldier, colonist, poet, political theorist, historian - had a close contemporary in the Chute family. Sir Walter Chute (1559-1617) is pale beside his namesake, but they had much in common - as comrades in arms and in Court, as political thinkers confronting Stuart absolutism, and as fellow-prisoners in the Tower of London. Chute's life contains at least two stories, and, if in future more comes to light about him, he could well become one of our most interesting characters.

Walter overlapped the lives of Philip, his grandfather, and of Chaloner Chute, his cousin. Neither of those two, strangely, left us much inkling of their private thoughts; their quotations which survive are too typical of their times to add a personal voice to our family story. But Walter's actions make him suddenly 'modern' to us. A bruiser of a boy, a fighter and duellist, not afraid to stand up to his father or even to his King. But complex also; worried by the new and revolutionary ideas that had begun to motivate him, trying to see beyond the excitement of iconoclasm, to understand where it was leading. We deduce this because Walter Chute was the man whom John Donne, the poet, chose as travelling companion for a year-long journey across Europe; at that date Donne was in turmoil of mind and emotion and needed someone he could trust to provide a balancing intellect - to 'bounce' ideas against, be an active sharer in his intellectual pilgrimage, and be competent to argue the minutiae of theology and cosmology with Catholic savants in Venice and Paris. .

Vaulting Between Ages

Born in the cosy, timeless Garden of England, Walter Chute as eldest boy obediently learned how to run the estates he was due to inherit. In his 30s however he broke away, and threw himself into mortal danger in the assault against the Spaniards, as our previous chapter relates. Eight years later, riding with Donne, he grappled in utmost seriousness with questions of science, religion, and human needs. Back in 1597 he was a brash, brave Elizabethan. In 1605 he was a new-age philosopher involved in questionings which tore apart the intellectual world, and to the powers-that-be were heresy and treason.

His life spanned a cultural leap comparable to that of our grandparents born in an era of horse transport who lived to see Ferrari win the Grand Prix. (Born, also, in a church-going age but living to see materialism enthroned.) Yet for him the leap was greater because we moderns are conditioned to embrace Progress, whereas his generation hardly knew the word. It was during his lifetime that Drake and Ralegh took exploration and colonisation across the oceans, that Spain's ambitions were humbled and England found itself a 'world power'; and that England also caught up with Continental Europe in challenging the mind-set of the Middle Ages.

Patriotism

Of Walter's 'two stories', the political one is the more easily told. It is a fragment of the dismal transition from Elizabethan to Stuart England, from a nation's pride, adventure and expansiveness under a dramatic queen, to its shame and squabbling under a drooling pervert of a king.

Our Revolution was no sudden outburst. For a whole generation before the Civil War and the beheading of Charles I, solid Englishmen had found it harder and harder to trust their age-old authorities of King and Church. Consider the years after 1603 in which Walter Chute tried to serve James I. He had been a fighter like his grandfather Philip, and in 1597 had followed Ralegh through the hail of gunfire in their assault on the Queen's enemies. The Chutes had become, as a rule, loyal and brave royalists. Philip had guarded Henry VIII; his son George became Cofferer to the Stuart Prince Henry; Walter's brother George enlisted in his teens to go and fight the queen's enemies in Ireland. Any Chute would have backed James I when he acceded in 1603.

So did many others, for England had been put through the mangle - the crushing of common law by the Tudors, the Reformation, war with Spain, Protestant-Catholic and English-Scottish hatreds. People had real hope of calm and compromise when the Tudor Elizabeth was followed by a king with all-embracing credentials: Scots-born of English royal blood with a Catholic mother but a Calvinist upbringing. Such a king would surely bind up wounds and redress the people's grievances. And in that great hope Walter Chute joined those who rode north to greet James VI of Scotland entering England as its King James I. Walter was knighted on the journey and at Court he was appointed ceremonial Carver to the King, a post he held for eleven years.

But in 1614 - disillusion! We find Walter elected on a Country Party ticket, the anti-Court faction, to a Parliament which the King had most reluctantly summoned so that taxes could be raised to finance his extravagant expenditure. *"Never had an election stirred so much popular passion as that of 1614. In every case where rejection was possible, the Court candidates were rejected.... Signs of an unprecedented excitement were seen in the vehement cheering and hissing which for the first time marked the proceedings of the Commons. But... the Commons refused to grant supplies until grievances had been redressed...*
the King, frightened beyond his wont at the vehemence of their tone" dissolved the session.
People called it the "Addled Parliament" for enacting no laws in the few weeks it lasted; but it set the tone for an era of violent Parliaments.

"Four of the leading members in the dissolved Parliament were sent to the Tower;

and the terror and resentment which it had roused in the King's mind were seen in the obstinacy with which he long persisted in governing without any Parliament at all." (Green's History of the English People, p.471)

Chute to the Tower

Sir Walter Chute was one of the four men thrown in the Tower for unruly behaviour.

What had happened to swing him, a courtier in daily conversation with the King, to take this violent lead in anti-Court politics? Disgust, perhaps, at its excesses, its extravagance and the preferment of pretty young men. Patriotic resentment, perhaps, at King James's crawling to Spain, the old enemy. Fury, at the debasement of public life under the king's proclamations of Divine Right and infallibility in legal matters?

Above all, we surmise, Walter Chute was outraged at the king holding Walter Ralegh in prison - a sop to Spain which Chute must have gone to the limit to plead against in Court. Ralegh occupied his time there by publishing histories and dissertations on the proper balance of powers between King and Parliament (a concept which infuriated the king). Chute was surely proud, when his turn came, to share the Tower with the great courtier who been his commander at Fayal and his brother George's in Ireland. Our ancestor's sentence was only four months, but not long after, the King sent Ralegh to the block. The legendary Elizabethan Age was done for.

Splintered Loyalties

Despite James I's crass conduct, many people felt unable to support Parliament against an anointed king. Loyalties solidified on both sides, and the passionate arguments between them tore most families apart. In the Civil War nobody could avoid taking one side or the other.

Lionel Chute in Essex saw it coming, and set sail for America in 1634 before the firing started. But among his cousins in Kent, the civil war had begun two decades earlier. On hearing of how his son Walter had attacked the Court in Parliament, and by implication had insulted his King, old George Chute was aghast. When Walter was sent to the Tower, his father saw no choice but to disown him. We mentioned Walter's disinheritance above, but must stress how utterly untraditional it was, at that date, to disinherit one's eldest son. An outraged letter from a leading politician to *"ould Mr Chute"* survives, begging him not to be so unnatural as to cut off his firstborn and *"throw him oute as a bastard from your nest"*. He takes leave to add the warning that *"it behooves yow to satisfy the world allso, who ... believe no ill deserving in your sunn"*. (i.e. Walter's stance must have won a lot of public support).

Cut Off With a Shilling

But the 80 year old was adamant. We saw his Will of 1614 (*p.137*). In it he says that Walter has already received *some* cash from him (though, for all we know, this may have been just a bribe to the Tower guards to give him a mattress), and he leaves all the great Chute estates in Kent and Sussex to his third son Edward, plus annuities to Edward's wife and children.

A Working Holiday with Donne

Walter's horizons had by now stretched well beyond his father's, and here begins his second story.

On 16 February 1604/5 a licence was granted to: "Sir Walter Chute knight and John Donne gent. to travaile ... with two servantes four nagges and iiij xx li in money". Thus in 1605/6 Walter became the one-to-one travelling companion to one of England's most learned poets on a philosophical journey across Europe.

Donne, by coincidence, had also been in the gunfight at Fayal, but a far more lacerating experience for him was his recent withdrawal from the Roman Catholic faith. Donne's family had obstinately held to it, despite persecution, for two generations since the Reformation. *"I had my first breeding and conversation"*, he wrote, *"with men of a suppressed and afflicted religion, accustomed to the despite of death and hungry of an imagined martyrdom"*.

John Donne in 1616

Indeed it took Donne many years to discover ease in his adopted Anglican faith, and then to become its first truly great preacher.

These two breaches - Donne's with his Catholic upbringing, and (a decade later) Walter's breach with his King - take us to the heart of the 17th century's intellectual turmoil, when the natural world was re-examined, and cherished beliefs and natural loyalties were overthrown. Thoughtful men had to reconstruct their whole understanding of life.

Heresy in High Places

The natural world of sun, moon and stars had long ago been explained `once and for all` by the Fathers of the Church, who constructed a cosmology out of Greek science, Roman medicine and Christian dogmas of Form, Hierarchy and Order. For centuries, Western Christendom had felt at home in this benevolent universe, where the only permitted question was whether you would obey the rules and save your soul. But now Francis Bacon, soon to be Chancellor of England, challenged such ideas as a mere invention of cloistered schoolmen, who spun intellectual webs with no relation to reality. He demanded new criteria for "explanation", and (by chance) these were starting to become available through the sudden growth of technology.

St Ambrose had declared: *"To discuss the nature and position of the earth does not help us in the life to come"*. This attitude no longer satisfied men in a century which furnished mankind with the telescope and microscope, the barometer, thermometer and micrometer, the pendulum clock and a balance weighing accurately to a 500th of a grain. The Church declared that by divine law the Sun moved round the Earth; Galileo was now to prove the opposite.

Another casualty was the metaphysical concept of dual natures - of Form and Matter, Accidence and Substance - which had papered over logical cracks in describing natural objects. To St. Augustine it mattered less whether a creature existed than what it symbolised. But now, if something existed, it *did* matter. Now you could measure specific gravity, atmospheric pressure and movements of planets. In any case symbolism, however piously intentioned, was a human, mental construct.

(It was over the symbol of kingship that Walter was to break with his father in 1614. The aged George believed that an Englishman could *never* oppose an anointed King, who ruled by Divine Right; i.e. *"salute the rank, not the man"*.)

Breaking the Mould

An eastern European today would be all too familiar with Donne's and Chute's dilemma. Having preserved itself by an `infallible` social dogma, Communism left trauma and chaos behind it when humanity outgrew the dogma and threw it out.

The mediaeval Church had feared that any questioning of the "how" in the universe - the measurement of causes and effects - would necessarily lead to questioning the "why" - the operation of a divine Creator. In 1633, the Inquisition threatened Galileo with torture for publicising his astronomical observations. A professor of Padua, invited by Galileo to see his astronomical proofs and discuss what they meant, is famous for having refused to look into a telescope. (*There is a psychological test question today: was he right to do so?*)

Cardinal and Savant

In a famous Renaissance painting, a finely-dressed Cardinal reads answers out of Scripture to a grovelling intellectual who pleads for forgiveness for his speculations. This is calculated to make viewers grind their teeth, assuming that it applies to the age of Galileo - who, to avoid torture, was forced to recant.

But what if one sets it in an earlier scenario - say the intellectual is a pagan medicine-man or even a Greek philosopher? The early Church (long before Aquinas) had to promote a theory of the world in which thunder was not caused by demons or by Zeus. Nature, after all, was the mainspring of pagan religion. What the Church concocted was a `spiritual` explanation of Nature, plausible enough to survive for centuries before the first telescope.

Galileo changed all that, and after him came Descartes and Newton. Nowadays we cannot conceive of a world without experimental physics - but the modern question is - have we become too obsessed with science and the material? What price have we paid for our `conquest of nature`? Having argued away the spiritual world, are we also about to destroy our own lives, even our planet?

Yes, But ...

Back now to 1605. Given his political radicalism, surely Walter would cry, with Bacon, "good riddance to mediaevalism" and embrace the `new philosophy` with delight. We find that he did not; and on this issue Walter becomes interestingly `modern`. When London's chattering classes (whom we saw reading Nashe) were becoming intrigued by Bacon's iconoclasm, Donne chose for companion a man who, to be worth talking to for months in the hope of enlightenment, must have shared his anxiety as to where all this `natural philosophy` was leading.

In 1605, though Galileo had not yet got far with his observations, no thinking man could ignore the public demand for a better explanation of the natural world - which would satisfy them by appealing to contemporary assumptions (as distinct from those of a former age) and seem to be 'truthful' and incapable of further analysis. But few men thought or felt as deeply as Donne - indeed his intellect and his feelings were often in conflict; he saw that humanity could not be satisfied with only one quality of explanation.

> *"The new philosophy calls all in doubt,*
> *The element of fire is quite put out ;*
> *The sun is lost, and the earth, and no man's wit*
> *Can well direct him where to look for it.*
> *And freely men confess that this world's spent ..."*

In other words 'philosophers' could produce a more 'scientific' explanation for the world, but for most people it would explain nothing, but merely cause distress, confusion, and a sense of loss.

Feeling

As the two men rode across Europe, these speculations were sharpened by Donne's agonising distance from his young wife.

As a man-about-town, Jack Donne wrote great love poems ("The Extasie", "Lover's Infinitenesse", "Goe and catche a falling starre", etc.) which rank among the greatest in our language. For him, human love became the mystical gateway to an understanding of divine love*, and he analysed it obsessively. He had eloped and married in secret, and his wife's family had him jailed, thereby cutting off his hopes of political advancement.

All his life he was passionately in love with her, and the reason he left her in England in 1605/6 was that their third child was still a baby and they badly needed income. His biographer believes Donne "felt that the time would soon be ripe to sue for public employment once more and that a journey to the continent would put him in touch with current developments abroad."

A colloquy to wonder at

We can begin to place Walter Chute when we appreciate that he was the man that Donne - learned, fiercely intelligent, full-blooded, ambitious for success, but endlessly analysing his own feelings, motives and personal worth - chose to be with when he left England for a year's self-education, racked by religious misgivings and the separation from his wife. He was as keen as anyone to discover 'the true nature of things' but would not be satisfied with half-answers. At their date, the great discoveries in physics, the cold mathematical universe of Descartes, the concept of 'progress' were still in the future. But already Donne aimed to meet French and Italian intellectuals (in Venice he breathed the same air as Galileo), to discuss the new science and its impact on orthodox Catholic societies.

Nothing can recreate the words of their colloquy, as the two men rode back to England; but this was surely the turning point in Walter Chute's life, and easily explains his later confidence in standing up to a mere King. A mind which had shared the daily experience of spiritual and philosophical debate with John Donne at that crisis in intellectual history will have been re-born like an astronaut today who has looked down on the Earth.

The new philosophy appealed to one human desire - to remove mystery - and led to our obsession with measuring what can be measured. But in Donne's and Chute's eyes it "left all in doubt". We can now appreciate their intuition of the vast areas that 'science' leaves unexplained.

---

* A surprising parallel will emerge when we reach the chapter on Desmond Chute in the 20th Century. Donne's image in "The Extasie" of two motionless lovers, only hands touching, with "eye-beams twisted" as their souls "negotiate":
> "All day, the same our postures were,
> And wee said nothing, all the day"

is echoed by Desmond's friend Stanley Spencer, another explorer of the mysticism of sex (though in earthier style), describing two figures in his painting ' The Turkish Window ':
> "a youth gazes up at the face of a woman who lays [apart] on the floor of the cage and gazes down at him. They could remain doing just that for ever"

SIR GEORGE OF IRELAND & STOCKWELL

In 1578 the Chutes of England founded their first branch overseas when Philip's grandson George, an adventurous teenager*, volunteered to join a punitive expedition into Ireland. He survived the fighting, won a knighthood, founded a Chute dynasty in Ireland and another in Stockwell, Surrey, married three wives, lived to the greatest age in a generally long-lived family, and was able to tell his father: "don't bother to leave me any of Grandfather's property; I have won all I need by my own effort". There are still gaps in our knowledge of his career, but what we can find is a life-long adventure and an undoubted success story.

Punishing the Rebels

In 1578 the Roman Catholic family of Earl Desmond of Munster in southern Ireland won the Pope's support for an invasion to unseat the "heretical Queen Elizabeth" of England. A tiny band of invaders landed on to the Dingle peninsula, expecting to provoke a massive Irish uprising against the English occupying forces. Among the queen's courtiers who recruited contingents to quash this "rebellion" was one Sir John Perrott (rumoured to be a 'royal bastard' in both senses). Young George Chute signed up in his service.

The outline of his Irish adventure will fit better in our next chapter "**Squires and Soldiers in Ireland**". At the end of it, his Irish wife has died and George leaves their elder son Daniel to solve land disputes and secure an estate. Here we will follow Sir George when he returned to England from Ireland, after being knighted in Dublin in 1608 by the King's Deputy.

Perhaps he had quarrelled with his sons, as he promptly bought himself the Manor of Stockwell (then rural but now 'inner-city'), in Lambeth, South London, across the Thames from Westminster, with money which he otherwise could have left to his Irish family.

Prince's Cofferer

In 1610 Sir George was nominated as Cofferer in the newly constituted household of Prince Henry, in which Sir Thomas Chaloner, uncle of the future Speaker Chaloner Chute, was Chamberlain and tutor to the promising and likeable young prince.

"Cofferer", keeper of the treasure-chest, was one of two senior finance men who controlled the revenues of the Prince's estates, over £40,000. Prince Henry died in 1612 (to England's great loss); Sir George therefore was no longer so close to Court in 1614, when his brother Sir Walter caused scandal by insulting King James I in Parliament.)

A Lively Old Man

With his titles and property in England, Sir George, now in his fifties, re-married not once, but twice. First a Herefordshire heiress Margaret Welford. She seems to have died in childbirth, as George soon persuaded Sir Martyn Barnham from Kent to let him marry his daughter Anne. But George was perhaps too old to father healthy children; 7 were born but most were weakly and few reached adulthood. The brass in old Lambeth Parish Church (*below*) to their little Margaret, is one of the earliest Chute memorials to survive. Today, alas, it is covered by a display board of the Garden History Museum, which took over the building to save it from dereliction.

> here lieth the body of MARGARET CHVTE (daughter of Sr GEORGE CHVTE of Stockwell in the Covn of Svrrey, KT, and Dame ANN his Wife) who departed this life the 2nd of March 1638 being aged 6 Years and One Monthe

From Subsidy Rolls of 1628 and 1642 we see that Sir George was much the richest landowner in his area. In March,1612 he had had spare cash to subscribe (among other speculations) to the Third Virginia Co. Charter.

The Longest-lived Chute?

When he made his last Will in 1647, George was little short of 90. He died within months, leaving prosperous descendants in Stockwell who kept the Chute name alive until c.1700.

He was alive and of sound mind in 1647; since in those days very few men survived beyond their 80's, he could hardly have been born much before 1560.

POLITICAL PRISONER AND THE LOST INHERITANCE

STONE WALLS DO NOT A PRISON MAKE

In 1642, when Cromwell`s Parliament was in full cry against the Crown and Established Church, the sleepy parish of Bethersden was riven by events which landed its respected squires in prison. Richard Lovelace, Cavalier poet and "the bravest, handsomest bachelor in the kingdom", was neighbour to **George Chute** of Surrenden Choute, and both were leaders of a Kentish Petition urging Parliament not to pass a Bill to abolish bishops. Their action was brave, because recently a similar petition advanced by Sir Edward Dering of Surrenden Dering had been ordered to be burned by the Common Hangman.

After a summary interrogation, Parliament committed Lovelace and Chute to the Serjeant`s custody in London jails. (A few miles east of Surrenden, you may visit the magnificent Godinton House, where George`s wife Eleanor (née Toke) went home to her parents` protection while he was locked up.) Lovelace, in "To Althea, from Prison", put romantic love and idealism into celebrated poetry:

> Stone walls do not a prison make
> Nor iron bars a cage;
> Minds innocent and quiet take
> That for a hermitage.
> If I have freedom in my love
> And in my soul am free,
> Angels alone, that soar above,
> Enjoy such liberty.

REWARDS OF ROYALISM

The Civil War split society as savagely in Kent as everywhere else, but the Chutes stood firm by their Royalist roots. Under Stuart kings, two Edward Chutes were High Sheriff, in 1635/6 - "a right worthy gentleman" - and 1671/2. The latter married into one of the rich textile families of east Kent, the Dixwells of Brome.

These families, including Austen (forbears of Jane), Oxendon (with a weird memorial in Wingham Church) and Dixwell (two baronets; one painted by Van Dyck), kept a tight grip on political power. It was said that to be elected in Kent you must have the textile families on your side. The Chutes joined this club by marriage, and were so much in royal favour that when Sir George, Kt. died of smallpox in 1664, having been promised a baronetcy, Charles II graciously conferred it later on his son George who had been born after his father`s death. (Records show the odd fact that the boy was not baptised until he was 20, a few days before receiving the baronetcy.) In 1696 he was MP for Winchelsea, Philip Chowte`s old constituency, which Sir George took over from an Austen. Two more Austens held Rye and Hastings; a Dixwell baronet held Dover. These magnates had the Cinque Ports well wrapped up, and their political cronyism was soon to prevail over ties of Chute blood.

A SLAP IN THE FACE FOR THE CHUTES OF THE VYNE

Sir George Chute, baronet and MP (1664-1721), was unmarried and the last male of his line. His aunt had married yet another Austen, and it was to her son Edward that he left all the Chute estates in Kent and Sussex. Edward Austen gave thanks in a flamboyant marble memorial to Sir George in Bethersden Church (see picture on p.178), now somewhat hidden behind the organ.

This bequest must have infuriated Sir George`s blood relations at the Vyne, whose funds were now gravely diluted by having had so many children. At that date it was still very much the accepted practice among gentry to keep property `in the family`, so we may wonder if, in the background, there was some family rift of political origin. Perhaps the Chutes of Kent were `Jacobite` Royalists who resented the Vyne`s public support of the Whig cause, or nursed a still older grudge against Chaloner Chute`s fraternisation* with the republican Commonwealth.

*Such labels tend to stick. Even though the Lobb Chutes and Wiggett Chutes were conspicuous Tories since before 1790, we find James Lees-Milne noting in his diary after visiting the Vyne on 17.12.1944:
"I think the Chutes were Parliamentarians which accounts for their puritanism today".

SQUIRES AND SOLDIERS IN IRELAND

1. **TREE: THE CHUTES IN IRELAND**

2. **SQUIRES AND SOLDIERS**

3. **A KERRY DANCE**

4. **GENERAL SIR TREVOR, THE KERRY BULL**

5. **CHALLONER - A LIFE CUT SHORT**

TRALEE   LISTOWEL

CHUTE HALL, TULLYGARRON, HOME OF THE FAMILY FOR SOME 300 YEARS

CHUTE FAMILY TREE 3: THE FAMILY IN IRELAND

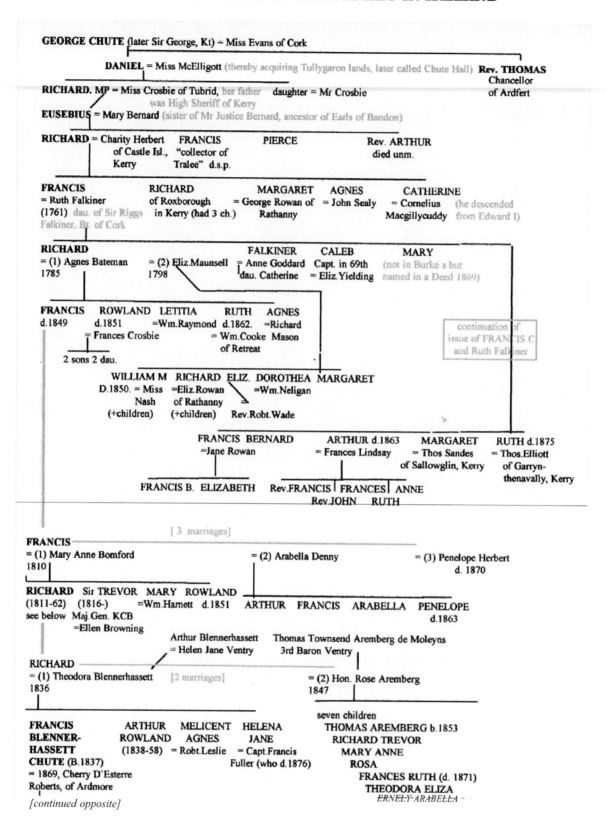

GEORGE CHUTE (later Sir George, Kt) = Miss Evans of Cork

DANIEL = Miss McElligott (thereby acquiring Tullygaron lands, later called Chute Hall) **Rev. THOMAS**
Chancellor
of Ardfert

RICHARD, MP = Miss Crosbie of Tubrid, her father daughter = Mr Crosbie
was High Sheriff of Kerry

EUSEBIUS = Mary Bernard (sister of Mr Justice Bernard, ancestor of Earls of Bandon)

RICHARD = Charity Herbert   FRANCIS   PIERCE   Rev. ARTHUR
of Castle Isl., "collector of   died unm.
Kerry   Tralee" d.s.p.

FRANCIS   RICHARD   MARGARET AGNES   CATHERINE
= Ruth Falkiner of Roxborough = George Rowan of = John Sealy = Cornelius (he descended
(1761) dau. of Sir Riggs in Kerry (had 3 ch.) Rathanny   Macgillycuddy from Edward I)
Falkiner, Bt. of Cork

RICHARD   FALKINER CALEB   MARY
= (1) Agnes Bateman = (2) Eliz.Maunsell = Anne Goddard Capt. in 69th (not in Burke's but
1785   1798   dau. Catherine = Eliz.Yielding named in a Deed 1869)

FRANCIS ROWLAND LETITIA   RUTH   AGNES
d.1849   d.1851   =Wm.Raymond d.1862. =Richard
            = Frances Crosbie   = Wm.Cooke Mason
                     of Retreat

continuation of issue of FRANCIS C and Ruth Falkiner

2 sons 2 dau.

WILLIAM M RICHARD ELIZ. DOROTHEA MARGARET
D.1850. = Miss =Eliz.Rowan   =Wm.Neligan
Nash   of Rathanny
(+children) (+children)   Rev.Robt.Wade

FRANCIS BERNARD   ARTHUR d.1863 MARGARET   RUTH d.1875
=Jane Rowan   = Frances Lindsay = Thos Sandes = Thos.Elliott
                          of Sallowglin, Kerry of Garryn-
                                                thenavally, Kerry

FRANCIS B. ELIZABETH   Rev.FRANCIS FRANCES ANNE
                      Rev.JOHN RUTH

[3 marriages]

FRANCIS
= (1) Mary Anne Bomford   = (2) Arabella Denny   = (3) Penelope Herbert
1810   d. 1870

RICHARD Sir TREVOR MARY ROWLAND
(1811-62) (1816-)   =Wm.Harnett d.1851 ARTHUR FRANCIS ARABELLA PENELOPE
see below Maj.Gen. KCB   d.1863
      =Ellen Browning

             Arthur Blennerhassett Thomas Townsend Aremberg de Moleyns
             = Helen Jane Ventry   3rd Baron Ventry

RICHARD
= (1) Theodora Blennerhassett [2 marriages]   = (2) Hon. Rose Aremberg
1836   1847

                                  seven children
FRANCIS   ARTHUR MELICENT HELENA   THOMAS AREMBERG b.1853
BLENNER- ROWLAND AGNES   JANE   RICHARD TREVOR
HASSETT (1838-58) = Robt.Leslie = Capt.Francis MARY ANNE
CHUTE (B.1837)   Fuller (who d.1876) ROSA
= 1869, Cherry D'Esterre   FRANCES RUTH (d. 1871)
Roberts, of Ardmore   THEODORA ELIZA
                             ERNELY-ARABELLA - -

[continued opposite]

DESCENT IN 19TH/20TH C. FROM:-

FRANCIS BLENNERHASSETT CHUTE = CHERRY D`ESTERRE ROBERTS

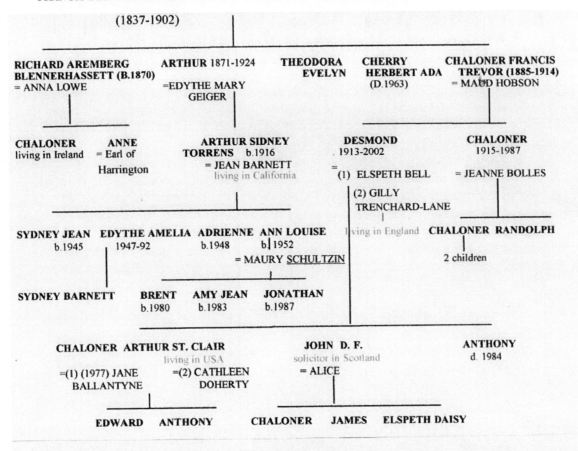

(1837-1902)

RICHARD AREMBERG BLENNERHASSETT (B.1870) = ANNA LOWE

ARTHUR 1871-1924 = EDYTHE MARY GEIGER

THEODORA EVELYN

CHERRY HERBERT ADA (D.1963)

CHALONER FRANCIS TREVOR (1885-1914) = MAUD HOBSON

CHALONER living in Ireland

ANNE = Earl of Harrington

ARTHUR SIDNEY TORRENS b.1916 = JEAN BARNETT living in California

DESMOND . 1913-2002 = (1) ELSPETH BELL (2) GILLY TRENCHARD-LANE

CHALONER 1915-1987 = JEANNE BOLLES

SYDNEY JEAN b.1945

EDYTHE AMELIA 1947-92

ADRIENNE b.1948

ANN LOUISE b.1952 = MAURY SCHULTZIN

living in England

CHALONER RANDOLPH 2 children

SYDNEY BARNETT

BRENT b.1980

AMY JEAN b.1983

JONATHAN b.1987

CHALONER ARTHUR ST. CLAIR living in USA =(1) (1977) JANE BALLANTYNE =(2) CATHLEEN DOHERTY

JOHN D. F. solicitor in Scotland = ALICE

ANTHONY d. 1984

EDWARD ANTHONY

CHALONER JAMES ELSPETH DAISY

[*Sources:* Burke`s Landed Gentry for the opposite page; the late Desmond Chute for the above. For the section below: Gerard Francis Chute of Listowel, who believes the "Rowland, gentleman of Tralee" at the head to have been the younger brother of Gen. Sir Trevor Chute, KCB

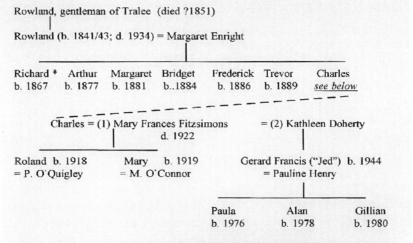

Rowland, gentleman of Tralee (died ?1851)

Rowland (b. 1841/43; d. 1934) = Margaret Enright

THE CHUTES OF LISTOWEL

Richard * b. 1867

Arthur b. 1877

Margaret b. 1881

Bridget b..1884

Frederick b. 1886

Trevor b. 1889

Charles *see below*

Charles = (1) Mary Frances Fitzsimons d. 1922

= (2) Kathleen Doherty

Roland b. 1918 = P. O'Quigley

Mary b. 1919 = M. O'Connor

Gerard Francis ("Jed") b. 1944 = Pauline Henry

Paula b. 1976

Alan b. 1978

Gillian b. 1980

Notes: * Dates of birth of the generation Richard to Trevor are deduced from their ages shown in the 1901 Census, and may be a year out.
There have undoubtedly been, and continue to be, other Chutes in Ireland whose ancestry is not known for these family trees. Some 25 Chutes appear in the directories for Tralee, Listowel and Cork.

SQUIRES AND SOLDIERS IN IRELAND

Since 1578, when young George of Bethersden went to fight for his queen in Munster, many Chutes have moved in and out of Ireland. George's son acquired an estate near Tralee in 1630 which he named Chute Hall, and there his lineage grew up for nearly 300 years. Though Protestants, they were good neighbours and sheltered Catholic priests in times of persecution.

But being land-owners who traditionally supplied officers to the British army, the senior Chute line fell foul of republicans before 1900 and were ultimately forced to quit Ireland. One went to California before the Great War; others, under death threat from the I.R.A., moved to England in the 1920s.

Some of the Chutes married as many as three times, so that children abounded at the Hall. Those who left home to make their fortunes became more identified with other local communities, and some married Catholic girls. They therefore met little nationalist hostility and many are thriving today in Listowel, Tralee and Dublin.

In this chapter we are forced to focus on the senior line at Chute Hall, as their outline genealogy, at least, was preserved in England when Dublin central records were torched in the 1920s. We know, alas, almost nothing of individual personalities.

County Kerry

The Kerry coast from Dingle to Tralee is often claimed as one of the most lovely landscapes on earth. But, being an easy entry for invaders since time out of mind, it has seen some of the bloodiest fights in history. Chute Hall (*below*) is still a place-name when you head out of Tralee on the Killarney road, just past the Ballyseedy

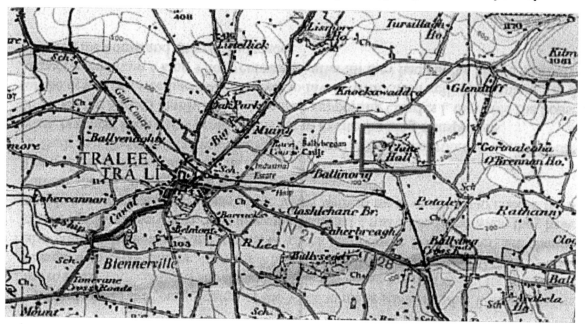

memorial. There, the family house used to hold relics from the distant past. Among Bronze Age immigrants were, surprisingly, musicians - one of whose Irish Horns was unearthed at Chute Hall. Long after, local folk developed the `Ogham language` and left curious inscriptions on standing stones; two of these remain standing on the former Chute lands (whither they were carried in the 18th century) though little else still stands to record the family's heritage.

The Rebellion of Desmond

Fifteen generations have now passed since George Chute, grandson of Philip, took up arms for the Queen against "rebellious" Irishmen in Munster. Still a teen-ager in 1578, George was fired up with the prospect of a Crusade. Ireland, he was told, must be rescued from the backwardness of Roman Catholicism, and English rule must be upheld if the Irish were ever to move forward into Protestant enlightenment. There was no time to lose, since Earl Desmond of Munster had appealed to the Pope and won his blessing for an invasion. A Catholic force would land at the Dingle, and the Earl prayed it would trigger a general uprising against England.

In Irish folk-memory, the 1579 campaign was an inhuman display of sadism by English brutes, brought up to despise the Irish race and to justify casual cruelty as being a fair blow against Popery. When the mutilated corpses had been dug in, English soldiers garrisoned the vulnerable Dingle area and backed it with a Plantation of English civilians.

After this ghastly baptism into adulthood George Chute found comfort in a Miss Evans from Cork, and stayed at Tralee. Children followed - Daniel the heir and Tom who took Holy Orders. Daniel evidently sowed wild oats until 1630, when he won the Tullygaron estate by marriage, and started building Chute Hall.

By then, his mother had died, his father had returned to England, and Revd. Tom had learned enough Gaelic for his mission to the locals. (This was prudent because Henry VIII's minions, sent out to convert Ireland to Protestantism, had only spoken English; that mission was doomed because the Irish, listening obediently, did not understand a word.)

In 1608, on his way home, George Chute was dubbed knight in Dublin for services rendered to the Crown. Since James I made income on the side by `fining` armigerous Englishmen, it is a fair guess that George paid cash for his honour.

At that date, the king's solution to the `Irish problem` was to bully the London Livery Companies into financing a massive Plantation of Protestants into Ulster. When they got there, the Londoners were angry to find themselves marooned among hostile natives and in largely uncultivable land, instead of in an idyllic paradise which had been promised.

Anglo-Irish and Proud of it

The Chutes however made a success of southern Irish life for over two centuries. As mentioned above, they stood out against the excesses of protestant sectarianism in the "penal days" by keeping a hiding-hole at Chute Hall for Catholic priests with a price on their heads. Their Kerry Dances (see below) are the stuff of legend; their hunts are in the history book.

But unlike many settlers who `went native`, the men of Chute Hall served the British Crown as county Sheriffs and became respected doctors, priests, lawyers and academics. Above all they upheld the strong Anglo-Irish military tradition, which over the years included such great names as the Duke of Wellington and Field-Marshals Lords Kitchener, Alexander and Montgomery. In the 19th C., Major General Sir Trevor Chute (the "Kerry Bull") commanded British forces in the Far East, and Francis Blennerhassett Chute married the sister of Field Marshal Lord Roberts V.C.

In this long tradition of Chute regular soldiers, one of the first into France in August 1914 was Lieut. Challoner Francis Trevor Chute of the Munster Regiment. Within days he became one of the Great War's first tragic victims (*p.157*). This did not deter his son Desmond, who was only a baby when his father was killed, from enlisting after 'Munich' in 1938 and becoming a tank commander in the 1939-45 war.

19th C. photograph of Francis Blennerhassett Chute with his family & friends

"A Bicycle Ball - one new thing under the sun"

The newspaper article "A Kerry Dance" reprinted here shows that though Chute Hall, that "fine old mansion", had no mod cons, this was no obstacle to a roistering seven-hour party, where as late as 1899 people were happy to sing for both Irish and British causes - "Wearing of the Green" and "Soldiers of the Queen" - to the music of a country damsel with a concertina. The Chutes had apparently decided *over breakfast* that the day would not be complete without a party, which could just be fitted in along with the day's hunting!

"The carefree hunting life", a historian wrote, "existed in most parts of Ireland ... Even in Kerry ... various gentlemen kept hounds; Sir John Godfrey of Kilcoleman Abbey had a pack and so had Arthur Blennerhassett of Ballyseedy and Francis Chute of Chute Hall whose huntsman, wearing an old red coat and ill-fitting breeches, would ride up and down the streets of Tralee blowing a twisted horn to advertise that there was to be a hunt.

"Francis Chute's cousin, Lord Ventry, kept a small pack of harriers at his home on the shores of Dingle harbour, where he also kept hawks and a pet seal."
(From *Twilight of the Ascendancy*, by Mark Bence-Jones, p.3)

The 'Fine Old Mansion'
Chute Hall itself was a stone-built house in Georgian style which never had electricity. It controlled a 10,000 acre estate that, besides farms, eventually included Tralee Docks. The ladies of the house

went into Tralee once a week by pony trap to do the shopping.

Behind the revelry and gay abandon, the men of Chute Hall were in fact such pillars of society that their English cousins were ready to give them the Vyne. In 1820 when Lobb Chute blood faced extinction, as neither William John nor Tom Chute had children, it is understood that William offered them the eventual bequest of his property provided they would make the Vyne their principal home. The cousins however preferred to stay in Ireland.

Chute Hall, September 1898

With hindsight this was a brave decision, because the Irish idyll was to end within that century. By the 1880s, tenants were withholding rent, farms were sabotaged and dead animals thrown at the door of the house. The harassment wore out Francis Blennerhassett Chute's health and he broken-heartedly left Tullygaron, dying at Southsea in England at only 65. One of his sons, Arthur, moved to America; the others, Richard and Challoner tried to bring up children in Kerry, but in the 1920s nationalists were making such imminent threats on their lives that the last Chutes of this, the senior, line moved away to Dublin and then to England.

Chutes in Ireland Today

In the vicinity of Tralee and Listowel there are still Chutes of the Chute Hall ancestry, twenty five or more, living and thriving in business and the professions. We have not been able to link them precisely to the 19th century 'tree' shown in Burke's because recent Chutes have not shown great interest in genealogy, and the records which might have helped us went up in flames nearly a century ago in the Dublin Post Office fire. Manuscript deeds can still be found in local museums, but their wayward script has so far defied comprehension.

In the 1920s, Chute Hall left the family ownership, gradually disintegrated and by 1950 had been dismantled by the neighbours. Some of its 17th century stonework is now visible in the walls of local farmhouses. But to show there are no hard feelings in Kerry, the local stable named its prize-winning mare "Chute Hall Lass".

(A whole book would be needed to do justice to the Chutes of Ireland; one of them should rise to the task.)

A KERRY DANCE.

Sunshine and shadow chasing each other across the green mountains and the deep hush of summer drooping over the garden. There is little of the "distressful country" aspect about this corner of Erin to-day. The orange lilies, the sweet peas, and the geraniums grow brighter than in "merrie England"; the eucalyptus, the mimosa, and the aloe strikes a tropical note. We gaze around from the depths of our deck-chairs in absolute contentment—a state of mind more common in this part of the world both to the "quality" and the proletariat than in the "busy mart."

A sound of bicycle bells breaks the stillness, and a moment later a party of youngsters is upon our fainéant group.

"Will you come to a dance to-night?"

No further preamble. Instantly the "donothings" are on the alert.

"A dance? When and where and by whom given?"

"Mr —— invites you all to Tullygarron Hall at half-past seven—afternoon dress; you must all come."

The idea is a novelty even in pleasure-loving Kerry. We accept the informal invitation with alacrity.

"We must be off now—we have to invite half the country still. The idea only dates from this morning. 'Twill be grand fun!"

And away they go, while we relapse into our deck-chairs and discuss this bolt from the blue. The host is the most popular man in the county. Tullygarron Hall is an empty house of vast dimensions some two miles distant from us. The youngsters said truly, "'Twill be grand fun!"

At 7 15 we muster at the gate—no foolish fashionable tardiness in Kerry. Here comes a crowd of guests, with ringing of bells and sounding of horns. We are swept along with the crowd, up the green lanes, then across the bog-road, where bog-cotton gleams silvery white on either hand, past two young priests, who gaze after us in astonishment, past country folk, who stand open-mouthed, past cottages and meadows bathed in the evening light, till the entrance gates of Tullygarron Hall are reached. We walk our bicycles up the steep drive, fringed with long grasses and hemlocks, and emerge on the broad terrace in front of the house. There the majority of the guests are already assembled, and a weirdly attired crowd we appear for a dance. The men have surpassed the ladies in variety of costume. Cycling suits predominate, but some choice spirits have combined evening and morning dress. A white dress tie worn with a tweed suit, a white waistcoat with gold buttons in conjunction with a tweed suit and a red tie—this latter is most suggestive of Margate sands we inform the complacent wearer—are among the finest "creations" while the white duck trousers and Norfolk jackets are not often seen in West End ball rooms, but find much favour at our "bicycle ball."

Tullygarron Hall is a fine old mansion with a spacious hall, columned and hung round with sporting trophies. The ballroom is dimly lit by primitive lamps, but the mystic light adds to the strangeness of the scene, and the floor is perfection. The "music" has not yet arrived, so those of the company, who are able, volunteer valses. When the "music" does arrive it is a surprise to the Londoner—a country damsel with a concertina. 'Tis delightfully harmonious with the entertainment, however, and we set to and foot it merrily to that instrument, which, though we up till then considered it cockney par excellence, had quite another sound and a charm of its own in Kerry.

Valses and barn-dances follow each other in rapid succession. Oh! but 'tis warm work dancing, and the claret and champagne cup, which flow in the old dining hall, are very pleasant accessories to the revel! It is cooling, too, to sit out in the garden—not on a prosaic seat—oh, no! a haycock has far more charm. A haycock, oh! ye uninitiated, is the beau ideal of a seat, for not only can you set down and its attendant ills at defiance by pulling out the top hay, but it is so delightfully fragrant, and softer than the downiest club arm-chair. There are also woods in which to wander; the summer night air is as soft as swansdown, and there is only enough moon to create a chiaroscuro which imparts a mystery and a glamour to everything.

Viens, suivons les sentiers ombreux,
Ou s'egarent les amoreux

A lancers is suggested, and we form a mammoth set on the terrace. The house with its illuminated windows makes a picturesque background, and the concertina sounds best in the open air. The fun waxes fast and furious. I should like to transplant one or two of the gilded youths who support themselves against the ballroom doors of London, to this Kerry revel of ours. I doubt even they could resist the entrain of the "bicycle ball."

Time, alas! speeds on. At last even the most untiring of us can no longer cry, "On with the dance," and songs are called for—the usual finale of an Irish dance. "Soldiers of the Queen," "Off to Philadelphia," "Tommy Atkins" (for "military" is well represented among us), and the ever delightful "Wearing of the Green" follow in rapid succession. But it is the local ditties that bring down the house. At the chorus we we all join in, link arms, and march round the room—a very comic sight:—

'Twas for ould Oireland we marched along with proide,
Drillin' in the moonloight along the mountain soide,
With grand demonsthration we thrampled down the gorse,
Then hurrah! for Captain Hickey and the Ballylooney Horse.

continued opposite

Hosts at the 1899 Kerry Dance were the brothers Richard, Arthur and Challoner Chute, pictured here in about 1913, when Richard had been placed on the roll for High Sheriff of Kerry, and Arthur was about to emigrate to California to grow oranges. Challoner, a Regular Army officer, was among the first into France in 1914 and within weeks he was killed after Mons, leaving a widow and two baby sons. One of the sons, Desmond (1913-2002) followed his father's career, and is pictured below on demobilisation in 1945. He was yachtsman in Malta, farmer in England, sensitive painter everywhere

KERRY DANCE - *CONT/*

" God save the Queen" " Auld Lang'! sung with hands crossed, bring the songs to a close. No not quite to a close. Some one starts " For he's a jolly good fellow," the host is quickly raised on many stalwart shoulders, and a scene of wild enthusiasm follows.

There is a time to come, and alas! a time to go. The bicycles are sorted out, and down the drive we start—fifty of us and more. We break into twos and threes for our dwellings are scattered, and but a small number set out over over the bog road. Surely there is one new thing under the sun, and that is a " bicycle ball" and the return therefrom. Compare our homeward journey, on the swift " bike" to the usual drive, cabbin'd, cribb'd, confin'd in cab or carriage. The bog stretches before us, around and behind us, as if to eternity. Over in the east above the mountains a faint light of dawn is seen, but the sky is still studded with stars. The air is gloriously scented; we drink it as we ride slowly, cautiously, for fear of obstacles in our path (we are all minus lamps), and also that we may enjoy the weird solitude of the scene to the utmost. It has been a night of nights—three o'clock and past ere we reach home. " Oh! the days of the Kerry dancing" we hum as we ride in at the gates. And now we add, in the words of the song :—

> Oh! to think of it, oh! to dream of it,
> Fills my heart with tears."

THE "KERRY BULL" - GEN. SIR TREVOR CHUTE, K.C.B.

Sir Trevor (1816-1886) reached the highest rank out of the many Irish Chutes who joined the British Army for service around the world. He was reputed one of the best drills in the army and would, by one account, `use the most terrible language to some...senior officers, and then at the top of his voice shout out "Very well, men ...if only you had officers to command you"` which `made a very deep impression`.

Trevor joined the army aged 16, served in the Ceylon Rifles, then in the 70th (Surrey) Regiment where in 1848 he came into conflict with his Irish fellow-countrymen by `serving during the troubles`. Thereafter he served with increasing distinction in India, Australia and New Zealand, where "throughout his career he revealed a remarkable talent for organising frontier operations".

Five years into **India** (becoming full-colonel at 38) he commanded his regiment during the Mutiny where he rescued the British officers at Peshawar and disbanded the mutinous sepoys. At Lucknow, as acting brigadier, `his initiative and resource in organising flying columns to disperse the mutineers and settle the country earned him the thanks of the Indian Government and an officer`s medal`. Behind these words we can visualise the heat, disease and moral uncertainties of that campaign; not to mention the arguments between civil and military, the supply shortages, part-dependence on native troops, and the 101 daily problems of running the operation. The Empire depended, for its security, on such super-tough men who asked no questions and achieved the near-impossible.

Trevor was spotted as an ideal frontiersman to `pacify` the Maoris, and by 1865 he was Major-General in Auckland commanding British forces in **Australia and New Zealand**. His campaigns are described in detail in the Dictionary of New Zealand Biography, which remarks that, until Chute came, the colonists of the day had despised the British regular soldier as not tough enough to cope with the bush warfare required to control the Maoris. Chute put them right by `conducting an action which, if rough, was bold, vigorous and effective`.

In 1865/6 he took up a task which his predecessor General had refused, and led a march to clear Maoris from bush lands flanking a planned Taranaki-Wanganui road. We give this as an illustration of his prowess.

The Forest March

From Wanganui, Chute marched his force through forests, over rivers, assaulting fortified villages, carrying on around Mount Egmont to Mataitawa; thence he made a rapid coastal reconnaissance northwards to Awakino, and finally marched his force back from New Plymouth to Wanganui.

`In six weeks, for the loss of nine killed and 26 wounded, Chute had marched his men 260 miles, had captured seven fortified *pas* and had reduced 20 villages`. Governor Grey commended him as displaying all the qualities of a great general.

The downside was the accusation of `undue severity` - of Chute destroying more cultivations, homes and cattle than the job warranted, and thereby aggravating the `Maori problem` for scores of years. Another says: "perhaps his only fault was his willingness to risk heavy casualties".

But the Kerry Bull was appreciated in high places; he went on to administer the **government of New South Wales** 1867/68, and to receive a K.C.B. In Australia he promoted the volunteer movement, supervising camp officers in "a rough school where rough tuition was needed". When the last British garrison was withdrawn from the State of Victoria in 1870, it was under Sir Trevor`s supervision, and in England he was promoted **full general in 1877**. He died on 12 March 1886 and his portrait was placed in the Alexander Turnbull Library at Wellington, New Zealand*.

---

* An engraving can also be found in a scrapbook in Norfolk Record Office, Norwich; file ref MC 166/260, 633x1

CHALLONER FRANCIS CHUTE - LIFE CUT SHORT IN WAR

Out of all the miseries of war, we single out a young wife, with a baby son and another on the way, who loses her husband in August 1914 within a fortnight of his battalion going to France. The War is expected to be "over by Christmas" but grows unimaginably - far beyond the experience of any of its generals - into the vast amorphous killing in Flanders. When nobody can see an end, what can such a woman hold on to?

Challoner (the Irish spelling) had had the good looks, talents and humour to succeed in any career; but as a Regular Officer in the Munster Fusiliers he was one of the first into France. Baby Desmond was a year old; Maud Chute was expecting little Challoner when war began and her husband went away, to an almost immediate death.

After Mons

The Germans had prepared every step in advance, even the number of days within which they would take Paris. But they had not calculated that Britain would fight, and when our small regular army crossed to France in 1914 as the British Expeditionary Force, the Kaiser supposedly ordered General von Kluck to: "*address all your skill and all the valour of my soldiers to exterminate the treacherous English and their contemptible little army*". Hence the BEF, having broken a German advance by their initial victory at Mons in mid-August, were happy to become known as "the Contemptibles".

But Germany called up more troops to Mons and the BEF were heavily outnumbered. Retreat is the hardest military operation to manage. Soldiers are exhausted and communication lines break down. In 1914 there were no field radios nor air reconnaissance. Once the telephone lines were left behind in retreat, messages had to be sent by bugle call or by motorcycle dispatch-rider.

The Munsters 2nd Battalion was sent forward to hold the enemy at bay and cover the retreat of the men from Mons, now exhausted from long marches with swollen feet in the heat of summer. The moment came at last when the Staff sent a rider to tell the Munsters at Étreux that they could withdraw. The rider was captured. A second rider was sent; the Germans shot him on the road.

Étreux

" At dawn the Munsters found themselves attacked by several German battalions and presently realised that their retreat was cut off. They made a good fight for several hours, hoping to hold out till help should come. But all the while their comrades in First Corps were marching away southward, utterly unaware of their desperate position."

Their colonel and most of the Munsters' officers were killed at Étreux; it was only when their ammunition ran out that, completely surrounded, the remnant of the heroic battalion surrendered. Within this rearguard action, our cousin defied fate with personal heroism. A fellow soldier later wrote to Mrs Chute in Ireland:

" Chuty, with his guns, which he handled with really wonderful skill, covered the withdrawal of my Company at mid-day. It was pouring with rain, and with entire disregard of personal comfort (characteristic of him) he lay down in 6 inches of water to manipulate his guns the better. Owing to the help of your husband's guns the company got safely through.

" Chuty brought his machine-guns back at the gallop along the road under a positive hail of lead. It was a splendid feat, successfully accomplished, and once again the guns were placed in position. We were now completely surrounded, and your husband crossed the road to try and find a target to aim at. As he crossed, he was shot...and fell dead. Up to the last he was cheery and full of spirits as ever...

" Yesterday the Germans allowed us to send out a burial party of our own men, and they found Chuty and buried him with the other officers of the regiment who were killed."

Étreux today is a dull little town. The best-kept part of it is the British War Cemetery where Chuty lies, among the cheery young men, officers and other ranks, who fought here and died because that dispatch never got through.

GV RI

HE whom this scroll commemorates
was numbered among those who,
at the call of King and Country, left all
that was dear to them, endured hardness,
faced danger, and finally passed out of
the sight of men by the path of duty
and self-sacrifice, giving up their own
lives that others might live in freedom.
Let those who come after see to it
that his name be not forgotten.

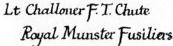

Lt Challoner F. T. Chute
Royal Munster Fusiliers

2ND BN ROYAL MUNSTER FUSILIERS
ETREUX 27TH AUGUST 1914.

"THE ACTION IS LIKELY TO BECOME THE CLASSICAL EXAMPLE OF
THE PERFORMANCE OF ITS FUNCTIONS BY A REARGUARD. THE
BATTALION NOT ONLY HELD UP THE ATTACK OF A STRONG HOSTILE
FORCE IN ITS ORIGINAL POSITION THEREBY SECURING THE UNMOLESTED
WITHDRAWAL OF ITS DIVISION BUT IN RETIRING DREW ON TO ITSELF
THE ATTACK OF VERY SUPERIOR NUMBERS OF THE ENEMY IT WAS
FINALLY CUT OFF AT ETREUX BY FIVE OR SIX TIMES ITS NUMBERS BUT
HELD OUT FOR SEVERAL HOURS THE REGIMENT ONLY SURRENDERING
WHEN THEIR AMMUNITION WAS PRACTICALLY EXHAUSTED AND ONLY
A SMALL NUMBER OF MEN REMAINED UNHURT. THE SURVIVORS
WERE WARMLY CONGRATULATED BY THE GERMANS ON THE FINE
FIGHT THEY HAD MADE. NO OTHER CLAIM TO A MEMORIAL NEAR
ETREUX IS LIKELY TO BE ADVANCED – CERTAINLY NOTHING WHICH
WOULD NOT TAKE SECOND PLACE TO THE MUNSTERS."

Above: A plaque in Étreux Military Cemetery.

*Left: Memorial, with Chute's name sixth in the list,
outside St Jude's Church in Southsea, Hampshire
(where his father F B Chute retired from Ireland after
harassment by republicans in Co. Kerry)*

EAST ANGLIAN CHUTES
IN THE 16/17th CENTURIES

___

1. FAMILY TREE - FROM ANTHONY TO:
   - LIONEL & THE AMERICAN BRANCH
   - ARTHUR & THE VYNE BRANCH

2. CHUTES IN "CROMWELL COUNTRY"

3. CHARLES, M.P. - PARLIAMENTARIAN

4. LIONEL AND ROSE OF DEDHAM

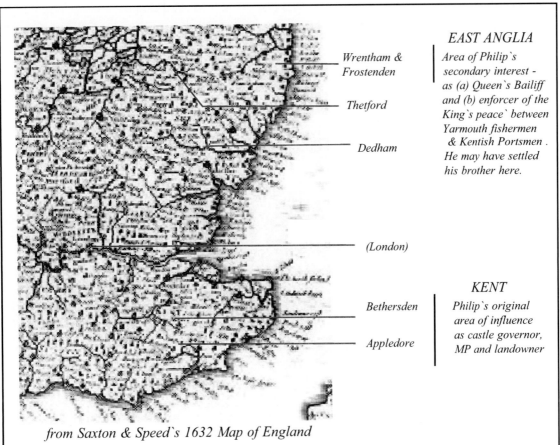

EAST ANGLIA

Area of Philip`s secondary interest - as (a) Queen`s Bailiff and (b) enforcer of the King`s peace` between Yarmouth fishermen & Kentish Portsmen . He may have settled his brother here.

Wrentham & Frostenden

Thetford

Dedham

(London)

KENT

Philip`s original area of influence as castle governor, MP and landowner

Bethersden

Appledore

from Saxton & Speed`s 1632 Map of England

Philip Chowte of Appledore bought Surrenden Manor at Bethersden and other properties in Kent from about 1540 on. In that year he became Queen Anne of Cleves`s bailiff at Frostenden in Suffolk, and his 3rd wife came from nearby Wrentham.
`Arthare Chewte` (Philip`s brother?) is recorded at Ellough in the same part of Suffolk.
Philip`s nephew Arthur had land at Wrentham c. 1600; this Arthur`s son Charles (father of Chaloner Chute the Speaker) was Member of Parliament for Thetford; his nephew Lionel married a girl from Dedham, whence they sailed with 3 children to America in 1634.

CHUTE FAMILY TREE 4 -
DESCENT FROM ANTHONY, BROTHER OF PHILIP

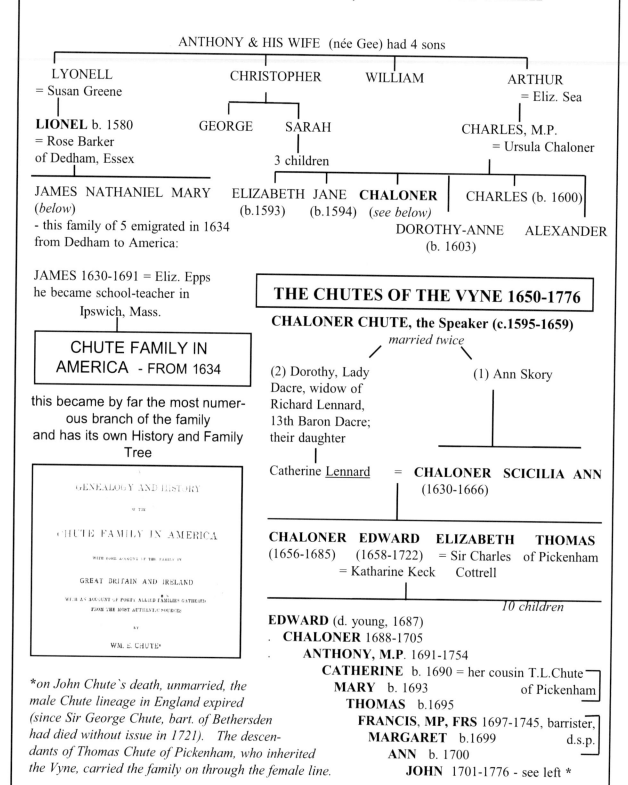

ANTHONY & HIS WIFE (née Gee) had 4 sons

LYONELL
= Susan Greene

CHRISTOPHER

WILLIAM

ARTHUR
= Eliz. Sea

LIONEL b. 1580
= Rose Barker
of Dedham, Essex

GEORGE   SARAH

3 children

CHARLES, M.P.
= Ursula Chaloner

JAMES NATHANIEL MARY
(*below*)
- this family of 5 emigrated in 1634
from Dedham to America:

ELIZABETH JANE **CHALONER**
(b.1593)   (b.1594) (*see below*)

CHARLES (b. 1600)

DOROTHY-ANNE   ALEXANDER
(b. 1603)

JAMES 1630-1691 = Eliz. Epps
he became school-teacher in
Ipswich, Mass.

CHUTE FAMILY IN
AMERICA - FROM 1634

this became by far the most numerous branch of the family
and has its own History and Family
Tree

GENEALOGY AND HISTORY

CHUTE FAMILY IN AMERICA

WITH SOME ACCOUNT OF THE FAMILY IN

GREAT BRITAIN AND IRELAND

WITH AN ACCOUNT OF FORTY ALLIED FAMILIES GATHERED
FROM THE MOST AUTHENTIC SOURCES

BY

WM. E. CHUTE*

THE CHUTES OF THE VYNE 1650-1776

CHALONER CHUTE, the Speaker (c.1595-1659)
married twice

(2) Dorothy, Lady
Dacre, widow of
Richard Lennard,
13th Baron Dacre;
their daughter

Catherine <u>Lennard</u>

(1) Ann Skory

= **CHALONER   SCICILIA   ANN**
(1630-1666)

CHALONER   EDWARD   ELIZABETH   THOMAS
(1656-1685)   (1658-1722)   = Sir Charles   of Pickenham
= Katharine Keck   Cottrell

10 children

EDWARD (d. young, 1687)
. **CHALONER** 1688-1705
.   **ANTHONY, M.P.** 1691-1754
CATHERINE b. 1690 = her cousin T.L.Chute
MARY b. 1693   of Pickenham
THOMAS b.1695
FRANCIS, MP, FRS 1697-1745, barrister,
MARGARET b.1699   d.s.p.
ANN b. 1700
JOHN 1701-1776 - see left *

**on John Chute`s death, unmarried, the
male Chute lineage in England expired
(since Sir George Chute, bart. of Bethersden
had died without issue in 1721).   The descendants of Thomas Chute of Pickenham, who inherited
the Vyne, carried the family on through the female line.*

THE CHUTES IN 'CROMWELL COUNTRY'

This curious portrait at the Vyne shows a thoroughly miserable old man and a confident-looking wife with a letter between them. Either she does not want to read it, or she is proud of the news. He looks ready to die. Modern historians (who like to turn things inside out in the manner of puppies or clothes-washing machines) would have it that they are Lady Dacre's ancestors.

In fact they are Arthur (born c.1547) and Elizabeth Chute, of Wrentham, Suffolk, grandparents of Chaloner Chute of the Vyne. She was of the Say, or Sea, family (related to Lord Say and Sele), a political clan of whom two became Speakers of the Commons.

Since her son Charles was the first of a long line of Chute lawyer-MPs, and her grandson became Speaker himself, it

Arthur and Elizabeth Chute, grandparents of the Speaker

seems perfectly fair that she looks us proudly in the eye. Before her, after all, the Chutes of East Anglia were socially of no great note. Arthur's father Anthony (brother of Philip the Standard Bearer) is still only a name without a profile, and his nephew Lionel was the school-master who emigrated to America.

CHARLES CHUTE, M.P.

Elizabeth, we guess, pushed young Charles into the Law in about 1580 as a stepping-stone to political advancement. Under her namesake Queen Elizabeth I, Charles became 'feodary and clerk of the markets of the Queen in the Duchy of Lancaster', and served as an MP for Thetford in 1592-3. Under James I, he worked in London codifying land registrations and, curiously, was one of only seven gentlemen allowed to visit Ralegh in the Tower. Till now, his father would still have been proud of him. But in 1634 Charles, perhaps still living at Kelvedon, Essex among the Puritans of 'Cromwell country', joined the Parliamentarian camp.

By then, of course, the political world was turning upside down; so if you treat the top picture as "allegory" and want a legend as to why old Arthur looks so disillusioned, you could say that the letter was from Charles

Charles Chute, MP for Thetford, husband of Ursula Chaloner and father of the Speaker

announcing he had thrown in his lot with Cromwell; and that Elizabeth's confident gaze represents the victory of political pragmatism over conservatism. Not a bad ikon for the Chutes of the Vyne to keep over their hearth?

FAMILY LANDMARKS IN SUFFOLK

The round-tower of All Saints Church, **Frostenden** (*left and below*) where on 8 September 1578 Lyonell Chute married Susan Greene. Ten years later, with their son Lionel, they could have watched from this tower as the defeated Spanish Armada fled northwards. In 1634 Lionel emigrated to Massachusetts.

Philip Chowte, Lyonell's uncle, had been appointed by Henry VIII in 1540 as Bailiff of Frostenden Manor for Queen Anne of Cleves, and held the post for life. He had weightier responsibilities in Kent, so did not normally remain in Suffolk himself; one deduces that his brother moved to this county as Philip's deputy, since Chutes are recorded up to about 1630 here and at nearby villages: <u>Wrentham</u> (home of Philip's third wife) where Lyonell's cousin Arthur owned land; at <u>Sotterley</u> and at <u>Ellough</u>, home of 'Arthare' and Margaret (*see below*).

Frostenden now lies some miles from the sea, but in the 16th C. it included salt-pans, important for salting the fish to be distributed inland. At the biggest local fish market, Yarmouth, Philip Chowte was the king's emissary in trying to end murderous disputes between Kentish & East Anglian fishermen.

The earliest known original Chute memorial (1607)
In Ellough Church (now disused) this small but elegant group of brasses in memory of Margaret Chewt has survived for four centuries. Surmounted by the "Chewt" coat of arms (*ringed left, enlarged below*) and her father's, a female figure with head-dress, its lineaments now defaced, stands above the inscription:

"Margaret Chewt, the faythfull loving wyfe of Arthare Chewt, gentleman, daughter to Christopher Playters, Esquer, who died at thage of 85, in ffebruarie 1607".

Inscribed 'CHEWT' at its head, the shield shows our 3 swords - but not the canton or the stars, since 'Arthare' did not descend from Philip (we deduce that he was his brother)

Dedham, Essex is a place of pilgrimage for the American Chutes.
Also for citizens of Dedham, Massachusetts, who occasionally come together
here in Essex and have generously donated funds for restoration of the church.

Dedham

In 1634 **Lionel Chute**, a man of 54 with a young wife Rose, née Barker (herself
from Dedham) and their children James, Nathaniel and Mary, the youngest only 15,
packed the family sea-chest and took sail for the three-month voyage to America.
The boat was crowded, the crossing stormy, the passengers sea-sick and ill-
tempered, and the medicine primitive. (We know that 200 years later, you could
not buy a transatlantic ticket in Bristol without also paying a costly U.S hospital
charge in advance). As to their landfall, maps in 1634 showed the interior of North
America blank - and therefore
haunted by monsters and evil
spirits (which were still very
strongly believed in).

Lionel may have been fed up
with England's civil unrest, or
fleeing the war to come, but
Rose, in accepting this unpre-
dictable but certainly tough
future for her home-making,
was a woman of rare courage.
How fitting that her descendants should have become by
far the most numerous of the
Chute clan, and to have gone
on to spread into all parts of
the globe.

*Exact replicas of the ships that brought the first settlers to
Virginia, moored on the James River.*

~ 163 ~

In the muniments room at Dedham Church is a copy of the old parish record showing James, son of Lionell Chute, baptised on February 2, 1614. On the same page you find three children baptised in 1614 from the Sherman family.

The Shermans, soon to become illustrious in the US, were among many who embarked from Dedham`s river port in Puritan times. In 1600 Edmund Sherman left his house to Dedham`s Free Grammar School (where, in time, the painter John Constable was to learn his

letters). The building still stands, complete with 18th century pupils` names carved in the brick. It faces the church porch from whose roof the Puritan preacher "Roaring Rogers" thundered his calls for repentance for 31 years from 1605.

The internal roof of the nave, under which the Chutes worshipped, is adorned today with escutcheons illustrating the church`s history. Among them is the Avery Oak of Dedham, Mass. Below, a fine pew-end carved with the first Great Seal of the American Republic (1787) prominently commemorates the generosity of the people of Dedham, Mass.

The Avery Oak
Dedham,
Massachusetts

THE COMMEMORATION PEW TO THE PEOPLE OF
DEDHAM, MASSACHUSETTS.

STAYING ON IN SOMERSET

1. THE EARLY CHUTES OF BRIDGWATER

2. ROBERT CHUTE`S `BREACH OF PROMISE`

3. JAMES HENRY : ACTOR-MANAGER
AT BATH AND BRISTOL

4. FATHER DESMOND - MISSION AMONG ARTISTS

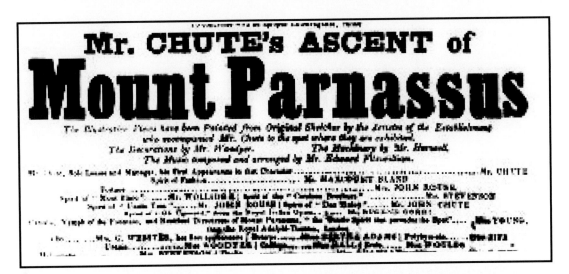

19TH CENTURY THEATRE BILL

James Henry Chute and the plan for his New Theatre Royal in Bristol, built 1867

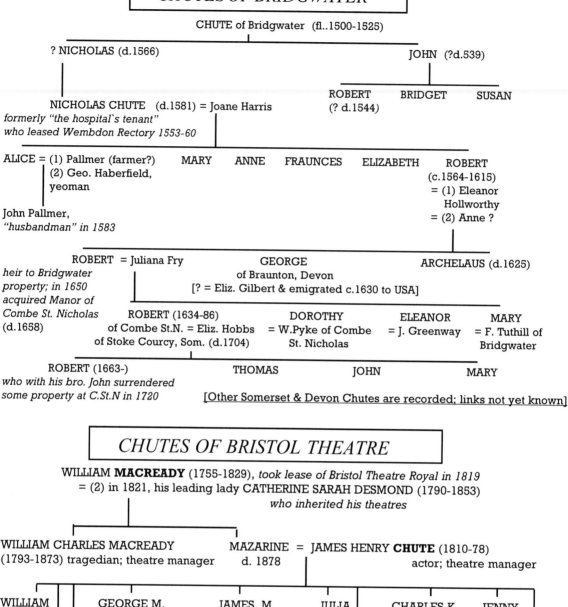

CHUTES OF BRIDGWATER

CHUTE of Bridgwater (fl..1500-1525)

? NICHOLAS (d.1566)   JOHN (?d.539)

ROBERT   BRIDGET   SUSAN
(? d.1544)

NICHOLAS CHUTE (d.1581) = Joane Harris
formerly "the hospital`s tenant"
who leased Wembdon Rectory 1553-60

ALICE = (1) Pallmer (farmer?)   MARY   ANNE   FRAUNCES   ELIZABETH   ROBERT
         (2) Geo. Haberfield,   (c.1564-1615)
         yeoman   = (1) Eleanor
                                                                                Hollworthy
John Pallmer,   = (2) Anne ?
"husbandman" in 1583

ROBERT = Juliana Fry   GEORGE   ARCHELAUS (d.1625)
heir to Bridgwater   of Braunton, Devon
property; in 1650   [? = Eliz. Gilbert & emigrated c.1630 to USA]
acquired Manor of
Combe St. Nicholas   ROBERT (1634-86)   DOROTHY   ELEANOR   MARY
(d.1658)   of Combe St.N. = Eliz. Hobbs = W.Pyke of Combe = J. Greenway = F. Tuthill of
                      of Stoke Courcy, Som. (d.1704)   St. Nicholas   Bridgwater

ROBERT (1663-)   THOMAS   JOHN   MARY
who with his bro. John surrendered
some property at C.St.N in 1720   [Other Somerset & Devon Chutes are recorded; links not yet known]

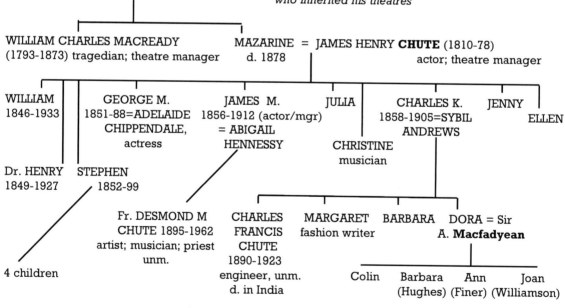

CHUTES OF BRISTOL THEATRE

WILLIAM **MACREADY** (1755-1829), *took lease of Bristol Theatre Royal in 1819*
= (2) in 1821, his leading lady CATHERINE SARAH DESMOND (1790-1853)
who inherited his theatres

WILLIAM CHARLES MACREADY   MAZARINE = JAMES HENRY **CHUTE** (1810-78)
(1793-1873) tragedian; theatre manager   d. 1878   actor; theatre manager

WILLIAM   GEORGE M.   JAMES M.   JULIA   CHARLES K.   JENNY
1846-1933   1851-88=ADELAIDE 1856-1912 (actor/mgr)   1858-1905=SYBIL   ELLEN
             CHIPPENDALE,   = ABIGAIL   ANDREWS
             actress   HENNESSY   CHRISTINE
                                               musician
Dr. HENRY   STEPHEN
1849-1927   1852-99

            Fr. DESMOND M   CHARLES   MARGARET   BARBARA   DORA = Sir
            CHUTE 1895-1962 FRANCIS   fashion writer   A. **Macfadyean**
            artist; musician; priest CHUTE
            unm.   1890-1923
                             engineer, unm.
4 children   d. in India   Colin   Barbara   Ann   Joan
                                                        (Hughes) (Finer) (Williamson)

EARLY CHUTES IN BRIDGWATER

In the 1500s, when parish records became obligatory, Bridgwater emerges as the Chute centre in Somerset. It was an old river port and market town, larger but perhaps of lower social esteem than lordly Taunton which had a Castle and Priory. After the Taunton Chutes had sold up and gone (reputedly selling their land to nobility but more likely to their Bridgwater cousins), a clutch of documents brings these cousins to life. For their `human interest` we will single out Widow Maude, née Chute (1555), and Robert Chute (1583).

A SOMERSET WILL OF 1555

"A HEIFER CALF AND MY BLUE APRON"

Imagine going through life with the name Vermyn. But in Huntspill, north of Bridgwater, one farmer did, and Maude Chute married him. As a `spare woman` she probably had to accept even a humble proposal of marriage. She died as a widow in 1555 and her Will is touching in its careful distribution of simple things.

She had £24.3.8 in property, and her concern was to distribute a few cattle, beans, malt, aprons, smock, petticoats, etc among her family, godchildren and friends. In this short document she spelt her own family name in 3 different ways.

Last Will & Testament of Maude Vermyn, widow, of Huntspill, Somerset, dated 21 January 1555/6, her "Inventory" (including cash and chattels) being valued at "xxiiij.li. iij.s. viij.d"

I commend my soul to the mercy of Almighty God and my body to be buried in the churchyard of Hunspill.

I leave to the mother church of Welles iiij.d. To the church of Hunspill vj.s. viij.d. and my best kerchief. To beginning of Our Lady service a cow, my beads, ij. rings and a neckerchief. To the maintenance of the church way vj.s. viij.d.

To my brother William Chute a heifer of iij. years of age. To Elizabeth Chute a heifer calf and my blue apron. To William Chute, Julyan Cute (sic) and Robert Cute a calf betwixt them. To my sister Johan Chut my best kirtle, a white petticoat, a cappe, a knitter, an apron, a neckerchief, my blue mantle and a smock. To Hew Alleyne half a bushel of beans. To every of my godchildren iiij.d. To the church of Suthbrent xij.d. To Ede Bond my red petticoat with a camlet bodice. To Julian Chut my violet coat. To John Clarke vj.d. To Nicholas Fiffer half a bushel of malt. To William Louen half a bushel of malt. The residue to Robert Vermyn my son, whom I make executor.

Witnesses - Sir John Fysshepole, curate there, Nicolas Fiffar, William Chute, John Westcott, with others.

[Text printed in "Mediaeval Wills from Wells", a volume in the records of the Somerset History Society]

Other 16th century Chute wills from the area of Bridgwater, Wembdon and Chilton enable us to reconstruct the family tree opposite, with the help of land deeds preserved in Somerset County Archives at Taunton. But one of our archives produced a nasty surprise.

Young Robert Chute's `Breach of Promise`

If you are a genealogist hunting for records of the lordly Chutes of Taunton, it is mortifying to meet an archive showing rotten (if not unprecedented) behaviour by their teen-age relative at Bridgwater.

In 1583 Robert Chute, aged 18-19, son of Nicholas, was haled to court for **Breach of Promise of Marriage**. Written depositions to the court attest the young Elizabeth Seelie's anguished claim that Robert had definitely pledged himself to marry her. He of course denied it, and (whatever he had or hadn't done with Elizabeth) managed to get himself a `better marriage` soon after - to the daughter of one of the witnesses for the defence.

The outcome of the legal action does not survive, but the statements made by others in his defence have a timeless charm: e.g. how could he possibly have said such a thing to a mere village girl when he was already promised to my daughter and I had undertaken to "*geve to her mariage one hundred pownd*"?
Chute records do not mention the Seelie family's side of the case apart from her father's comment
"*Mr Seelye articulate did tell this deponent that he did marvaile whie Robert Chute was so greate a stranger unto him*",
but Robert's father Nicholas did let slip to a neighbour that "*he thought his sonn wold be but a bad howsband himselfe*".

For those who want to get at the gory detail of the case, and are prepared to test their skill in reading 16th century script, a section of the court record is provided above.

Robert's legitimate descendants in Somerset went on to include lords of the manor at Combe St. Nicholas and substantial taxpaying landowners at Wells; also the earliest Chute emigrant to America. In "Leaves on the Tree" (p.203) we outline the family's broad range in Somerset and Devon, but little is known of their personalities, so we will now leap 250 years, across a gap in family records (which we invite anyone to fill). After the Chutes sold the manor of Combe St. Nicholas in about 1720 and disappeared from local records, we guess that some of their comfortable inheritance helped to educate our next character, James Henry Chute.

James Henry Chute - Actor/Manager

Which of the Chutes in our history gave the greatest pleasure to the greatest number? John Chute of the Vyne, perhaps - with his wonderful Staircase and Tomb Chamber.

However, what about a man who, with his like-minded sons, dominated a city`s stage for nearly a century both as actors and theatre managers, bringing the best plays and players before the public and making Bristol the `final stage before the London West End`? Today`s Bristol Old Vic - inheritor of Chute`s **Theatre Royal** - still enjoys that status.
But James Henry Chute, a big hearty man with a huge moustache and unwavering optimism, ran <u>three theatres</u> concurrently, the Theatre Royal in Bath and two in Bristol, on famously high principles.

J. H. Chute

A writer declared in 1925: "There is no building in Bristol that has given so much pleasure to our generation as the **Prince`s Theatre**. It was our fairyland when we were children. It has proved our delight ever since."   That was the second Bristol theatre that Chute ran; he himself built and owned it, and his sons and his daughter-in-law carried it on until the 1930`s.

"Bristol owes much to the Chute management, and has always been aware of the fact. (It) has been characterised by the production of good plays by first-class artists, and with this excellence ... the Chute management has a clean record. Good art and good living have been combined on our stage. A greater blessing for a large city would be impossible to find". This verdict reminds us of the years when theatre had to struggle against people who thought it, on principle, disreputable.

It also reflects Chute`s remarkable skill in bringing out the best in individual actors and singers, and creating so happy an atmosphere at Bristol that the top stars like Henry Irving and Ellen Terry, Clara Butt and Beerbohm Tree, played under him, becoming his friends and admirers. Many such great signatures

can be seen on the letters preserved in the fascinating Chute collection at Bristol University`s Drama Department.

Runaway Marriage
James, born in 1810, had been a roving actor and a particular favourite in Dublin, when he joined the Bristol company; it was managed by Catherine Desmond, the widow of William Macready (died 1829) who ran two Theatres Royal at Bath and Bristol. James wasted no time in finding himself a girl, and she was a winner.

Catherine had a daughter Mazarine, and the legend says that James ran off with her. But her mother forgave their marriage when the young man proved he could handle contracts and also supervise plays. He became Catherine's right-hand man until her death in 1853, after which he took over both theatres' leases as actor/manager.

Bringing Out Actors

Seeing his bluff portrait, one can easily believe the report that the part of Falstaff particularly suited him. You might not expect a man of his build to have also been "the most expert swordsman in the profession", so here (in the words of a playwright Rennie Palgrave) is one of many tales recorded of Chute's management, to show his skill in handling actors.

A new leading man, Vernon, was rehearsing a stage fight for a forthcoming play, and Chute was on the stage watching. "Not that way, Mr Vernon", he presently said, "you would be disarmed". Pardon me, Mr Chute," replied Vernon, "I rather pride myself upon my rapier practice".

His manager, holding forth his hand for the other foil, instantly engaged with Vernon and, after a few passes, sent the other's foil whizzing into the Pit. Vernon really blushed, for the other actors had now gathered on stage for a rehearsal.

"I was hardly prepared for such vigour, Sir", he said, and "Bring Mr Vernon his weapon", rejoined Mr Chute. A stage hand passed up the foil, but (guessing what might follow) sat down in the Pit. Again the foils crossed, and after a slightly longer interval away went the actor's foil into almost the same spot as before. Without a suspicion of "I told you so!" the manager resigned his foil and turned up the stage.

"Thank you, Sir, for a valuable lesson" cried the defeated swordsman handsomely.
"We are none of us too old to learn", observed Mr Chute gently, and added:
"You see, someone in front might have known as much about it as you and I".

That subtle blend of discipline, tact, reason and encouragement could scarcely be bettered.

Frenchy hands

Another actor called Chute "a fine looking man, deep in the chest, broad in the shoulder, with twinkling eyes, that can be severe ... his hands are Frenchy in their action, and he is never seen without a pair of gloves - which I am told he has never been known to put on."

Father of Ten

"Greatly proud of his numerous offspring, Mr Chute was their companion as well as father, but, affecting an inability to recall in correct rotation the names of his ten children, he numbered them; and in that way he always addressed them at home. "Number five", he would say, "if you are going into the study, ask number seven to come to me"."

His Very Own Theatre

Theatres lit by gas and candles were notoriously exposed to fire, and in 1862 the Theatre Royal in Bath was burnt to ashes. Chute rebuilt it at his own expense.

An incurable optimist, he lived at the limit of his income; indeed he was forced to do so by the parsimony of the Bristol theatre's proprietors - who would not replace the unsafe gas pipes or even instal mains water in case of fire. After Catherine's death he did all these modernisations and internal enlargements at his own expense, though he was still only a lessee; it very nearly bankrupted him.

To be his own master in Bristol he built in 1867 - at considerable financial risk - a **New Theatre Royal** in the more fashionable Park Row, with double the seating capacity of the old theatre. His sons later renamed it the **Prince's Theatre** to avoid confusion when they gave up the lease on the old theatre in 1884. It flourished under Chute family management until the 1930's, but was destroyed by a bomb ten years later.

Curtain

In 1878 James and Mazarine died within a few months of each other, having produced ten children, acted in and managed three major theatres, and left a first-class reputation in the theatrical world.

Desmond Macready Chute

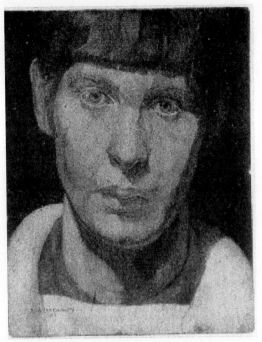

As war loomed in 1914, this introspective self-portrait of Desmond Chute, musician, painter, craftsman and intellectual, sadly contemplated a world on the verge of self-destruction. We remember him especially as:

(a) the only Chute to have his work honoured in a national art collection - his drawing of Eric Gill is in the National Portrait Gallery;
(b) notable for his gift, from an early age, of patiently helping fellow artists through mental crises which threatened their creativity.

For example, we take Stanley Spencer and Eric Gill for granted as major artists of their time. But they were famously tangled characters, and it was Desmond's support and mediation which guided their vivid self-searchings out of psychic danger and into spiritual harmony.

Being the only son of actor-manager James Macready Chute, Desmond was expected to take over the Bristol Theatre. After a Catholic education (his mother's faith) at Downside where he was Head of School, and a course in painting at the Slade, he emerged as an all-round artist - musician, painter, engraver. Though tall and accounted good-looking, he was shy, hating bright lights, and, by accident, found a vocation on meeting **Stanley Spencer**. The 24-year old painter from Cookham, Berks., full of a vision of Christ dwelling in Cookham and working His redemptive life through its villagers, had been sent to Bristol to work as a hospital orderly, before war service overseas. He hated the place, the 'living by numbers', the endless disturbance. We have Spencer's imagery of his meeting with the 20-year-old Desmond:

"I had a visit from a young intellectual ... who, like Christ visiting Hell, came one day walking to me along a stone-coloured passage with coloured glass windows all down one side and a highly patterned floor... I had a sack tied round my waist and a bucket of dirty water in my hand...

"The usual visitors passed us orderlies by, as they would pass a row of bedpans, (but) the nearer he came, the more deferential his deportment, until at last he stood and asked me with the utmost respect whether I was Stanley Spencer."

To Spencer the meeting was "a godsend"; "he appreciated the mental suffering I was going through". Becoming a close friend, Desmond entered the painter's visionary world, and by finding the concept Spencer needed - that his servitude at the hospital could be offered as a personal sacrament in Christ's service - "is now regarded" (a biographer says) "as largely instrumental in restoring Stanley's confidence in painting".

Spencer later wrote "The colour of Chute's hair is a brilliant rust-gold ... he reminded me in character of John the Baptist... he has a mind so quickened by God that you can do nothing but live when you are with him.

"Sometimes when we have been out for a walk - wonderful walks - I would begin to ask him about some particular novelist and he would go through a whole novel quoting pages and pages, quite unconsciously ... I used to sit looking out of the wide-open window and listen to him translating Homer and `Odyssey`, the `Iliad` and Cyclops and the men escaping under the sheep, oh my goodness, it really did frighten me. I have looked at different translations of Homer, but nothing to approach Desmond's..."

———

In 1918, while Spencer was serving overseas, Desmond chanced to find **Eric Gill** (calligrapher, engraver and stone-mason) working on his `Stations of the Cross` carving in Westminster Cathedral.   Their instant rapport led to Desmond joining the **Ditchling Community**, near Brighton, where the Arts & Crafts Movement had brought together artists in wood, stone, silver, cloth and print. This was not just a revival of the mediaeval guild, for quality control and promotion of its members` work. It was a quasi-monastic group of men working according to their beliefs as Catholics. Here Desmond learned stone carving and wood engraving under Gill, and with him became a founder member of the `Guild of St Joseph and St Dominic` set up at Ditchling in 1920.

Outsiders called them "married monks", and suspected them of using religion to cloak their dangerous sexual and psychological problems. Clearly they were an odd bunch. Gill, one of the great engravers and stone-carvers of the 20th C. but accused of incest and child-abuse, undoubtedly needed analysis and a steadying hand. He later wrote to Desmond how unable he felt to express "how much I owe you and how much I learned from you ...and am inspired by you". This echoes Spencer`s apprehension of Desmond`s mind "so quickened by God".

Desmond Chute at 21

Chute left the Community in 1921 to pursue a wider vocation, under the guidance of a famous visionary Father Vincent McNab. After ordination as priest in 1927 he was advised, to protect his tubercular lungs, to move to the warmth of Italy. He and his mother were granted a 5-minute audience with the Pope, but Pius XI was so impressed by the young priest that they spent half an hour together, while Abigail knelt beside he son "in ecstasy"

In 1931, Desmond`s mother Abigail died, and in gratitude to them Gill undertook to sculpt a public memorial to her, for it was she - when she saw there was no hope of bringing Desmond back into the world of theatre - who had given the Guild money to buy land at Ditchling Common for its workshop and cottages. In the memorial group at a Bristol cemetery (*below*) Gill`s 1932 sculpture is central. After Desmond`s death and burial in 1962 at Rapallo, other hands carved the smaller stones, dedicated to his memory (*left*) and of his aunt Annie.

Eric Gill c.1938
TO

**Desmond Chute`s
portrait of
Eric Gill**

(National Portrait
Gallery)

~ 173 ~

Father Desmond at Rapallo in 1958

While serving as priest in Rapallo, Desmond met Yeats and Max Beerbohm, and was an active member of the Tigullian Circle of writers, musicians and artists surrounding Ezra Pound. At Christmas 1955 the BBC broadcast a radio play by Desmond entitled "Poets in Paradise".

To conclude: - why, given his extraordinary range of talents as a young man, in music, literature and the arts of drawing, wood-carving and sculpture in stone, did Desmond not grow into greatness as an artist, far beyond that one drawing in the National Portrait Gallery? One friend (Walter Shewring) judged him incapable of the selfishness or intellectual hardness needed for producing important `creative art`; Desmond`s sensibility reached out towards all the detail of God`s creation: "He was essentially a Catholic priest, living a full life with wide spiritual sympathies extending alike to the dignities of a departing social order, to the intellectual subtleties of the Mozart *Concertante* or the *Anathemata* of David Jones, to the traditional workman and to all trades with their gear and tackle and trim, to the victims of war and the harried cats and dogs of Genoa". Between 1939-1945 even the Blackshirts of Mussolini and the occupying Germans gave him exceptional freedom of movement. After the war he rebuilt at his own expense the Chapel of the Redeemer in Rapallo, destroyed by a British bomb, adding a memorial to a priest who had then been killed in the confessional: *inter remittenda peccata animam pro ovibus posuit* (even while remitting sins, he gave up his life for the sheep).

Two of Desmond`s many woodcuts on view at Ditchling Museum, Sussex

TRIBUTES TO A GREAT THEATRE FAMILY

ERIC GILL`S MEMORIAL SCULPTURE
in memory of
Desmond Chute`s mother

Abigail Philomena Chute (d. 1931)

who prolonged
the Chute era of
Bristol theatre
management
for almost 20 years
after the death of
her husband
James Macready Chute

(memorial in
Canford Cemetery,
Westbury-on-Trym,
Bristol)

below: extract from a
PLAYBILL ANNOUNCING THE OPENING OF BRISTOL THEATRE ROYAL* FOR THE SEASON STARTING SEPTEMBER 12TH 1853

After the play, on the opening night,

God Save the Queen, by the Whole Company.

To conclude with an apropos Extravaganza, called

Mr. CHUTE's ASCENT of
Mount Parnassus

The Illustrative Views have been Painted from Original Sketches by the Artists of the Establishment
who accompanied Mr. Chute to the spot where they are exhibited.
The Decorations by Mr. Woolgar.   The Machinery by Mr. Harvell.
The Music composed and arranged by Mr. Edward Fitzwilliam.

Mr. Chute, Sole Lessee and Manager, his First Appearance in that Character.................................Mr. CHUTE
Spirit of Fashion.................................Mr. HARCOURT BLAND.
Fortune.................................Mrs. JOHN ROUSE.
Spirit of " Mned Elinu ".....Mr. WOLLIDGE | Spirit of the " Corsican Brothers "............Mrs. STEVENSON
Spirit of " Uncle Tom "......Mr. JOHN ROUSE | Spirit of " Don Holyr "...Mr. JOHN CHUTE
Spirit of " Il Trovatore " from the Royal Italian Opera......Mr. EUGENE CORRI
Cambe, Nymph of the Fountain, and Resident Directress of Mount Parnassus, " the Gencie Spirit that pervades the Spot".....Miss YOUNG,
from the Royal Adelphi Theatre, London.
Clio.........Mr. C. WEBSTER, his first appearance | Euterpe........Miss BERTHA ADAMS | Polyhymnia.........Miss TIPS
Urania..........Miss WOOSTER | Calliope........Miss HALL | Erato.........Miss WOOLLS
Melpomene......................Mrs. STEVENSON | Thalia.........................Miss ADAMS | Terpsichore.........Miss C. TIPS

---

* under the management of James Henry Chute. A Mr John Chute was also on stage.

EPILOGUE

Today's Chutes are too widespread, too adventurous, to feel the strength of 'family' as it used to be experienced - when each clan had its shared objectives, shared territory, and perhaps its shared hatreds. But our narrative has ended, serendipitously, with a chapter where a "Chute era" existed and left its mark - where the whole community at Bristol felt nostalgia at its passing.

In an after-dinner speech in 1907, the Bishop of Clifton said: "The President (J.M. Chute) is a great public educationalist. He largely controls the public factor for good in our midst". This is not a common view of the commercial theatre. However, as the historian of the Prince's Theatre wrote*, the Bishop's remarks were more than generous praise of one man; they reveal the true importance of that institution.

" In the age before television, before radio, before the cinema, the gramophone record and the major development of the public library lending system, when the University College was still a weak and small institution, the programme at the Prince's Theatre must have, in a very real sense, corresponded closely with the intellectual map of Bristol. The plays, operas and their music were almost the sole intellectual nourishment available. The result was that for the crowds that attended the funeral of James Macready Chute in 1912, and for the many members of the audience who wrote to the newspapers on its anniversaries, the Prince's was more than a theatre.

"It was something which had opened up for them a new world of the imagination. Prince's patrons of all ages... confess to the life-long influence the theatre had upon them."

The Prince's was destroyed in an air-raid in 1940, but now - "There seems scarcely a Bristolian who was alive and sentient by 1940 who does not recall with affection all sorts of shows but especially the Prince's Pantomimes. When they speak of these performances now, some forty, fifty, sixty or more years later, the light of that magic dances again in their eyes. A theatre which is so vividly recalled over forty years after its destruction was certainly special. Buildings alone rarely generate such love. What people remember is an age of innocence full of great stars, an intellectual awakening, a place where they were touched by a glory that has stayed with them all their lives.

"It is this that makes the Prince's important in the history of Bristol. And perhaps the Prince's was fortunate too in the way that it ended - in a fury of flame, having just played host to one of England's greatest stage personalities. It avoided the sordid fate as a bingo hall, car showroom or supermarket which befell so many of its contemporaries across the country.

" James Henry Chute, George Macready Chute, James Macready Chute and Abigail Philomena Chute, who believed so thoroughly in the value of the drama, would not have wished it otherwise. They and their beloved Prince's have no public memorial in Bristol. As long as anyone who remembers the Prince's lives, they do not need one."

* Don Carleton, in *"The Prince's of Park Row"*, publ. by the Bristol Branch of the Historical Association 1983, *reproduced here by kind permission of the author and the publisher*

APPENDICES TO PART TWO

After the General Index and Register of Chutes, a simplified tree
"CHUTE FAMILY BRANCHES" is shown inside the back cover

---

from the Manuscripts

Rex commisit Philippo Choette terram que fuit David Basset ... in Winifrod ad se sustentandam
in servicio regis, quamdiu regi placuerit.
[1234; King Henry III leases land in Winford, Somerset to Philip Choette for king's service]

...Damus et concedimus dilecto servienti nostro Philipo Chawte armigero...
[1545, July; Henry VIII's Patent to Philip `Chawte` as governor of Camber Castle]

Commend to my Lord's favour "a sapphire to be taken of my gyfte as a poor present, wisshing it to be an
oryent diamonde, and so it were worthe gramercie, but as it is, King Henrye the eight ware it in a ring".
[1564 June 10th; Philip Chowte to Lord Robert Dudley - favourite of Q. Elizabeth I]

I hear that as before on Thursday were committed to the tower Sir Walter Shewte, Mr Nevill,
second son to my ld. of Burgavenny, Mr Hakings and Mr Wentworth lawyers ... H.M. is very angry ...
All is out of frame. God put it in again.
[1614, June 12; Sir John Throckmorton to the king's Secretary of State]

Sir Walter Cheut, a carver to H.M. was so ill advised as to justify his unmannerly speeches by
a letter to the king. Mr Christopher Nevill, a younger son of my ld. Abergavenny, spake as
despitefully as the former, and Wentworth, another lawyer, delivered out of Daniel and Ezekiel
very harsh collections against kings and princes. These...were soon after the dissolving of the
assembly committed to the Tower...   *[1614, June 16; Sir Ralph Winwood to the same]*

Could I ever believe that a father would disinherit his sunn, his first born, whom only the law
of God terms the Lord's ... yet what hath Watt Chute done ... why should you throw him oute
as a bastard from your nest ... no cause can be so operative as to make nature forgett nature,
without great curse inherent potentially...   *[1614; Sir John Holles to George Chute]*

`A Game at Picquet` *[a satirical squib circulated in 1656, in which leading politicians including Cromwell
defend a degree of hazard and/or cheating as part of the fun of the game]*
Mr Chaloner Chute says: "There is such cheating that I will play no longer."

1680, November the 26th. The Lords spent a whole day on a remnant of a cause between
my Lady Dacre and her grandchild Chute.   *[Col. Edward Cooke to Earl of Ormonde in Dublin]*

5 Jun 1731. Francis Chute, collector, to the Commissioners of HM Revenue, Chests of silver stolen from
the Danes. *[Curious item in Derbyshire R.O. Some 800 years had passed since Derby was in `Danelaw`]*

SOURCES AND BIBLIOGRAPHY
(To supplement references given in text)

General

Burke's `Landed Gentry` and its predecessor Burke's `History of the Commoners` supply the traditional Chute descent from Alexander. It is repeated in Berry's Hampshire Genealogies and on the parchment taken by Lionel Chute to America in 1634.

Historical Manuscripts Commission Reports, Harleian Society volumes (incl. Visitations), and State Papers. Specific references from these MSS which we use herein are given in "Leaves on the Tree" below or in our main text, but indices to such MSS can be found on open shelves in the British Library. *(To save space, several known Chute/Chowte/Chawte/Choute references have not been quoted in this book.)*

Victoria County Histories of Hampshire, Kent, Surrey, Sussex.

Parish Records of Baptisms, Marriages, Deaths (many reachable via Internet).

Individuals and Branches

Vyne branch: see under Appendix to First Part p.76.

The Battle of Hastings, ed. S. Morillo (Boydell, Woodbridge 1996-9) re Norman shipbuilding.

History of the Norman Conquest, by Edward Augustus Freeman (1859-1879),1st Edition, vol 3.

Pipe-Roll of the Bishops of Winchester (a) 1301/2 and (b) 1410/11; Ed. Dr M.Page (Hants.C.C.)

Rev. J. Collinson: History of Somerset; re mediaeval dignitaries.

Philip Chowte: see list on p.183 below.

Hasted's History of Kent (c. 1790): re Philip and the Bethersden/Surrenden/Hinxhill Chutes.

J.A.Froude's History of [Tudor] England (1879) Vol X, Elizabeth; re Rebellion of Desmond.

Life of Ralegh, by Stephen Coote; re (i) Azores expedition & (ii) reprisals against Desmond

Life of John Donne, by Prof. Bald; re (i) Azores expedition & (ii) travels with Walter Chute

Dictionary of National Biography: (i) Chaloner Chute, Speaker, & (ii) Anthony Chewte, poet.

The Twilight of the Ascendancy, by Mark Bence-Jones (Constable); re the Anglo-Irish.

Blomefield's History of Norfolk, Vols. 3 ,4, 6 & 8 (indexed refs to Bigods/Wygotts).

Church Guides: Appledore, Dedham, S.Pickenham, Bethersden, Sherborne St. John, Moulton; and (for Wiggett antecedents in Norfolk) Guist, Heydon, Guestwick, Wood Dalling.

Bristol Theatre: See p. 204 for bibliography. Many Chute memorabilia in the Varcoe Collection, at Bristol Univ. Drama Dept. Library.

Memorial to Sir George Chute, baronet in Bethersden Church, Kent; with, above, Enlargement of shield displaying Chute arms of 3 swords & mullets, plus Philip's Canton with a Lion and a Baronet's `Red Hand of Ulster` in the centre

LANDED GENTRY

A modern reader may well be surprised by the curious devices which the Chutes adopted to dignify their ancestry, also by their interest in heraldry, their family tree based on eldest sons, and their insistence that any owner of the Vyne must be named Chute. These, however, prove a particular concept of "genealogy", wholly social and glaringly unscientific, which was of great importance in its day. The Chutes wanted it clearly understood that they were "landed gentry".

This term became sanctified after 1830 in huge social registers published by Burke`s. But it was not mere snobbery; it had had a legal validity for centuries. Back in 1066, King William interpreted his victory as divine approval for the Norman race to rule England. To him, a "gentleman" was nothing to do with gentleness; it meant `one of our race` (Latin *gens*) - i.e. Normans plus the continental allies who had helped to baptize his new kingdom with Anglo-Saxon blood. A member of this master race could, within the feudal framework, qualify for land and a place in local government.

Move on to 1415, and the famous rallying-call of King Henry V before Agincourt, as Shakespeare imagined it:

"We few, we happy few, we band of brothers; For he today that sheds his blood with me Shall be my brother; be he ne`er so vile, This day shall **gentle his condition.**

"And gentlemen in England now abed Shall think themselves accurs`d they were not here; And hold their manhoods cheap whilst any speaks That fought with us upon St. Crispin`s Day".

Here we have a King bribing men of humble birth with a unique chance, if they stayed and fought, to jump the queue in status. The social scale had been rigid after 1066, but Henry V was in a new, fragmented world. Kings had learned to distrust the nobility, and increasingly depended on the gentry as a class of countrymen owing them personal loyalty. Racial purity had lost out to intermarriage, and you could now become a gentleman by (a) identifying yourself with the ruling class and (b) acquiring enough wealth to buy an estate. Land-ownership was deemed to give you a stake in the nation`s stability (and until the 20th century, a measure of property gave you the right to vote).

Land - the centre of genealogy.

Before `genes` had scientific definition, a `family` paid no regard to the stream of DNA entering its blood through wives in every generation. What mattered was legitimacy for land ownership. A man inheriting the Vyne must have the name Chute. Nobles had borne names taken from their Norman possessions, and did the same in England, e.g. Robert Devereux, Earl of Essex, of a family from Évreux plus a county they acquired after 1066. Land had originally been won by the sword and defended by the sword, so of course the eldest son had inherited; he was the first son to grow the muscle to wield a sword and protect his father`s land and livestock. Gentry who acquired land would naturally follow the same practice as the nobles, to whom "genealogy" meant a succession of brawny eldest sons with the right *ipso facto* to inherit the family`s land.

Legal Disability of Women

Why, in that violent world, pay regard to wives in the family tree? After all, they could hardly wield a sword, and they often died in childbirth or puerperal fever. Their genetic contribution - which of course far outweighed the genes of the "male line" - gave them no legal status. This prejudice persisted long after the sword was replaced by land registration, and we see that, in the BCHR, the early Chute records, a wife`s Christian name is often not given, when her father`s usually is. In one generation, shown overleaf, three wives are openly differentiated according to their relative social clout.

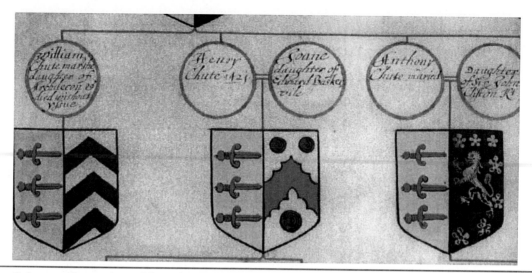

Only one wife named out of three. Henry, above, took a Baskervile wife; hers was a prestigious family, so Joane is named. Anthony's father-in-law, Sir John Clifton, was a mere knight; his rank is quoted but not his daughter's Christian name. As for William - he married the nameless daughter of a nameless archdeacon.

We deduced that the Chutes were armigerous by c.1450, at latest, but it is possible that Philip Chowte joined the fashion among gentry who came to power in the 1500s, and did some creative genealogy. Many "new men" felt inadequate without some trappings of nobility; if they lacked long-term estate records to prove Norman ancestors, they quietly invented them. After 1603, all these prosperous *armigers* caught James I's eye when he ran short of cash. He raised taxes on social dignities and defined them by law, sending out heraldic officials to 'visit' each county and check who was claiming noble or gentle rank. Hence this **preamble to a 1610 Visitation**, with its sharp sting in the tail:-

> "*The King's Most Excellent Majesty being desirous that the nobility and gentrie of this his Realm should be preserved in every degree as well in Honour as in Worship, and that every Person and Persons, bodies politique, Corporate, and others should be known in their Estates and mysteries withoute confusion and disorder, hath authorised us Robert Treswell, Esq., Somerset Herald, and Augustine Vincent, Rouge Croix, Officers of Arms, as Marshalles and Deputies to Clarenceux King of Arms of the South parts of this Realm of England, not only to visit all this county of Salop, to peruse and take knowledge, survey, and view of all manner of Arms, Cognizances, Crests, and other like devices, with the notes of the Descents, Pedigrees, and Marriages of all the Nobility and Gentry therein throughout contained, but also to reprove, controll, and make infamous by proclamation all such as unlawfully and without just Authority, vocation, or due calling do, or have done, or shall usurp or take upon him or them any name or Title of Honour or Dignity as Esquire or Gentleman or other as by his Highness gracious Commission under the greate seal of England more plainly may appear. . .*
> "*Know ye therefore that we the said Somerset and Rouge Croix, for the accomplishment of His Majesties desire and further of his Highness Service that way, at this present making Survey within the said County, have found these Persons whose names are under written presumptuously without any good ground or Authority to have usurped the name and Title of Gentlemen contrary to all right and to the Ancient Custome of this Land and the Usage of the Law of Arms, which name and Title they are from hencefourth no more to use or take upon them upon such further paine and perill as by the Right Honble the Earl Marshal of England shall be inflicted and laid upon them.*"

Under Charles II a man who falsely claimed noble ancestry in a court case was fined the colossal sum of £500. It had again become vital to know exactly who was Upper Class.

LEAVES ON THE FAMILY TREE

For those with special interest in family history, this section gives extra detail on the Chutes in England.
    (The burning of Dublin records in the 1920's left us with far less data for the Irish branch.)
As explained above, our approach is to take on trust the family tree from Alexander as given in Burke's, save for cases of manifest error, on the grounds that it is presumptuous to reject long-held traditions which, as yet, cannot be proved either way. Gentry family records pre-1500 are thinner than those of the great landowning nobles, and depend on snippets of data which emerge from MSS. It is helpful to find that when Chute names (including Chewt(e), Chawte, Chowte & Choute - but not those spelt "de Chut" nor Shute) occur in Historical MSS, they are almost always of `our` family. However, as modern technology (maybe even DNA sampling) brings new evidence to light, we should be better able to correct demographic data and flesh out biographies.

The sequence below accords with the family trees shown on earlier pages. To the left of each name is a figure-group to identify the individual, representing the number of a person's generation starting from Alexander, followed by his/her presumed order of birth in that generation. (We change from Roman to Arabic digits when Roman figures grow too big for convenience.) It has not been thought necessary to extend this identification coding to the Irish or Bristol branches nor to the Lobb Chutes and Wiggett Chutes.

Tree 1. Chutes at Taunton; Alexander to Edmond (Tree No. 1; p. 104)

It was the practice of the day to date events by reference to the reigning king. We quote any such date-references which occur in the received genealogy. D.s.p . (decedit sine prole) means died without issue.

		Reigning King
1.	**ALEXANDER**, of Taunton, Somerset, England; dated "1268" (death?); left 2 sons:	Henry III
2.i	**JOHN**, m. Jane, dau. of Sir John Bampfylde, Kt.	Edward I
2.ii	**RICHARD**	
3.	**CUTHBERT**, son of John, m (1281) Christian, dau. of Sir John Chideake. He d. 1308	Edward II
4.i	**JAMES**, son of Cuthbert, m. dau. of Richard Greenfield (Grenville?)	
4.ii	**PHILIP** 1332 m. dau. of Sir John Britton,Kt.	Edward III
4.iii	**ANTHONY** m. Anne Treforth, d.s.p.	
5.i	**GEORGE**, son of Philip; recorded at Taunton in 1334; d. 1344 having m. (1) dau.of Thomas Tirrell, (2) dau. of Chas. Squire	
5.ii	**JOANE**, dau. of Philip, m. Sir John Carminow, Kt. (of an old Cornish family)	
6.	**AMBROSE**, son of George. *[Unusually, only this one child has been recorded in generation 6. Did his siblings all die in the Black Death? If so, the Chutes had a lucky escape!]* He m. Anabell, dau. of Sir John Chichester, Kt. (probably from the Devon branch of this prominent family, which was later ennobled for its military success in Ulster)	
7.i.	**EDMOND** 1379, m. Dyonice, dau. of Henry Stourton.	
7.ii	**CHRISTIAN**, m. Ralph Menell.	
8.i	**WILLIAM**, son of Edmond, m. dau. of "Arcedeckne" (i.e. an archdeacon) d.s.p.	Richard II
8.ii	**HENRY**, about 1420 m. Joane, dau. of Edward Baskerville. (This family, of Erdisley Castle, Hereford, claimed Plantagenet blood and were Hereditary Champions of the King of England; they were 21 times Sheriff of Hereford.)	

NOTE re 8.ii Henry. Irish Chutes hold a curious tradition that a French **"Chevalier de Chute"**, related to us, was chief escort to his Princess Katharine when, after Agincourt in 1415, King Henry V chose her as bride and she followed him to England. His early death in 1422 left her a widow with a baby, the future Henry VI; the Chevalier allegedly remained to protect her until she married Henry Tudor. (By Henry Tudor, she became Henry VIII's grandmother).
This tale is unsupported by standard history books, but it is so odd that it could have some basis.
One might do more research into 8.ii Henry, husband to Joane Baskerville, given that *her* family were hereditary King's Champions, and see if he went to France on any such mission.

8.iii **ANTHONY**, m. dau. of Sir John Clifton, Kt. and had son   Henry VI
9.iii **CHRISTOPHER CHUTE** of Dorset, who m.
      Ammerica, dau. of Richard Wellgrove (?Waldegrave?)
8.iv **ROBERT**, unm. *[erroneously claimed in BCHR to have*
      been Serjeant at Law and Baron of Exchequer]
9.i **ROBERT**, Esq of Taunton 1438, son of Henry (8.ii),   Edw IV/Richard III
      m. Alice, dau. of Morrice Berkeley, Esq
      (from the Berkeley Castle family)
9.ii **ANNE** m. Sir John Isley St Maur - also recorded as Bentley or Scutley
10. **CHARLES** (Sir Charles Chute, Knt.)   Henry VII
      m. dau. of Sir John Cheney, Knt. (also spelt Cheyne)
      [membership of this important family yielded the Chutes dividends,
      both in a transfer of land in Sussex and in patronage given to Philip
      Chute by a later Cheney, who was Lord Warden of the Cinque Ports.]
11. **EDMOND** "of Sussex", in 1502 stated (though wrongly) to have "sould the manor of
      Taunton to Lord Denham, of whom descend the Earls of Bridgewater".

[Note: In the period covered by the above paragraphs on this page, there seem too many generations for the time-frame. The received `tree` is repeated here, though somewhere a brother who inherited the property may have been shown as a son. Our hunch is that in fact "10.Charles" and "11.Edmond" were either brothers, because the move to Sussex ought to have quickly followed the Cheney marriage to Charles, or were even the same person - since no wife is recorded for Edmond even though he was a landowner & a father.]

Chutes in Kent/Suffolk: - Edmond to the brothers Philip, Anthony & (?) Arthur (p.104)

12. **ROBERT**, son of Edmond;   m. Jane, dau. of John Lucas. They had issue:-
13.i. **OLIVER**,   m. dau. of Redd, of Kent
13.ii **CHARLES**, of Malling, Kent m. dau. of John Cripps (or Crispe) of Birchington, Isle of Thanet
13.iii **LYONELL**, m. dau. of John Butler
13.iv **WILLIAM**,   m. dau. of John Badlesmere, merchant of Tonbridge

sons of Charles (13.ii)

14.i ANTHONY, "of Kent" m. dau. of _Gee, of Kent. The only known detail about him is that he was appointed gunner in the Tower of London, 14 November 1529, at 12 pence per day. See p. 192 ff.
      [The similarity of the names Gee and Sea in wives of Anthony and his son Arthur might look suspicious as a record; but both are correct. John Chute of the Vyne included Gee heraldry in a blazon in the Tomb Chamber, and Elizabeth Sea (in double portrait with Arthur at the Vyne) is independently attested

14.ii PHILIP (c.1506-1566/7), of Horne's Place, Appledore, Kent. (His house and chapel can be visited.)
      We read that Sir Thomas Cheney had built himself c. 1525 a castle-sized house at Shurland, Isle of Sheppey, where he kept *"ordinarilie eight score serving men, besides retayners, gentlemen and others that were ready for all types of service, or danger of invasion, numbering at least 400 persons"*. From the patronage he later gave Philip, we may guess that Philip had been in this retinue and won approval there.
      When Camber Castle, near Winchelsea, Sussex, was built in 1539/40, perhaps including stone from former monastic buildings, Philip as a local dignitary became its first Governor. (He had been given tenure of dissolved friaries at Winchelsea & Faversham, Kent, which the King later passed to Sir Thomas Cheney.) Winchelsea was one of few Sussex ports to supply ships for Henry VIII's invasion of France in 1544; Philip as its M.P. won the honour of bearing the King's Standard at the Siege of Boulogne. That same year he was awarded lifetime Captaincy of Camber Castle; under the royal Patent (held in Kent Co. Records, Maidstone; quoted in 1544 State Papers, Vol. I, Item 1035 (para. 142)) he was granted, backdated to January, a wage of 2 shillings a day, with duty to employ *"8 souldiers and 6 goners under hym at 6d. a day each"*. This peace-time wage was 1/3 of what he was paid during the French campaign, when Philip got 6s. a day and Rogers, Captain of the King's men at arms, 10s. Philip was given a Christmas bonus of 45s. 6d. by King Henry in 1545, and he continued to receive local appointments under Edward VI (1547) and Queen Mary (1555) as well as holding unbroken his post as Captain of Camber and "keeper of the waters of Camber and Puddell".
      The Dudley MSS contain letters from Philip to Q.Elizabeth's favourite Lord Robert Dudley : one on Jan. 27 1559/60 reports French shipping movements, portending invasion of Scotland; another on June 10 1564 (or before) sends Dudley a sapphire *"to be taken of my gyfte as a poore present, wisshing it to be an oryent diamonde and so it were worthe gramercie, but as it is, **King Henry the eight ware it in a ring**"*.

Main Sources on Philip:
State Papers of Henry VIII and Edward VI (British Library)
Sir John Winnifrith's `History of Appledore` (publ. Phillimore 1973/83)
Army Historical Research p.188 "The Siege and Capture of Boulogne 1544" with Notes by Lt.Col.J.H.Leslie
     (in the National Army Museum, Chelsea, London)
Archaeologia Cantiana Vol 49, article by Dr F W Cock, re Appledore and Philip's tomb.
Hasted's `History of Kent`.
Parliamentary Register, House of Commons 1509-1558; Ed. S T Bindoff; Volume with List of Members, p.647-8.
re Camber Castle (with diagrams) : - Victoria County History, Sussex and English Heritage Guidebook;
Charter to Philip with endorsements is kept in Kent County Records Office, Sessions House, Maidstone.

Heraldry. Initially :- *gu seme of mullets or three swords barwise ppr the middlemost encountering the other two*;
    1544 augmentation:- *a canton per fesse ar. and vert, thereon a lion of England.*

We have assumed in our text that the Chutes must have been armigers by the date of the Cheney marriage in the 1400s, but MSS relating to Philip call him "Mr Chowte" up to 1544 after which he becomes "Philip Chowte, Esquire". This must leave open the question of how `ancient` his initial armorial actually was. (This is distinct from the question of whether he added mullets to a pre-existing blazon)

Philip married 3 times: (Sources disagree on the order and date of these marriages, but this sequence fits the facts best.)

1. **Joan, née Ensing**, dau. of Thomas Ensing, MP for Winchelsea, and widow of Peter Master (d.1526/32); she seems to have brought a son Thomas with her, and may have borne Philip a daughter;
2. **Margaret** (who died 28.9.1555) dau. of Sir Alexander **Culpeper** (or Colepepper) of Bedgebury, from one of the richest families in southern England; she bore Philip 5 sons & 1 daughter;
3. **Elizabeth Girling**, of Wrentham, Suffolk, who bore him 1 son (died in infancy). Philip's will included the poor of Wrentham among benefactions.

> The Chute connection with the Wrentham area dates from Philip's appointment as Queen's bailiff at Frostenden See p.192-3 for our guess that Anthony moved to Suffolk as Philip's deputy, to enforce Henry VIII's order to suppress the incursions into Yarmouth by fishermen of the Cinque Ports. Anthony's son Arthur and the unexpected "14.iii Arthur" certainly lived near Wrentham, as later did 15.12 Lyonell and others mentioned on p.193.

Philip's Bequests (Will proved 1 Feb. 1568). His main heirs were:
George - all the household stuff & Philip's property at Iden, Appledore (i.e. Horne's Place) & Kenardington.
Edward - lands at Herst manor, Chilham, Godmersham & Brede.
Anthony - estates at Bethersden (incl. Surrenden manor) & Seddlescumbe.
    The residue went to George, apart from
Step-son Thomas - lands at Playden, given "on condition that he make no claim to the Bethersden property".
    [Note. Since most of the Kentish properties ended up in George's hands, and Anthony the poet advertised himself as "poore", a major reallocation of lands must have followed. However, the estate was too large for one owner, as Winnifrith *(op. cit.)* says the Chutes` Appledore lands fell before long into a sorry state. Cogger's 1628 map of the Chute Estate in Appledore, found dusty & crumpled by Dr Cock when clearing out a cupboard in the Sessions House, Maidstone, is copied in Winnifrith.]

14. iii ARTHUR, married to Margaret née Playters. Unless he and "Anthony" are in fact the same, he is unknown in family history except for the tomb inscription at Ellough, Suffolk to: *"Margaret ... faythfull loving wyfe of Arthare Chewt, gentleman..."* (see p. 193). This tomb seems to be the earliest surviving Chute memorial brass.

The Bethersden Roll does not show Arthur, but as Margaret was born in 1522, her husband could have been either (i) a brother of Philip and Anthony or (ii) the same person as Anthony" - of whose person we know so little, and whose name could well be a misprint for this historical "Arthare". The memorial makes no mention of children.

Tree 2. Descent from Philip (p. 127)

15.i (Sir) EDWARD (shown as Philip's eldest son in BCHR, but not treated as such in his father's will)

15.ii. GEORGE of Surrenden Choute & Bethersden, m. Elizabeth Gage of Bentley, Kent (of the Firle Place family). High Sheriff of Kent in 14 Eliz (1572/3) per Berry's Hants Genealogies pp 164-7.
Somehow acquired lion's share of father's land bequests, including Bethersden Manor which had been bequeathed to 15.iv Anthony. See below re quarrel with son Sir Walter. He d. 1618; his Will of 1615 ("George Chut") is held as item 1/3982 at Lambeth R. O.; left no property to his two elder sons, but all the Kent properties to Edward. A difficult man? *[How did VC H Surrey come to hold wrong belief that he owned Stockwell before his son George?]*

Under a commission dated 30th June 1590, George Chewte was among 6 gentlemen sent "to look over and perambulate a certain great quantity of salt marsh and lands called the Camber Beach and Camber Salts, to enquire as to the number of acres of the ancient metes, limits and bounds, and within what liberties, parishes and manors lying ... and to make a plot or map." (State Papers 1590)

In 1599 there was fear of a Spanish invasion. On Aug. 4th 1599, letters from the Privy Council to Lord Cobham named George Chute as one of the gentry in Sussex required to supply "lances and lighthorses" in a general mobilisation against the Spanish.
See MSS of the Rt. Hon. R.J.Savile Foljambe of Osberton, in HMC Vol 15, Appx. Part V, p. 142.
(This implies that the Chutes still had substantial property in Sussex as well as in Kent .)

In the Duke of Manchester's Coll. MSS (HMC 8th Report) item 137 dated Michaelmas 1609.
Pells Office memo. (Kent and Sussex) relating to the sum of £66.3s.4d. being the composition made with Geo. Chute, esq and others for a recognisance of 200 marks acknowledged by Geo. Harper 22 May, 30 Henry 8, for the Surveyor of Woods. (Parchment Latin)

In 1614 "George Chute of Bethersden" had property valued at £1900. Hatfield House MSS, Vol.22, p.13

15.iii BLOUNT, died young

15.iv ANTHONY Chewte, first of the family to appear in the Dictionary of National Biography.
- Poet, attorney's clerk, writer (anonymously) of a treatise on the virtues of Tobacco; acknowledged author of poem "Beawtie Dishonour'd" - text in British Library. Allegedly (so Nashe says) purser with the Portugal Expedition 1585. Attached himself to the poet/satirist Gabriel Harvey (1550-1630) who got himself in dispute with Thomas Nashe (1567-1601) against whom Chewte evidently wrote polemic verses in 1593. (See DNB.) The 1594 letter in which he advertised himself as a *"poore Gent without friends... etc."* is quoted by the editor of Nashe's collected works and described as "to Burghley in the Lansdowne MSS printed in Corser's Collectanea, iv. 396" (not checked further by me). D.s.p.

15.v. son, name unknown;

the above 5 were sons by Margaret

15.vi ELIZABETH (poss. dau. of Joan, née Ensing) m. John Taylor of Shadockhurst, Kent; d.1600.
15.vii ANNE, (dau. of Margaret); m. Sir Walter Waller of Groombridge, Kent. Further detail can be seen in Mormon Register.
15.viii THOMAS (assumed to be son of Joan, née Ensing)

Issue of 15.ii George and Elizabeth: order of sons' birth given here as shown in BCHR:

16.i (Sir) **WALTER**, soldier adventurer and politician; no issue. See below.
16.ii (Sir) **GEORGE**, soldier, **founder of the Irish and Stockwell lineages**
16.iv **JAMES**; seems to have reached adulthood (shield in BCHR) but d.s.p.
16.iii **EDWARD** of Surrenden Choute/Bethersden, who m. Lydia Gibbon(s) and had 11 children.
(See Bethersden Lineage below p. 188)
16.v **THOMAS**, seems to have d. young (no shield shown in BCHR); and daughter
16.vi **ELIZABETH** (d. 1649, per Gage family record)
who m. (1) William (or Robert) Fitzwilliam of Mablethorpe; (2) Sir E.Tyrwhitt of Stainfield.

16.i (Sir) WALTER. See "Swashbuckling against Spain" p.138 for the joint venture of Ralegh and Essex under Admiral Howard against Fayal in 1597, in which Walter Chute participated. The record of this daredevil exploit which we quoted was written by Sir Arthur Gorges, Ralegh's ship's captain. The rest of W's career, as we know it, is summarised in "Sir Walter Breaks Ranks" p.140.

He is well worth further research. Sources for our information to date are set out opposite.

Sir Walter Chute - background

1. <u>Lineage:</u> The BCHR shows him as eldest son of George Chute of Bethersden but no dates are given. Donne's biographer Prof. Bald, one of our few independent sources on Walter, says (his p. 148) that Walter was slightly Donne's junior; i.e. born after 1572. This is questionable, because Walter's younger brother George went to Ireland as soldier in 1578, so he was born not after 1560; thus Walter must have been born by 1559, making him, in fact, Donne's senior by at least 13 years. If he went on the Fayal expedition in 1597, he was older, at 38, than most of the "raffish young bloods" who volunteered.

(Note. We deduced that Walter's grandfather Philip (c.1505-1565), whose first wife Joan née Ensing died young, married Margaret Culpeper by 1537 and that George, their eldest, was born c. 1538/9 and d. in 1618 at age 79/80. If *his* 2nd son, Sir George (the Ireland one) was b. 1560, it would just be feasible to find him at the age of 87 writing the Will dated Sept. 1647. Hence we date Walter 's birth at <1559.)

2. <u>Education & Travels.</u> He entered Cambridge University in 1587; at age 28 he would have been untypically mature; but this is explained by Prof. Bald's statement that Walter "had been at Hart Hall" (an Oxford College with a high proportion of Catholics). He was also "at Gray's Inn", for law study.

The 1597 story as written up by Sir Arthur Gorges contains no mention of Chute that we could find. It is quoted extensively in Stephen Coote's 'Life of Ralegh'. Prof Bald says Walter " had served with some distinction in the Islands expedition of 1597."

There is a possibility that Walter was the "Ensign Chute from Flushing garrison" who carried an official letter in March 1602. (De L'Isle Coll. Vol III 1603-7). This would tally with a letter recorded by Pearman in Arch. Cant. as written on 6 June 1600 from R. Whyte at Penshurst to Sir Robert Sidney, Governor of Flushing, in which occur the words "Mr Chute hath lost his eldest son in Ireland, his second is with you and the 3rd. He understands by them the desire you had of a good nagge." (Sidney's bailiff at Penshurst had muddled the order of the Chute sons.)

Prof Bald admits "practically nothing is known of the travels of Chute and Donne", though he says: "that Donne and Chute went to Paris may be taken as certain". It would have been logical for Donne, with his obvious interest in scientific phenomena, to visit Venice to meet its 'natural scientists' (just before Galileo began his demonstrations) as well as to study its commercial methods and unique republican constitution.

3. <u>Duelling.</u> Bald remarks that "Sir Walter Chute also visited Paris in 1611 or 1612, when he fought a duel with William Becher". In fact this was in 1610, when a letter dated October 6 from Sir Thomas Edmondes in Paris to Wm. Trumbull, the King's Sec. of State, said "At Lord Wootton's departure Mr Beacher...taking unkindness against Sir Walter Chute for refusing to satisfy him the remainder of some money which he had lost to him at play, called Sir Walter into the field, in which encounter Mr Beacher was wounded, but has recovered."

4. <u>Carver to the King</u> Walter was recorded by the letter writer John Chamberlain to the diplomat Sir Dudley Carleton (Hist. MSS Comm. Chamberlain letters i. 534) as having offered to members of the 1614 Parliament (see para 5. below) "his service to the King, which might stand them in stead in regard that he is so neere the King that he cuts all the meat he eates, and hath much entercourse of speech with him which he commonly setts downe when he comes home for feare of forgetting, and therin hath don the house many goode offices, which he will continue so long as he continues his place, which by this course [opines Chamberlain] me thincks shold not be very long".

5. <u>Addled Parliament.</u> Walter sat as MP for East Retford, Notts. - presumably a seat owned by some magnate, just as was Taunton, for which Donne sat in this same Parliament by patronage of the Master of the Rolls. (But Donne, who needed royal favour to get the Court position he earnestly desired, said nothing against the King.)

Duke of Rutland MSS from Welbeck Abbey include (pages 132-9) a Summary of Proceedings of the Addled Parliament by Sir John Holles, later 1st Earl of Clare; this confirms that **"four gentlemen, Hodgkins and Wentworth lawyers, with Sir Walter Chute and Mr Christofer Nevil were ... sent to the Tower"** and explains how Chute had spoken.

Separate brief accounts were given in letters written on 12th & 16th June 1614 to Wm. Trumbull by Sir John Throckmorton & Sir Ralph Winwood, held in the Marquess of Downshire Coll. MSS Vol. IV.

Prof. Bald records that in debate of 3 June 1614 "Chute also spoke against the Scots" on a motion which attacked the King's Scottish favourites, saying ... "that these who consumed the King had no freehold among us; they paid no subsidies, they consumed both the King and kingdom in prodigality, in all riot and dissolution of apparel and other superfluities, no mean contented them, that the pensions forth of the Exchequer came to 70,000 li. and above, that the King hath given to one man 1000 li. per annum old rent, which was more than Queen Elizabeth had given to all her servants in 44 years".

Chute's speeches in this and other issues, and the fact that he afterwards wrote directly to the king in his own defence, made his dismissal and imprisonment almost inevitable. One of the lawyers, who had hinted in Parliament that there might be a "Sicilian Vespers" [i.e. assassination by a popular uprising] of the Scots favourites, was imprisoned for a year; but Chute was only held for four months (Bald, p.288).

6. Disinheritance. In the Holles family MSS collection (Historical Manuscripts Commission) is the ref: to Sir John Holles (who, we learn from Bald, had also served with Donne and Walter Chute in the 1597 Islands Expedition, and who also recorded the proceedings of the 1614 Parliament) writing to "ould Mr Chute" to try and dissuade him from disinheriting his eldest son.
Holles wrote: "Could I ever believe that a father would disinherit his sunn, his first born, whom only the law of God terms the Lords, nay almostt uppon any demeritt, yet what hath Watt Chute done ... why should yow throw him oute as a bastard from your nest, spoile him of his birthright, nay of his honor, and reputation in the world ... No cause ... can be so operative to make nature forget nature, without a great curse inherent potentially ... Give me leave to tell yow that it behooves yow to satisfy the world allso, who ... believe no ill deserving in your sunn".

Disinherited he was; the 1614 Will shows it. Father George at 75 was too old to forgive *lése majesté,* but "the world" seems to have been on Walter's side in the dispute.

7. Later Life. At present we have no knowledge of Walter Chute's later life or his means of income. "Walterus Chute, miles" (=soldier) was buried Dec. 29, 1617 at St Martin in the Fields. (Harl. Soc. Church Registers 1898 - Vol.25). He had no children.

16.ii Sir GEORGE (c.1560-1647) lived slightly longer than his father (both passed 85) at the end of an adventurous career which brought him considerable wealth. The BCHR only shows his English marriages, but The General Armory entry reads: "Chute (Sir George Chewte or Chute, of Stockwell co. Surrey; knighted by Sir Arthur Chichester, Lord Deputy of Ireland, 14 Oct. 1608)". This confirms the deduction on which we based the story on p.145, etc. If he was old enough to fight in Ireland in 1578, but lived to write a last Will in 1647, he must have been born c.1560.

Ireland. It was therefore, we deduce, as a teenager that in 1578 he *"went into Ireland with Sir John Perrott and Sir Walter Blackley to suppress the rebellion of Desmond"* (Burke's). A small Catholic invasion party landed at the Dingle, and some accounts (e.g. Stephen Coote's in his Life of Ralegh) are horrific of how the English butchered these irregulars and their supporters. The poet Spenser, a secretary in the English force and famous glorifier of Queen Elizabeth, wrote that the normal rules of humanity did not apply in the Munster campaign since war had not been declared. An exhaustive account of Desmond's Rebellion - over 100 pages - can be read in Vol.X of J.A.Froude's `History of England from the Fall of Wolsey to The Defeat of the Spanish Armada` (1879).

George was among those "planted" in Co. Kerry, tho' his lands became "alienated" in one of the many squabbles in Ireland over non-compliance with promises by the Crown or by tenants.

He married a Miss Evans from Cork (p.148 for Irish Family Tree, after Burke's). In 1630 their elder son Daniel married Johanna, the MacElligott heiress, and took over her family lands at Tullygarron near Tralee, naming their new house **Chute Hall**.
The dates look odd, but we are boxed in by Burke's genealogy. If George came as a soldier-settler in 1578, you would expect him to marry young and have had a son by, say, latest 1583; if so, Daniel waited till he was 47+ before wedding his heiress in 1630. Burke's does not mention a first wife, so Daniel was perhaps sowing wild oats for many years before marrying Johanna - or were there interminable legal problems for new settlers? The latter might explain the odd fact that Daniel had to pay £1000 before he could settle in his new wife's property.

One deduces that George's wife, née Evans, had died by 1608, since he then returned permanently to England, aged 48-50, being knighted on the way (14.10.1608) by the King's Deputy in Dublin.

Cofferer to Prince Henry (the elder son of James I, who died young). In 1610, as we learn from a letter (23 Oct.) of Sir Wm Browne in the Downshire Coll. (Vol.II) of Histo-rical MSS, "they are about to establish the Prince's household who is henceforth to live on his own revenues ... in all £40,000 a year [from property]...
"It is thought Sir Chas. Cornwallis shall be his treasurer, Sir Thos. Challenor, chamberlain ...and

Sir George Chute, cofferer..." A coffer is a treasure chest, and only an already rich man would be trusted not to dip his hands in the till. It may have been the offer of this prestigious post which tempted George to leave the Irish outback and return permanently to England. We do not know how much contact he maintained with his sons in Ireland after 1608, but the rumpus which led to alienation of the original Chute lands , and to Daniel having to pay that large sum to take over the MacElligott lands in 1630, may have disenchanted George with the idea of staying in Ireland.

Wealth. George's wealth is further attested by his purchase of Stockwell Manor, his investment in the Third Virginia Company Charter, March 12, 1612 and by two surviving records of royal taxation:-
Subsidy Rolls   (i) for the year 1628-9 (3rd & 4th Charles I) under Lambeth show Sir George Chute, Kt paid "XLs" on "lands worth X pounds"; and
(ii) for the year 1642 (17th Charles I) under Stockwell, Sir Geo. Chute Kt paid £4.16.0 subsidy on lands worth £12". In 1642 he was Lambeth's richest landowner; the next richest in Lambeth had lands of £10 and the next richest in Stockwell owned £8.

Re-Marriages.   Sir George, in his fifties, re-married twice in England; his 'eligibility', i.e. wealth and dignities, was in social terms more important than his age. His English wives were -

(1) **Margaret**, sole heir of Thomas **Welford**, of Wisteston Court, Marden, and Broadfield Court, Bodenham, both in Herefordshire (d. 1614; memorial in Marden Church with, reportedly, Chute arms).
　　　　Was it a sign of his wealth, or of his decency, that when Margaret died he did not pocket her inheritance, as legally he could, but designated their only child **Anne** as "heir to her mother", i.e. to the Herefordshire properties?　　　　[*Note: Chute as a middle name still appeared at Marden as late as the 19th C.*] Though Anne survived, Margaret may have died in bearing her, since Sir George soon re-married:-

(2) **Anne**, dau. of Sir Martyn **Barnham** of Hollingbourne, Kent, baronet.   She bore him seven children though, perhaps because of her husband's considerable age, several were weakly and died young.   In a 1648/9 Deed she is "Dame Anna, relict of Sir George Chute" ; her Will was proved in PCC in 1656.

(The Barnham family owned manors of Upper & Lower Bilsington in Romney Marsh with the charming chivalric duty of "*holding by the serjeanty of carrying the last dish of the second course to the king's table, and of presenting three maple cups at coronations*". Ref. Teichman Derville 'L.& L. of Romney Marsh')
.
Like his father, Sir George was long-lived. Aged about 87, he died in August 1647 possessed of properties in Stockwell, Newington & Walworth.
　　　　He evidently knew the lawyer Chaloner Chute (later to become the Speaker) and another lawyer from the Keck family (that of Edward Chute's wife Katharine) since they witnessed legal deeds for him. He also knew the Chaloners well through serving the Prince alongside Sir Thomas Chaloner.
　　　　Victoria CH for Surrey is surely wrong in saying he got Stockwell from his father in 1618. His father George (who had no apparent reason to buy it, seeing that he had acquired the bulk of Philip's property in Kent/Sussex) mentions nothing of Stockwell in his Will. The Will, pictured in our main text, only mentions the Kent/Sussex lands, which he left to Edward. *Was the VCH writer mis-led by the curious fact that George senior's Will is archived in Lambeth, not in Bethersden?*

Burial. In his Will Sir George "desired to be decently and without ostentation buried in Lambeth Parish Church where his predecessors, owners of the manor of Stockwell, have a right of burial".

This original Parish Church of St. Mary, standing on Thames-side beside the Archbishop of Canterbury's Lambeth Palace, is now converted into a museum of garden history. As a result, though all memorial plaques in the church were fully recorded, many are now covered over by display boards; among them is the brass tablet of 1638 to little Margaret, dau. of Sir George & Anne Chute, fixed below a white marble tablet to Archbp. Hutton. Despite Sir George's request, no other Chute tomb is mentioned in that record (held in Lambeth Records Office) where Margaret's tablet is item 121.

For descent through 17.iv George, son of Sir George & Ann Barnham, see 'Stockwell' p.191.
The Stockwell Chute dynasty lasted beyond 1700, as shown by Deeds surviving in Lambeth archives. Its assets appear to have gone through Chute heiresses to the Parker family.

NOTE ON THE BETHERSDEN, SURRENDEN & HINXHILL PROPERTIES

Hasted *"History of Kent"* (1798) Vol 7 says concerning "the manor of Old Surrenden, alias Bethersden... Sir Anthony Aucher...in the sixth year of the same reign [of Edward VI, i.e. in 1552/3] passed it away to Philip Choute, esq. ... in whose descendants this manor continued down to Edward Choute, esq whose name was frequently spelt, and usually pronounced Chewte...when from its long continuance in them and improvements they had made to this antient mansion, it had gained the name of *Surrenden-Choute*.

  "He [Edward] removed his residence to Hinxhill*, the manor of which he had purchased, where he kept his shrievalty anno 11 king Charles I [i.e. 1635 or 1636] and where his son Sir George Choute likewise resided; who was succeeded in ths manor of Surrenden by his son George Choute, esq. who in 1684 *[this date is wrong]* was created a baronet, and afterwards resided at Lovelace in this parish, of which he was only tenant, and dying there s.p. in 1721, devised this manor by will to Edward Austen, esq. of Tenterden, afterwards baronet, who soon afterwards sold it to Thomas Best, esq. of Chatham ... [so that in 1798] Thomas Best, esq. now of Chilston [is] present owner of it." *[Sir A Aucher was a maternal ancestor of Jane Austen]*

*Under "Hinxhill, usually called *Hinxsell*, and in very antient times written *Hengestelle*... an obscure parish" in Chart and Longbridge Hundred, Hasted says (page 562) that Edward acquired it "sometime after the death of Charles I". This is impossible if, as above, he kept his shrievalty there under Charles I. This seems to be one of the confusions between the Edwards (and Georges) which make the Choute lineage hard to pin down. Hasted (p. 565) "Sir Edward Chute [sic] was buried at Hinxhill in 1624 though there was no "memorial".

Winnifrith says the Chutes never lived at Appledore after Philip's death; Horne's Place became a rented farmhouse. However, in 1593 one Pascall Sloman, yeoman of Appledore, made a Will appointing George Chute executor & leaving him "a black stoned colt"; Walter Chute was bequeathed "an ambling bay nag".

16.iii EDWARD (c.1580-1640), brother of Walter & George, received the Kent/Sussex properties under their father George's Will. He became High Sheriff of Kent 1635-6.
He bought Hinxhill Manor (E of Ashford) and went to live there with his 1st wife **Lydia**, dau. of Thomas Gibbon(s) of Bethersden; they had 11 children:-

- George (17.vii) & Edward (17.viii) - see below - who left descent;
- Anthony, Philip, Elizabeth, Lydia and Eleanor, who apparently did not;
- Anne who m. Thos. Knatchbull, esq.
- Elizabeth who m. Edward Master, esq. of Streetend, Willesborough, Kent *(Hasted vol. 7, p. 572)*
- Mabella who m. Francis Bettenham on 19 March 1649, and
- Alice who m. Edward Roberts on 20 Jan. 1650 *(latter 2 from Willesborough Parish Records)*.

> Cambridge Univ. records show George, Edward and Philip entering Emmanuel Coll: 1627-29

Lydia died in 1631 aged 46. On 12.8.1633 Edward, 53, m. (2) **Thomazine** Criche, widow, 52.

> Hasted says of " FRID, usually called the Frid farm, corruptly for the Frith", a manor in the northern part of Bethersden parish: "Thomas Gibbon... resided here in the reign of King James I and left two daughters his co-heirs; the youngest of whom Lydia entitled her husband Edward Choute, esq....to the possession of this manor." This explains why the Memorial to Sir George Choute, bart. is in the "Frid Chancel" (as Hasted calls it) of Bethersden church. (Lydia was related to the author of 'The Decline and Fall of the Roman Empire'.)

17.vii GEORGE, 1611-50, m.(1632) Eleanor, dau of Captain Nicholas Toke (1588-1680) of the nearby Godinton Park; George "was of Surrenden in Kent" and (acc. to Pearman in A.C.) "was an ardent Royalist, he delivered the Kentish Petition for the restoration of Bishops etc. which raised the wrath of Parliament. In 1642/3 Resolution made that George Chute now in the Serjeant's custody be discharged from further restraint, and ordered that he shall he bailed".

Richard Lovelace's famous poem including **"Stone Walls do not a Prison Make"** was written while he and Chute were in prison for their complicity in this *"Petition from Kent praying for a Restoration of the Bishops, Liturgy and Common Prayer, and a Good Understanding between King and Parliament"*. It was delivered on 28 March 1642 to Parliament which (attacking the Anglican Church while Charles I was still king) voted it seditious and ordered it to be burned by the hands of the common hangman. Lovelace again presented the Petition on 30 April; the Speaker asked from whose hand he had received it, and Lovelace replied "Mr Geo. Chute delivered him the Petition the next day after the Assizes". ['Reputed the handsomest man in England', L. was Chute's neighbour at Lovelace Place in Bethersden but, twice imprisoned and fined for Royalist activity, he gradually sold all his Bethersden properties .]

A portrait of George and Eleanor was loaned to the National Portrait Gallery in 1866 by Wm. Wiggett Chute. The picture had disappeared from the Vyne before the 1956 inventory. (Pearman in AC says it was at Godinton, the Toke family home, in 1889; there is no sign of it there now.)

17.viii EDWARD married on 17 July 1654 Elizabeth, described as "daughter of Sir Basil Dixwell of Brome [Broomhouse], Bt. by Dorothy, dau. of Sir Thomas Peyton, Bt. of Knowlton." (Sir Basil was painted by Vandyck; in NPG collection).

> There is confusion among Edwards. An Edward Chute was High Sheriff of Kent in '11 Charles II', i.e. 1671, and Pearman in A.C. says that his "grandson was Sir George Chute, Bt." (who died in 1721). Sir George Bt's actual grandfather was George, not Edward. However his grandfather's brother 17.viii Edward, who m. Eliz. Dixwell, is said by Pearman to have died of smallpox at 25, which would not leave him alive to be Sheriff in 1671.

Edward 17.viii according to Pearman in AC: *"died of the small-pox at 25* and was buried in St Bride's Church. He bought Hinxhill Court, and gave his daughters* [Elizabeth & Eleanor below] *£3000 each"*.

18.vii ELIZABETH m. Sir Jacob Oxenden, Kt. The Oxendens, who appear in Jane Austen's letters, were by 1700 baronets, of Diane Park, Wingham and Broome House, Kent. (There is a famously extravagant memorial to the Oxendons in Wingham Church.)

18.viii ELEANOR m. Sir John Wyldman, Kt. whose father was an Alderman of the City of London but, per the BCHR, was not an armiger. *[A conflicting marriage record says "Mrs Elina Chute née Westrowe m. John Wildman Junior of Beckett, Berks, bachelor aged c.26, on 5 Sept. 1676"]*

---

children of George and Eleanor (nee Toke):

18.v Sir GEORGE *"of Streatham, Surry and of Surrenden, Kent"*. (If indeed of Streatham, he must have been given property there by 18.i George.). Born c.1640; married, Apr.1661, **Cecilia**, dau. of Ralph **Freke** of Harrington, Wiltshire. Knighted in July 1660; shares a ledger stone at Bethersden with his son; in its Parish Register the vicar wrote: *"Goe sleepe Sir George. Where's such another Can equall thee? or th' Squire thy brother?"*

Pearman says he "died of smallpox at 23*, buried at Bethersden, Will proved 1664".

> Notes:
> 1. Cecilia Freke's sister married an Austen. See next page re bequest to the Austen family.
> 2. The "Squire thy brother" is not recorded in any genealogy; presumably, in the parlance of the day, it referred to a brother-in-law.

18.vi ELEANOR (named by Pearman but not shown on BCHR)
m. William Gerard, Esq.

---

* These two successive early deaths from smallpox seem odd; more confusion ?

19.ii Sir GEORGE CHUTE, BARONET   born June 1664 after his father George's death. Immediately before being created Baronet by Charles II on Sept 17, 1684, he was baptised at Bethersden, aged 20 (why not as a child?). Described in the accolade as "of Hauxfall Place"; the baronetcy may have been given in fulfilment of a political promise originally made to his father. Pearman says he "pulled down Hinxhill and retired to Bethersden", but dies not explain why. At Lovelace in Surrenden where he resided under its new owner, "he was only tenant" (Hasted).

He was M.P. for Winchelsea (Philip the SB's old constituency, and one of the Cinque Ports) Nov. 1696-1698. He took it over from a Robert Austen, deceased.

> (The Chutes, Austens and Dixwells had the Cinque Ports well wrapped up, as in the 1695-6 Parliament, Sir John Austen, bart. was MP for Rye; Robert Austen, esq. was MP for Hastings, and Sir Basil Dixwell, bart. was MP for Dover.)

Sir George died without issue on February 4, 1721, this Baronetcy thereby becoming extinct. He devised his whole estate to Edward Austen, Esq., a political ally and relative of his aunt's husband*.

There is a fine marble memorial to Sir George, bart. in Bethersden Church; look behind the organ. He is buried, beside his father, under a ledger stone in the nave.
There is also a ledger stone to one Thomas Worrall whom the unmarried baronet evidently held in unusually close personal favour.

> *The Austens were a Tenterden family of long standing with wealth from textiles who, per Winnifrith, died out locally in the 19th C. It was said that to gain a Kentish parliamentary seat, one must win the favour of the textile magnates. Edward Austen later became a baronet. The Austen cousins in Hampshire were friends of the Lobb Chutes of the Vyne. It is not known if any cash from the original Philip Chute fortune ever filtered through from Edward to Jane the novelist. As noted earlier, Sir Anthony Aucher from whom Philip bought Surrenden Manor, was a maternal ancestor of Jane Austen.

19.iii CECILIA CHUTE 1668-1675, is a name mentioned in Kentish sources, but her parentage has not yet been established.

AN OVERPOWERING AUNT?

Consider this case. An unborn baby loses his father from smallpox. When he grows up, he is the first - for many years - of his wealthy family not to take a wife. But he has a gravestone prominently laid in the family church for his male servant who has died young.

He is in his 50's and decides to make a Will. In another county he has cousins - a father with several sons, only one of whom could own their family estate. At that date the gentry normally kept land and money 'within the family'; but it is not to his blood-relations that he bequeaths his vast estate, but to the son of his mother's sister, of a quite different family who are already wealthy in their own right.

The case of Sir George Chute, Bart might tempt one to see his mother's sister (born Judith Freke), as a ruthless harpy who dominated her young and widowed sister Cecilia and her orphaned son. So much so that in adulthood the son (a) shied away from women all his life and (b), having no children himself, was bullied by his aunt into leaving to her son Edward Austen all the widespread Chute estates in Kent and Sussex - i.e. not to his blood-cousin Edward Chute who had all those sons at the Vyne.

Is that why the Bethersden Chutes died out? A situation which would have appealed to Edward Austen's later relative, Jane Austen, the novelist of middle-class manners. Unproven but just a thought...

THE BRANCH AT STOCKWELL MANOR, LAMBETH

Children & Descendants of Sir George Chute (16.ii) & Anne, née Barnham (pp.125,187)

17.i **Philip** and 17.ii **George**, twins, died young
17.iii **ELIZABETH**, b. 1623, d. young in 1627, buried at Sonning (info. per LeNeve, nowhere else)
17.iv GEORGE - first surviving son - see below
17.v **WILLIAM**, described as "of Willesden, Middlesex"
17.vi **FRANCES**, who m. (1) John Tufton, esquire; (2) Henry Fitzjames, esq. of Dorset
    [Note: One source says she was not Anne's but Margaret's dau. from previous marriage - if so, the hard-working Anne suffered one less pregnancy]
17.vii **MARGARET** who died aged 6 in 1638, commem. by the brass tablet in Lambeth Parish Ch.

17.iv GEORGE was old enough in 1640 to receive a land lease. Two years later, his father was paying £4.16s. tax on lands worth £12 (the wealthiest in all Lambeth) per Subsidy Roll 17th Charles I (1642). Son George went on to do several land deals, recorded in deeds at Lambeth Records Office. In 1669 he could afford to pay the huge sum of £4,570 to buy copyholds in Streatham. (To one of these, his cousin 18.v George Chute later moved from Bethersden). He married: -
(1) in 1650 **Sarah Style** of London; marr. settl. deeds in Lambeth Records Office. They had 4 children of whom only George and Sarah survived infancy (see below); mother Sarah died after some 8 yrs of marriage. George re-married, to -
(2) in 1660 **Margaret**, dau. of Thomas **Hussey**, grocer, and widow of Lawrence Coles.
    BCHR says <u>their</u> dau. Margaret died young, but this seems to be confusion with the earlier girl commemorated at St Mary's.

children of George and Sarah Style

18.i. GEORGE (born 1651/2, d. by 1687) - see below
18.ii **CHRISTOPHER** d. young
18.iii **CHARLES** d. young
18.iv **SARAH**, m. Robert Parker of Ratton in the

> *The 4 generations from 15.ii George Chute of Bethersden, armiger, to 18.i George and 18.iv Sarah, as shown on the BCHR, also appear in the 1662-3 Visitation of Surrey (as preserved in Harleian Society Vol. 60, which reproduces the MS signature of 17.iv "George Chute" confirming the pedigree).*

parish of Willington, Sussex, Baronet. (An elaborate heraldic shield recording Parker and Chute lineages is added as postscript to BCHR) They had 5 children, among whom Philadelphia Parker and Sir Geo. Parker Bt. were party : (i) to a Petition as to property rights heard by the House of Lords Nov.16, 1692 *[the official report, incidentally, refers to "Katherine Chute, the widow", a name of which we have no other record]* and (ii) to a 1696 Order in Chancery, held in Lambeth R.O.

18.i GEORGE seems likely to have been the 'Mr Chute' who stood in 1681 for election to be one of the two Sheriffs for London.
In 1674 he m. **Joanna St. John**. Her father Sir Walter St. John, Baronet, had estates in Lydiard, Somerset and Battersea, Surrey; he insisted that all the Chutes' estates in Lambeth, Stockwell, Newington, Walworth and Streatham be mortgaged to his family in the marriage settlement. On 28 June 1675 he gathered a social party of several knights and an independent barrister to witness the marriage settlement deed (doc. ref: 1/3937 in Lambeth R.O.) After all that fuss, George/Joanna produced but one child, their daughter
    19.i Joanna Chute, who eventually m. a Sir Peter Soames of Heydon, Essex, Bart.
George died at the age of about 35 - unusually young for that family; had he caught the Plague in London, or was it smallpox, like the Bethersden Chute casualties?

With 19.i Joanna, the Chute name in Stockwell expired.

What became of their great estate we do not know, though VCH Surrey says the Thorneycroft family owned Stockwell Manor under Wm. & Mary, i.e. after 1688.
Some land at Stockwell was still in Chute hands in 1707 when 18.i George's widow Joanna, now living in the smart quarter of St James's, Westminster, disposed of a lease (doc. ref:1/3920 at Lambeth R.O.).

Tree 4 (p.160): Descent of 14.i Anthony, down to the Vyne Chutes (p.194)

Anthony, elder brother of the famous Philip, the Standard Bearer, is strangely elusive. This is unfortunate, since he is the traditional ancestor of (a) the American Chutes and (b) Chaloner Chute's line at the Vyne. Of Anthony himself, the only record known (found by a Canadian Chute researcher, and mentioned on p. 182 above) is one showing him employed as a gunner at the Tower of London. As to his descent, the College of Heralds find so little 'proof' that Lyonell was his son that they are unwilling to grant the American Chutes legitimacy to bear Chute arms.

This need not surprise us. Anthony was born c.1500 before parishes had to keep records, and the Chutes, after centuries at Taunton, were taking time to find a role and put down roots in S.E.England. Without a settled address you might well leave no record unless, like Philip, you became a national figure. When Anthony's sons did settle down, they left ample records; in the late 1500s we find them on the East Anglian coast, in a cluster of villages round Wrentham* in Suffolk (the town where Philip found his 3rd wife).

Tradition does not explain why Anthony, or at least two of his sons, moved there. Until evidence emerges, we have made our provisional hypothesis, using clues from Philip's career (p.183). Historians of the Cinque Ports say that Henry VIII resolved to end the centuries-old vendetta between the Portsmen of Sussex/Kent and the fishermen of Yarmouth in East Anglia, which harmed national security. The trouble stemmed from the Portsmen's rights, age-old in practice and confirmed by Kings Henry II and Edward I (who needed the Portsmen's loyalty) to fish in the North Sea herring grounds and run fish markets at Yarmouth.

Thus it was in the Ports that Henry VIII's edict must be published and enforced. The enforcers must have included Philip Chowte, M.P. for Winchelsea and protégé of Sir Thomas Cheyne, Lord Warden of the Cinque Ports. It would be hard enough at any time to strip an ancient right from these semi-pirate fishermen who lived in the Marshes on the edge of civilisation. But the Portsmen already had cause to feel resentful. Their coastline was silting up, they could not build the larger-draft vessels required for modern naval warfare, and they were losing this prestigious industry to the deeper water ports of Hampshire to the west. Without it, they forfeited income and much of their claim to special privileges.

So when we find Philip & Anthony, men of Sussex/Kent, having unexplained connections with Suffolk, a plausible reason emerges. As one of the king's enforcers, Philip could order his local fishermen not to go near Yarmouth, but they were in such a bloody-minded mood that someone had to be stationed on the coast south of Yarmouth to deal with any mass disobedience (or call for help if needed). That is just where the king gave Philip his post at Frostenden manor (*valley of frogs*) under the guise of bailiff to Queen Anne of Cleves; his salary could be used to finance the operation of an armed patrol vessel. But Philip could not be in two places at once. One way to keep a check on the fishermnen would be to pay his brother Anthony to set up home in Frostenden as Philip's deputy with King's Warrant. With 4 sons, Anthony could be an effective coast-guard.

---

* Wrentham was a vigorous Puritan centre under the Brewsters of Wrentham Hall. Might this explain Charles Chute's defection in middle age from the royalism of his father, to the cause of Cromwel,? (p. 161.)

Anthony's sons (the order of their birth is unclear):-

15.9. CHRISTOPHER, of whom the only known record is a letter dated 1578, concerning mines in Wales, in the Hatfield MSS, Vol. 2, p.185, in which a William Humphrey recommends to Lord Burghley that "treasure be got from the earth without time wasted" and that "the money collected for the works may be employed by Christopher Choute who is well able to deal in the matter."

15.10 WILLIAM (nothing known but his name).

15.11 ARTHUR was probably born c.1547, as deeds in Ipswich Records Office show him buying and selling lands in the Wrentham area from 1567 to c.1585. He m. **Elizabeth**, dau of Henry **Sea** of Herne, Kent. John and Anthony Chute (18th C.) held that her family was related to that of Lord Say and Sele, which produced two Speakers of the Commons. Arthur & Elizabeth were grandparents of Chaloner Chute the Speaker; their double portrait, aged 80 & 70, hangs over a fireplace at the Vyne.

15.12 LYONELL m. Miss Greene of Ipswich on 8 Sept, 1578 at Frostenden. They lived at Brampton, near Wrentham. Date of his death unknown. His Will was dated 24 July, 1592 (proved 1st Aug.); 'Arthur Chowtt, gent.' witnessed it. Lyonell was father of:-

16.7 LIONEL - FOUNDER OF THE AMERICAN CHUTE FAMILY. Born c. 1580, m. (c.1610) Rose, dau. of Robert Barker of Dedham, where he was local schoolmaster. Had 2 sons & 1 dau., and emigrated about 1634 to Ipswich in the newly founded colony of Massachusetts, and was teaching in school there in 1636. (Curiously, a 'Lionel Chute' witnessed Wills at Dedham up to 1638. Surely not his father?) He died 1645 in America, and his widow re-married a Matthew Whipple in 1646.
The AMERICAN CHUTES, outside our scope, are fully researched by Cousin Jackie in New York.

Lionel`s children **James** (bapt. 1613/14) and **Mary** (bapt. 1619) are named in Dedham records.

16.8 **GEORGE**

16.9 **SARAH** m. - Greenlawn, Esq, & had 3 children

16.10 **CLEAVE**

16.11 **JUDITH** m. John Adkinson (or Edmondson) & had 7 children.

parentage uncertain

16.12 **CHARLES, M.P.** (c.1570-1651) Son of Arthur & Elizabeth. Portrait at the Vyne. He m. Ursula, dau. of John Chaloner (acc. to Berry; others say dau. of William Chaloner). MP for Thetford 1592-3 (35 Eliz.) as Charles Chewte. Of Kelvedon, Essex,and Fulham. Brought up his children in Kensington. There is no record of him in any later Parliament - at least not for Thetford. In 1601 Feodary and Clerk of the markets of the Queen in the Duchy of Lancaster. (See CWC History.) Seems to have lived past 80, as his Will at PCC was proved in 1652. Under James I, he was one of the few men allowed to visit Sir Walter Ralegh in the Tower, per the following extract from MS at Hatfield in the Cecil Collection.

SIR G. HERVEY, Lieutenant of the Tower, to LORD CECIL.

1604, July 30. I have received your letters by Lady Ralegh, and have thought it my duty to put you in mind that upon the prisoners' return from Winchester the Council ordered that Lord Cobham, Lord Grey and Sir Walter Ralegh should each have two servants, one to attend, and the other to go about their business. This was observed till the Council gave warrant for divers other persons, whose names I send herewith, to have access to them; since which time Sir W. Ralegh, besides his men of allowance, has drawn unto him a prea- cher and 3 boys in ordinary. It may be that the warders, not finding their names in the list, have stayed such at the ward till they have acquainted me therewith: whereupon I have ever permitted them to come to him.

The persons named in the schedule as permitted to have access to Sir W. Ralegh were:
The Lady Ralegh: *Sir Car. Ralegh : *Sir S. Carewe : his physician: Sir Alexander Brett: Mr. Peter van Lore: *Mr. Arth. Aston : *__Mr. Char. Chewt__: *Widow Money : Mr. Shelbern : 2 servants that attend him, i.e. Peter Hart and Talbot a Schoolmr. [Those with an asterisk are annotated as "names crossed out by Cecil"; not clear if this means that they were no longer to be allowed access to the prisoners.]

Other Chute Records in Suffolk

1. The Ellough Memorial

An **Arthare Chewt**`s widow Margaret (d. 1607) is buried in Ellough Church, now disused, standing not far from Wrentham and Frostenden. Nothing else is known of him, but her tomb displays traditional Chute heraldic arms of 3 swords barwise (without canton) above which is clearly written CHEWT. The words are hard to decipher today, but were clearer when the author of Suckling`s `History and Antiquities of Suffolk` described them in Vol I, p.55:

`There is a small brass effigy of a female, placed within the communion rails, the linbes of which are nearly obliterated. The inscription, in more perfect condition, commemorating :*

"Margaret Chewt, the faythfull loving wyfe of Arthare Chewt, gentleman, daughter to Christopher Playters, Esquer, who died at thage of 85, in ffebruarie 1607"

is accompanied with the Chute arms "gules, 3 swords barwise, arg. hilted or." and the Playter arms.`

To have an engraved brass memorial at that date implies that the surviving family of Playters and/or Chewt were wealthy. (The Playters family, patrons of the Ellough living, included knights and later a baronet.) One supposes she returned to her family village after his death, so the inscription gives no clue as to where the Chewts lived and it does not mention her having children; but it tells us that she was born c. 1522. This implies: (i) that she married Arthare c. 1542 and (ii) that Arthare was by then an established gentleman in Suffolk, though we have no record of his owning land there in his own name. If Arthare was born c. 1510-20, he could easily have been Philip`s younger brother. Or, as we have hinted, he might have been confused in the record with Anthony

2. Unidentified Chewte in Suffolk 1612 Visitation.

"Alexander Sherman of Bruisyard [3 m. NE of Framlingham] m. Elizabeth dau. of _ Chewte of Soterley in Suffolk and hath issue Frances a dau." NB. Sotterley is only 2 miles from Wrentham & Frostenden.

By 1668 there is no Chute entry in Suffolk Visitations, so presumably they had all left the county.

16.12 CHARLES and Ursula née Chaloner had 6 recorded children:-

(a) Mentioned in C.W.Chute` History of the Vyne` as baptised at St Mary Abbot`s Church, Kensington :	(b) Mentioned in other H.R.O. document (31M57/1097) as baptised in Fulham Parish Church:
17.21 CHALONER, the Speaker (c.1595-1659)	**17.18 ELIZABETH** (bapt. 8.10.1593)
17.22 CHARLES bapt. 1600	**17.19 JANE** (bapt. 7.1.1595), m. John Bowles, 1633
17.23 DOROTHY ANNE bapt. 1603	**17.20 ALEXANDER,** m. Eliz. Holbecke, 1628.

17.21 CHALONER , THE SPEAKER (c.1595-1659) - pp.18 ff. above.

For his life & legal career see C W Chute `History of the Vyne` (1888) pp 71-75. Here we summarise.

Leased Sutton Court, Chiswick from Lord Mayor of London, who had been granted it when Parliament took it from the Dean and Chapter of St Paul`s Cathedral .

Lay Rector of St. Nicholas Church, Chiswick; presented 5 bells.

Elected to Parliament for Middlesex 1656 & 1658/9.

On 29 Jan 1659 *"Mr Chaloner Chute was chosen Speaker of this Parlem. an Excellent Orator, a man of great parts and generosity, whom many doubted that he would not joyne with the Prot[ector`s] party butt he did heartily."* (Bulstrode Whitelocke Diary)

He tried to decline the post on grounds of poor health but Members were insistent that he accept.

In the event, the "incessant fatigue of office" in conciliating between violent factions in parliament caused his speedy retirement. When he was ill at Sutton Court , *"some members of the House by order went from the House to visit their Speaker Mr Chute which was a great honor to him, & he had so much gained the affection of the house that he swayed much with them"* (Whitelocke, March 19)

He died on 14.4.1659 at Sutton Court. Buried at St Nicholas, Chiswick (near other Chaloners).

Sources: C.W.Chute op cit. (copy in H.R.O. Winchester).	Parliamentary Reports 1659.
Diaries of Bulstrode Whitelocke.	Dictionary of National Biography, which quotes other sources.
Manning's Lives of the Speakers (publ. 1851) pp 334-6	Records of St Nicholas Church, Chiswick etc.

CHALONER, the Speaker m. (1) **Ann née Skory,** widow of William Plase. Her Skory pedigree, according to John Chute, descended from a 13th C. Sir Richard de la Launde of Cornwall, and in recent generations included Lanyon and Earl of Hertford. She died young but they had 3 children:

18. 9 CHALONER (II) (1630-1666) Married his step-sister **Catherine Lennard,** dau. of Lord /Lady Dacre
.   (**Lady Dacre**, widow, became CCI`s 2nd wife in 1650, the year after he committed to buy the Vyne).
.   CC II was MP for Devizes in 1656 & 1658/9. Was among the MPs whom Oliver Cromwell tried on 22.9.1656 to exclude as 'unfriendly' to the Protectorate. Quotation in CWC's History, p.78.

July 1659: a Commissioner for Militia in Middlesex & Co. Southampton. Jan 1659/60: an assessor for Wiltshire, for a Tax for Maintenance of Armies and Navies. For a day in May 1661, sat as MP for Haslemere, but was unseated. MP for Westminster; 28 Jan. 1662 was ordered by the Commons to be apprehended in custody of the Serjeant at Arms and forced to defend himself, after various MPs denounced him for speaking *"reproachful words against the Honour and Justice, and in breach of the Privilege of this House".*

.   Kept his father's London house "at St Martin in the Fields"- doubtless because Lady Dacre had barred him from the Vyne - thus his children will have been brought up in London.

Re: Dispute with Lady D, see House of Lords MSS for 1679, pp.152-4, item 209 with notes & 13.11.1680. His Will, in HRO, protests he never intended to keep anything from Lady D to which she was entitled. The armour in his portrait is said (CWC notebook) to be Civil War armour given him by Richard Cromwell.

18. 10 SCICILIA

18. 11 ANN, who m.   (1) in 1648, Christopher, son of Sir Edward Salter
                              (2) Henry Barker, of The Grove, Chiswick, i.e. the Chutes` neighbours there. His grandfather's portrait hangs at the Vyne; the family is described on p.65 of doc. 31M57/652 in HRO. Henry was trusted friend of CC II, whose Will gave HB the custody of Chute children in event of their mother`s death.

Children of CC II and Catherine née Lennard:-

19.4 CHALONER III (1656-85)   Bewigged portrait at the Vyne. Profession if any not known. The letter sequence mentioned under Edward below proves that CCIII's death was sudden and unexpected.

> [The courtier whom he petitioned to let him go to Flanders was the "transvestite" Lord Cornbury, grandson of 1st Earl of Clarendon. Unlikely that Cornbury wanted more than a ringside view in Flanders; he traded on his Hyde family link to James II, but quickly deserted the king when Wm. of Orange landed; when later his cousin Queen Anne sent him to govern New York, he allegedly wore women's clothes at a state function.]

CCIII's Letters are briefly quoted in CWC p.79.   In Historical MSS Coll. - Duke of Rutland, Belvoir Castle the editor's intro. mentions CCIII and his attentions to the Countess of Rutland's sister Lady Bridget Noel, and describes her lifestyle. Relevant letters are:

> 1681 Nov. - gossipy letter from CCIII to Countess of Rutland.
> 1681/2 March 10, April 18 & 20, from Viscountess Campden to her dau. the Countess of R, disapproving CCIII's addresses to Lady B.N.
> 1682 May 19, CCIII to the Earl of R's secretary about dress for a wedding
> 1682 13 July CCIII to the secretary about water pumping to Belvoir Castle.
> 1684 Apr 29, July 1 (from camp at Leffenes), CCIII re military service in Flanders under Louis XIV.
> 1685 July 16, CCIII to the Countess saying he had gone to Tower Hill to see Monmouth beheaded; describing scene and reporting what Monmouth said.

19.5 EDWARD (1658-1722)

Educ: Winchester & New College (Fellow 1678). Influence of his cousin, Lord Keeper North, got him a clerkship under Charles II's Sec.of State Sir Leoline Jenkins. (See CWC p. 80 ff. for text of letters).
Letter from Roger North of the Middle Temple to Sir Wm. Trumbull, James II's Sec. of State, quoting EC's poverty and seeking a job, is dated Sept.23, 1685 in Marquess of Downshire Coll. of Hist. MSS.

Patronage moved fast, since by Nov.17, 1685 (when CCII died) Trumbull had already given EC a job in
> Paris; there is even a letter (Feb 1686) discussing the handling of his baggage to France.
Two letters of Nov.19th (from Samuel de Paz and Owen Wynne) refer to the change in EC's fortunes and
> how he will have "other thoughts than those of going to Paris".
He succeeded to Vyne just in time not to work under James II.
He wound down the correspondence with Belvoir initiated by CCIII, completing with a horse-talk letter (March 19, 1689/90) to Earl of Rutland which explains how the Basingstoke Monteith had been financed.

Edward owned the Vyne 1685-1722; his improvements include collection of furniture and tapestries and the restoration of stained glass to Chapel (note the Chute/Keck arms upper-left in window).

m. 1686 **Katharine Keck**, widow of Ferdinand Tracy (by whom 2 children*). Her father **Sir Anthony Keck** (1630-95), barrister of Inner Temple, knighted 1688/9 on becoming Commissioner of the Seal, MP 1691 for Tiverton, was described by Roger North: *"a person that had raised himself by his wits, and, bating some hardness in his character which might be ascribed to... the gout, he was a man of polite merry genius"*. Katharine's mother Mary was a Thorne heiress. Docs. in H.R.O. detail the marriage settlement and payments which cleared the Dacre "debt" and enabled Edward to marry Katharine.

> Having feathered her nest, Sir A seems still to have left great wealth to his son Francis, but F's children John & Mary left no grandchildren; hence (i) the former Dunch estates at North Baddesley (see explanation on next page) reverted to the Kecks' Chute cousins, and (ii) a Tracy nephew of Francis got a substantial bequest on condition that he took the name Keck. (The latter's descendant Susan Tracy Keck (d.1835) of Great Tew m. Francis Wemyss, Lord Elcho on 18.7.1771)

> *One of them, John **Tracy**, appears to have been Edward's god-son as well as step-son. Acc. to Horace Walpole's editor, his son was a barrister named John Tracy Atkyns (d. 1773); hence Walpole expected claims by Tracys and Atkyns's to the Vyne on Anthony Chute's death.

Edward kept racehorses at the Vyne, won the Basingstoke Monteith, and as "staunch supporter of the House of Hanover" became High Sheriff of Hampshire 1699.

Edward d. 18.4.1722; buried at St. Andrews Church, Sherborne St. John, where various Chute/Keck funerary hatchments are still displayed. There is now no trace of Edward's, Katharine's, Anthony's or John's graves, which seemingly were overlaid during Wiggett Chute's 19th C. restorations. (So also was the "vault on the south side of the chancel, under the communion rails", where Lobb Chutes were buried.)

Among **assets the Chutes gained from the Keck marriage** were (a) presumably the Nottingham estates named in Edward's Will but otherwise unexplained (Darleton Manor, Kingston & Dunham, W. of Lincoln) and (b) the Great Tew leases which John Chute was able to re-sell, and (c) North Baddesley Manor, N of Southampton, which had circuitously reached the Chutes as ff. - Katharine's brother Francis Keck had m. a Dunch heiress (a strong Parliamentary family connected by marriage to Richard Cromwell); he thereby acquired the Dunch estates; but when their children died childless, these estates devolved, under Francis's old Will, on his nephew Anthony Chute. [This seems grossly unfair to the Dunch family; but before that date the male Dunches had expired, leaving 4 dau. to inherit; so the Dunch name had gone.] On Anthony's death intestate they passed to John, who then sold (i) in 1762 the 50-acre Rownhams estate for £1000 to the brother of Sir Robert Walpole's chaplain, and (ii) in 1767 the balance of the manor to a Mr Thos.Dummer of Cranbury Park. The M27 garage "Rownhams" is therefore situated on part of a former Chute property. Another part of Francis Keck's estate went to John Tracy (Edward Chute's stepson), as stated above, on condition he took the name Keck.

19.7 THOMAS (c.1660-1701), of whom Lord North "took especial care". Juvenile portrait at the Vyne. Clerk of the Crown in Chancery from 1695-1700. Letters seen in which (all else having failed) he petitions King Wm III, on his retirement from the job, for back-payment of many years' fees due to him for appointing magistrates, etc.; his petition was refused!

In J H Baker's "The Order of Sergeants at Law" p. 419, the Call of Edward Ward in 1695 is quoted; in Ward's words *"Saturday the 8th of June 1695 ... and then I took the oaths to the government, and the sergeant's oath, which were ministred to mee by Mr Chute, Clerke of the Crown in Chancery..."* (On the preceding evening, Ward had ceremonially taken his leave of the Inner Temple when *"I treated the hall which was very full with burned wine, bisquetts and sack".)*

Thomas Chute, favourite grandson of the generally detested Lady Dacre, became her heir, but also married money. The family of his wife **Elizabeth Rivett,** heiress, is listed in "East Anglian Pedigrees" (tho' she and her father are not personally mentioned). They seem to have been lawyers, as one Rivett provided a legal Opinion for John Chute. They owned *inter alia* the advowson of Moulton St Michaels, near Diss, which passed into the Chute family; in due course J.S.Wiggett, E.R.Chute & T.D.Chute became rectors there.

Thomas is most notable in the family for acquiring the Pickenham estate in Norfolk in 1700. He and his wife Elizabeth are buried at South Pickenham. (See p. 198 below)

Their dau. **20.xi ELIZABETH** m. **Thomas Lobb** of Cressingham, the manor adjoining Pickenham; it was their son Thomas who, as

21. THOMAS LOBB CHUTE, inherited the Vyne in 1766 after the male Chute lineage failed. He was born Lobb in 1721; m. **Ann Rachael Wiggett.** They both d. in 1790 and were buried at Pickenham. He was one of the Vyne's major benefactors; see p.39 above and p.199 below.

---

continuing : Children of CC II and Catherine née Lennard

19. 8 BENJAMIN, d. young

19. 6 ELIZABETH, who m. Sir Charles Lodowick Cottrell, Knight, the Master of Ceremonies to Queen Anne. They had Cottrell issue: **Jane;** **(Sir) Clement,** scholar and antiquary; **John,** a colonel: **Stephen,** a doctor of civil law; & **William** who became a bishop in Ireland.

Sir Charles's brother-in-law was named Dormer. Succeeding generations, as Cottrell-Dormers:- (a) owned and developed the famous Oxfordshire gardens of **Rousham,** which made William Kent's reputation in England as landscaper; (b) remained hereditary Ms of C. at Court until, in 1797, Sir Clement C-D was dismissed for calling George III "a silly old fool". Later Cottrells took Chute as middle name (e.g. Clement Chute Cottrell, Indian Army, 1850)

10 children of Edward Chute and Katherine née Keck:-

20. i EDWARD (b 1687, d. young)

20. ii CHALONER IV (1688-1705) b. 4.10.88, died aged 16 on 5.5.1705 at Rotterdam, where his father had sent him to study mercantile commerce. (The Chutes at last waking up to the economic needs of a large family!) Memorial tablet in Cathedral Ch: of St Lawrence, Rotterdam read: *"HSE Chalonerus, Edvardi Chute de la Vine in comitatu Hantoniae apud Anglos armigeri filius natu secundus..."*

20. iii CATHERINE b. 1690 who m. her cousin Thos. Lennard Chute, son of Thomas Chute and Eliz. Rivett of Pickenham. Their son **Thomas** (bapt.1713) d.s.p.; he could be the "TC 67" on the barn at S.Pick.

20. iv ANTHONY (1691-1754). Owned the Vyne for 32 years; uneasy relations with everyone. Stood unsuccessfully for Hampshire as a Walpole Whig in 1734. Sat for tame government boroughs in the Isle of Wight, voting regularly with the Administration until his constituents (allegedly) petitioned for his removal.

MP for: Yarmouth, I of W. 8 March 1737 - 1741
        Newport, I of W.   1741 - 1747.

Letters from him, his father & others on political matters are in Jervoise Coll: at HRO (44M69/G2...)

Ann   **Mary**
(attributions per Vyne inventory 1956)

20. v MARY b. 1693 d.s.p. Portrait at the Vyne

20. vi. THOMAS, b. 1695, d. young

20. vii. FRANCIS (1697-1745), Chancery barrister (K.C. 1736), Fellow of the Royal Society 1742, intellectual, wit. Recorded as poet in Giles Jacob's "Poetical Register" (1723). J.Gay published Chute's "The Petticoat, an Heroi-Comical Poem" in 2 books, 1716; it went to 2 editions. FC presented a Silver Chalice in 1739 to Ewhurst Church near Kingsclere (VCH Hants IV, 248). Glos. Records Office has (D4582/7/9) a ballad *"written by Mr Francis Chute in compliment to Mr and Mrs Tracy with whom he passed his Christmas in....1720...at Stanway"*. Some of his conversations were preserved in Spence's Book of Anecdotes. Cambridge Univ. Library, Houghton Papers Coll: has 3 letters from him (1733) to Sir Robert Walpole.

Briefly M P for Hedon (Heydon), Norfolk, pro-Walpole, 1741- 4th March 1742; he was unseated on a petition by rival candidates (pro-Pulteney) that he lacked the necessary local property qualification. (Notes to Horace Walpole letters Vol 35, p.20). HW found him a fine public speaker, reporting to Mann on 10 Dec. 1741 that in Parliament Chute had spoken with `vast and deserved applause` on the Address. On his death in April 1745 (which decided John to return from Florence), HW described F.C. as *"a most rising man and one of the best-natured and most honest that ever lived"*..

His wife **Ann** was godmother to Ann, 2nd child of Thos Lobb Chute & Ann Wiggett. As a widow, `living at Somerset House`, she met HW in 1754. She re-married, but her new husband (Paulet) is said to have ill-treated her. Some of her bank statements survive in the Public Record Office.

20. viii MARGARET b. 1699, d.s.p.

20. ix ANN born 1700, accompanied brother John to the Continent for 12 months 1739... See article in "Originals Abroad" for her relations with John. Was godmother to a Cottrell; and her 1747 Will (as "spinster of Sherborne St John") made a bequest to "dear sister Tracy". Portrait at the Vyne (above).

20.x JOHN (1701-1776) Aesthete and architect. Life and main sources covered on other pages. The papers at HRO (5M50...) of Thomas Puckridge, Agent for the Thistlethwayte/Whithed family's Southwick and Norman Court estates, explain that "the method of providing money for Whithed & Chute abroad was for Puckridge to pay Samuel Cranmer, goldsmith and banker of Fleet Street, sometimes by sale of bonds; Cranmer then paid Sir John Lequesne in Paris or elsewhere and he gave Chute letters of credit enabling him to draw money, usually on Sir John Lambert." Anthony Chute seems to have had power of attorney in England for F. Whithed abroad. (Refs: 50M50/ 2097,2102,2104,2106,2219, 2584, dated 1739-1747 & 1766.)

CHUTES OF PICKENHAM

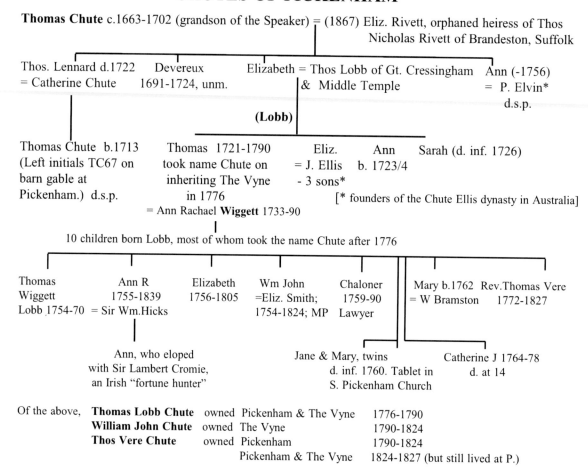

Thomas Chute c.1663-1702 (grandson of the Speaker) = (1867) Eliz. Rivett, orphaned heiress of Thos Nicholas Rivett of Brandeston, Suffolk

Thos. Lennard d.1722 = Catherine Chute

Devereux 1691-1724, unm.

Elizabeth = Thos Lobb of Gt. Cressingham & Middle Temple

Ann (-1756) = P. Elvin* d.s.p.

(Lobb)

Thomas Chute b.1713 (Left initials TC67 on barn gable at Pickenham.) d.s.p.

Thomas 1721-1790 took name Chute on inheriting The Vyne in 1776 = Ann Rachael **Wiggett** 1733-90

Eliz. = J. Ellis - 3 sons*

Ann b. 1723/4

Sarah (d. inf. 1726)

[* founders of the Chute Ellis dynasty in Australia]

10 children born Lobb, most of whom took the name Chute after 1776

Thomas Wiggett Lobb 1754-70

Ann R 1755-1839 = Sir Wm.Hicks

Elizabeth 1756-1805

Wm John =Eliz. Smith; 1754-1824; MP

Chaloner 1759-90 Lawyer

Mary b.1762 = W Bramston

Rev.Thomas Vere 1772-1827

Ann, who eloped with Sir Lambert Cromie, an Irish "fortune hunter"

Jane & Mary, twins d. inf. 1760. Tablet in S. Pickenham Church

Catherine J 1764-78 d. at 14

Of the above, **Thomas Lobb Chute** owned Pickenham & The Vyne 1776-1790
William John Chute owned The Vyne 1790-1824
Thos Vere Chute owned Pickenham 1790-1824
Pickenham & The Vyne 1824-1827 (but still lived at P.)

Thomas Chute acquired the <u>Pickenham estate</u> in about 1700, and Chutes held it for 144 years, longer than any family since the lordly Nevills who had it before 1496. It was evidently a luxury estate for a dignitary to retire to, rather than an economic investment, as from 1496 to 1700 there were 8 sales, averaging 1 every 25 years (Nevill, Methwold, Bradbury, Hobart, Methwold, Player, Fisher, Atkyns, Chute). In 1700 it was "of no great extent" (WLWC) but by the time Wm.Wiggett Chute inherited it in 1827, it had been much enlarged, since:
(i) In 1724 it was joined to the neighbouring Lobb estate of Cressingham when Elizabeth née Chute inherited Pickenham from her deceased elder brothers, and it became the property of her husband Thomas Lobb. *(Lobb tombs can be seen in Great Cressingham Church.)*
(ii) In the later 1700s, Ann Rachael née Wiggett's father William Wiggett, Mayor of Norwich, who loved Pickenham, bought more land for the family there. (He and his wife have memorial tablets in S. Pick Ch.)
The <u>house</u>, built by Fisher &Atkyns 1685-89 was of brick, smallish (see Caroline's memoir) and dilapidated when WLWC began to rebuild it in Palladian style after 1827. He sold it in 1844 for £108,600 to finance his rebuilding of the Vyne. In c.1900 its latest owner, a button millionaire, demolished the Palladian house, building a monstrous 60-room Edwardian 'Hall' for a visit of the Prince of Wales for a week-end's shoot.
In 1883, Pickenham <u>estate</u> covered 5135 acres. It remained a financial burden, being poor agricultural land, fit mainly for shooting. WLWC's successors - Applewhaite, Mills, Taylor, Moreton - had to pour money in to keep it going. Its present owner (2005) is largely absent, in his native Malaya and elsewhere.

The **Hall** (no visitors) is at South Pickenham village, where the **Church** is a little gem, with its 'Round Tower' (former look-out & beacon); in its chancel, many Chute, Lobb, Wiggett tombs/memorial plaques can be seen.

---

*there is a curious legend among American Chutes that the Elvins were somehow related to the Indian Pocahontas!

THE LOBB CHUTES

Thomas Lobb Chute, though one of its major benefactors, is a shadowy personality at the Vyne, leaving minor traces, e.g. his name in Sherborne St John Church porch as patron, and in the list of initial subscribers to the Basingstoke Canal. He probably devoted most of his time to Pickenham, where his Wiggett parents-in-law came to live; its local historian provided the quotes about his appearance, his attitude to servants, and his fondness for servant girls. Yet we assume he dearly loved his wife Ann Rachael, as he only survived her death by six months.

William John Chute, M.P.

He and Eliza come into most books on Jane Austen; also Jane's Letters and Caroline Austen's memoir. The "Vine Hunt" is discussed in detail in Brig. Hope's `History of Hunting in Hampshire` and in James Edward Austen-Leigh's "Memoir on the Early Days of the Vine Hunt, by a Sexagenarian" (Spottiswoode, London 1865), now out of print but copied as Item HP103 in HRO. JEAL wrote that at Harrow, WJC's fag was Spencer Perceval, later the murdered Prime Minister. After Clare Hall at Cambridge, WJC lived in Angers, from which experience he spoke French with a very good accent. He was an unusual mixture of high culture, intelligence and boyishness. In the 1790 Election when he & Heathcote stood for adoption as candidates, a letter from Wither Bramston, his brother-in-law, says *"the cry of all the Farmers & Yeomanry who are the strongest Bodies of the Voters, are all for Heathcote and Chute."* (HRO ref. 20M64/5) Bramston duly added to a letter of his wife (ref. 20M64/6) *"Last Thursday was the most glorious day I was ever witness to in that County, and plainly proves that the County of Hants is neither to be bought with Ministerial money, the influence of the House of Peers or the faction of Party, but that the independent gentlemen of the County will have their own Members ... Heathcote and Chute for ever, Huzza."*

Eliza's diaries covering many years 1794-1840 are held at HRO in the Austen Family collection, ref: 23M/93/70 ... (not in the Chute collection, though Rachel Chute seems to have had them at the Vyne when she wrote the articles we reproduce above). They are a historical study in themselves - and a delightful one. Her letters and her passport add to the picture of an energetic and cultured woman for whom the Vyne had been a prison.
- After WJC's death we find her organising journeys for herself across England demanding beds and hospitality at a series of country houses. It was the done thing for gentry to stop over at each other's private homes since hotels were not decent. Arrangements were made via the Mail Coach, which must have been reliable. E.g. her letter 30 August 1826 from Williamstrip, Glos: *"We are now bending our steps homeward after ten days at Witcomb, three at Malvern and two at this place from where we go for one night to Crudwell and two to Avondale".* She then proposes to spend a night at Oakley Hall and *"we shall be with you for tea between eight and nine o`clock. Mr Thomas Chute is with us and my maid... Caroline and I sleep together. If any inconvenience to receive her, you must let me find a letter from you directed to me at the Post Office Andover, where I shall enquire."* (HRO ref 31M57/969)
- Her family of **Smith,** which descended from a successful Lambeth timber-merchant, lived at Stoke Park near Devizes, for which her father Joshua was MP. Their once famous house, now `Earlstoke`, has been turned into a prison. One of her three sisters became Marchioness of Northampton. Eliza's marriage contract clearly preserved her financial independence (unusual at the time) which was just as well, given WJC's tendency to ignore unpleasant realities. (Her mother Sarah wrote to Eliza at her marriage not to be too timid with Mr Chute.) An instance of Eliza's loftiness towards the Austens (p.49) was when Jane & Cassandra, who had been offered a carriage from the Vyne to go to a dance in Basingstoke, were not invited into the dining room but were left waiting out in the hall while the Chutes finished dinner! Similarly, Eliza was cool towards Dr Workman, telling Caroline "it is not brilliant" when they got engaged, though it was good for her to have a protector. But there is irony when Eliza's official posture contrasts with her good nature. She can hold her husband accountable for every penny he borrowed from her, but on the same page of accounts she can be giving generously to a beggar, a poor sailor, or a "Turk". She distributed soup to the needy in winter, set up and ran a Sunday School, restored the church tower, and was remembered with affection.

Rev. Thomas Vere Chute was (per Brig. Hope) "a better sportsman and a far bolder rider" than his brother. He joined the Militia while in charge of Pickenham; became a priest (Rector of Pickenham 1810-1827), & in Feb.1816 had a call from his sister in Gloucestershire as the person most likely to change young Ann's mind when she eloped with Cromie. Ann was the only child of Sir Wm. Hicks, the man who made terrible faces (p.89). Both Caroline Wiggett and Caroline Austen tell of Tom's attachment to Mrs Wheeler. His 1826 letter to Wm. Wiggett, declaring him heir, describing the estate and explaining his legacies to the Ellis's, is at HRO. WLWC wrote "He, like many others of the family for several generations suffered much from gout and like many others when the attack had passed, and even before ... did many imprudent things. A bold & hard rider to hounds, and frequently on young horses, he had many falls and at last had one very severe fall which was believed ... immediate cause of his death." .

THE WIGGETT CHUTES

This Norfolk family owned the Vyne from William Lyde Wiggett Chute (1827) onwards. Its history up to 1880 can be read in CWC `History of the Vyne` and in the Memoirs of WLWC and of his sister Caroline.

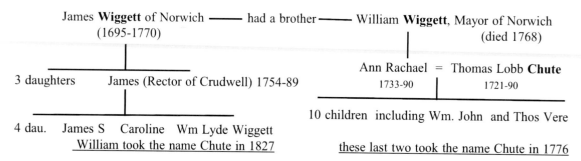

William`s elder brother **J S Wiggett,** did not take the name Chute but was given the living of **Great Moulton, Norfolk**, inherited by the Chutes from the Rivetts (the family of the 17th c. Thomas C`s wife). There JSW built an Italianate rectory which (though reduced in size by an embarrassed successor, and now divided) can be seen in modified splendour today. Later, Rev. Edward Russell Chute (p.202 below) and Rev. Theophilus Dacre Chute followed him as incumbents.

William Lyde Wiggett Chute M.P. (1800-1879)

Born in Crudwell, Wilts, youngest child of Rev. James Wiggett (lifetime rector) and his wife Rachel Lyde. She died in 1802 leaving James unable to cope with large family - hence his appeal to Wm. John Chute, already William Wiggett`s godfather, to adopt Caroline. The Rectory is now a smart hotel. William inherited both Chute estates in Jan. 1827. The Shooting Lodge at Pickenham is probably where he lived in the 1830s while the architect Donthorne (who "victimised" and overcharged him) gave the dilapidated Pickenham Hall its Palladian make-over. He was Tory MP 1837-47 for West Norfolk (his fellow-MP was Wm. Bagge) but, after selling Pickenham, gave up the seat as soon as he could.

WLWC raised a £25,000 mortgage on the Vyne estate in 1833 and began restoring village houses at Sherborne St John, though he could not live at the Vyne until Eliza died (1842). In 1844 he sold Pickenham for £108,600 (q.v.); he released the Vyne from mortgage and began its comprehensive reconstruction.
His Memoirs (copy in HRO) cover early Wiggett history , his memories of W J Chute, and a full description of his building work at Pickenham, in Sherborne St. John and at the Vyne. Whereas WJC never cut down a tree and let ivy cover the Vyne 2 ft. thick, WLWC stripped and repaired it and used masses of trees from the estate, plus his own brick-kilns, in completely rebuilding the village and estate.

A sociological condemnation of WLWC`s enclosures, etc. at the Vyne appears in *"The Woman`s Domain"* by Lummis and Marsh (Penguin Books 1990); but the book gives a sympathetic survey (pages 91-118, `The Vyne, Community and Change`) of the period of Jane Austen, Eliza Chute & Caroline Wiggett at the Vyne.

From Wm. & Martha`s 11 children, we focus on Chaloner & Russell, whose lineage are of particular note.

Children of Chaloner William Chute and Eleanor Portal

Rachel Eleanor	1876-1968	JP
Charles Lennard	1879-1956	Baronet
John Chaloner	1881-1961	Archdeacon
Anthony William	1884-1958	Archdeacon

All brought up at the Vyne, but on CWC`s death went with their mother to the Portal home; there they all stayed until Charlie reached his majority in 1900 and inherited full possession of the Vyne.

Rachel Highly intelligent, musical, literary and humorous but, being a girl, not given university education. Served with VAD in Great War; became first woman J.P.; active in the Girls Friendly Society. Unmarried.

Sir Charles: Brilliant scholar in mathematics and classics at Eton and Magdalen, Oxford. After his father's early death, had to wait until age 21 to inherit the Vyne - meanwhile the Vyne was run by Trustees. Career at the Bar was interrupted by Great War (Military Cross); after which he concentrated on public work.

      Joan, his wife, was shy and nowise Charlie's intellectual equal; unhappily they were childless, but she cared for the Vyne extremely well even in hard wartime conditions, and incidentally left some fine needlework. Shortage of money obliged them to lease the Vyne to a girls' school through the 1920s, after installing central heating. Charles was created baronet 4 July 1952 for public services. He died October 1956; some said it was due to exhaustion from public service, not unlike Chaloner the Speaker in 1659. He had first offered the Vyne to any member of the family who felt able to sustain its maintenance; none could. He bequeathed the Vyne to the National Trust, having tried to arrange for its use under NT ownership as a diocesan clergy home (this object did not prove feasible but Alcester received a bequest). Left a short memoir, now at HRO. Sherborne St. John recreation ground, a Basingstoke school, and a room in Winchester Castle are named after him.

> James Lees-Milne (Diaries 16/17 Dec. 1944) visited the Vyne for the National Trust on a cold rainy Saturday during the War when the 65-year-old Charles - then holding all the top public positions in Hants - came home exhausted from work and in no mood for social jollity. JLM judged him schoolmasterly, "abrupt, contradictory and snubbing" and Joan picked at her skirt like "a superannuated schoolgirl"; JLM left the Vyne "worn down by the Chutes; I decided I hated country houses". (A reviewer of the diaries said that JLM *records with the steely conviction of a camera shutter snapping, but rarely stops to examine*". In fact he got on better with the Chutes on his post-war visits in 1946/48, when Charles was under less pressure.)

Joan went in widowhood to live at Sherborne Cowdray and died in 1959; she presented Chaloner Chute's silver tankard, received from the grateful bishops, to the Speaker's House in Parliament.

John ("Jackie"), Mathematical scholar at Eton and Balliol; keen games player (soccer, tennis, cricket) and enthusiastic pencil-sketcher. Lost an eye playing cricket. Was tutor to the future Lord Bridges on a tour to Asia; became assistant master, then house tutor, at Eton 1906-36 and was so popular that his Old Boys held annual reunions for 50 years. Eton, short of clergy in the 1914 war, pressed him to take Holy Orders. Later he became Rector of Piddlehinton, Dorset (an Eton living) and Archdeacon of Sherborne; elected Archdeacon Emeritus of Salisbury 1961. Had his mother's dark Portal complexion and her international outlook.

      Mamie, his wife, musician and humorist, was a universal favourite. (Her uncle was Bishop Durnford of Chichester, her brother Admiral John Durnford was a Mayor of Chelsea, her nephew John Barker became executor to the last Chutes of the Vyne.) As a widow she lived with a series of small dogs at Buckland Newton, Dorset, then at Middle Farm Cottage, Bramley, near the Vyne. The family - *see picture* - gave her birthday parties at the Vyne until she was 92 (died 1979).

Anthony; shy scholar, celibate clergyman; Winchester and Magdalen Oxford, where he became Fellow and Dean of Divinity 1925-29. From 1936, Rector of Basingstoke; in 1948 its Archdeacon. Hon. canon of Winchester Cathedral.

    (right) Capt. Anthony Vere Chute (son of Lawrence Vere of Wissett, Suffolk, and father of Robin, Chaloner and Richard) proposing the toast at a birthday party at the Vyne c. 1978 for Mamie Chute, born April 1st 1887; she is at the back, far right. Tony's wife Daphne in uniform is pictured "1940" at the bottom right corner of our back cover.

Since Chaloner William had no grandchildren, and we have lost trace of any descent of his brother, Revd. Devereux - whose elder dau. Maud m. Henry de Rosenbach Walker (*memorial shield at Sherborne St John Ch:*) - Wiggett Chute blood now seems to survive only in the descendants of Edward Russell Chute, Rector of Moulton St Michaels, Norfolk.

Revd. Edw. Russell Chute (1846-89) m. Mary Nina Firth, and brought up four sons at Moulton :
    Frederick Russell (1875-1917) - Pioneer in Alaska (?engineer or husky-dog trainer?)
    Edward Lennard (1876-1949) - W.African Police, Tobacco-farmer in Rhodesia
    Lawrence Vere (1878-1948) - Chinese Customs, then Pedigree Pig-farmer in Suffolk
    Mervyn Lyde (1881-1961) - Railway Engineer, Fur Farmer, Conservationist, High Sheriff.

After ERC died young, his widow (there being no clergy widows` pensions then), felt obliged to re-marry to support her sons` education.. Her 2nd husband, ex-Col. A.D Smith R.M., fancied her but not her sons; he cut short their education and effectively drove them away; they dispersed to far places and only returned to England to fight in the Great War; when FRC was soon killed *(memorial in Witley Cemetery, Surrey)*.
    Len   m. Ethel Seymour, no children
    Vere   m. Nora Carruthers; had one son Anthony Vere (d. 1990) and 3 grandsons.
    Mervyn m. (1) Frances Armour (d.s.p. 1927) and
             (2) Emerin Keene (d. 1978) by whom 2 sons; 8 grandchildren, one of whose weddings is recorded below.

These are tabulated in **THE WIGGETT CHUTE FAMILY** on p. 74. They mostly fall outside the period covered by this book

A VYNE WEDDING IN 1994: JAMES DEVEREUX CHUTE AND HIS SISTERS

"SOMERSET CHUTES" OF BRIDGWATER, COMBE ST. NICHOLAS & BRISTOL

Further research is needed to find genealogical links between:

a. **The Taunton Chutes**, i.e. Adam Chut and the presumed descent via Alexander to Edmond;

b. **The Bridgwater Chutes** (c. 1500) who moved on to Combe St. Nicholas, Somerset in 1650, surrendered some of their property there in 1720, but may have kept leases on C St.N church lands up to 1775;

c. **Devon Chutes:** There are a dozen 16/17C. parish records of Chutes in Devon, not yet researched, and PCC Wills of Robert Chute 1759 (Will made in "Devon") and Edward Chute 1791 (Will at "Exeter");

d. **The Bristol Theatre Chutes**, 150 years from James Henry (1810-78) to Father Desmond (1895-1962).

(a) **Taunton** came to prosperity later than Bridgwater, a bigger market town with a river port. Taunton had a historic castle, but its pre-Norman population was small and dependent on the monastery. No Chute deeds survive for Taunton (mostly bishop`s land). A sceptic might suggest that Edvard`s descendants, with their maritime background, made their money in Bridgwater, but that Taunton`s *social* prestige rose and by 1500 it was a more `dignified` place to have sprung from. In any case, the impossible legend that Edmond "sold Taunton Manor to an ancestor of the Earls of Bridgwater" must be a garbled recollection of a land exchange between the various local Chutes. The Bridgwater lineage went on to be comfortable landowners at Wells & Combe.

(b) Somerset parish records (starting like the rest of England`s in the 1500s) show 5 - 6 generations of Chutes at **Bridgwater, Wells and the Manor of Combe St. Nicholas.** Wills in Bridgwater and/or Wembdon include - John Chuytt 1539, John 1562, Nicholas 1566, Nicholas Chute, gent. 1581, Henry 1592 (he is not otherwise known), Robert 1615, Archelaus 1625, Robert (?=Fry) 1658, etc. up to Eliz. 1670. Baptism of George C at Bridgwater in 1597 is followed by those of his 2 children. Marriages incl. Mary C = Thos. Hore, Bridgwater 1627. Combe Land Conveyance by Robert & John 1720. One such paper shows the Chute heraldic shield (though it could have been added later), so they are `ours`, but we cannot top or tail them in the family tree.

(c) **Devon.** The names Robert and Edward Chute recur at Exeter from 1704 to 1800. An Edward C signed Combe St Nicholas parish leases in 1759 & 1775; this suggests a connection between our Somerset & Devon branches, though we cannot identify *that* Edward, and no genetic link has been found. At Exeter, a Robert C of St Paul`s Parish was made freeman of the City in 1740, and an Edward C, apothecary, appears in property deeds 1748 - c.1800 for St Sidwell`s Parish. These seem to be the ones whose Wills are mentioned above. The Will of George C proved `in Devon` 1 June 1597 could be of Archelaus`s brother who moved to a leased house at Braunton; if so, it was a different George C (=Eliz. Gilbert) who emigrated to New Jersey in 1630.

(d) **Bristol Chutes.** J.H.Chute`s birthplace, which in the 1861 Bristol Census he gave as "Stoke, Hampshire; July 4, 1810", is usually interpreted as Alverstoke beside Gosport. However, no Chute is found in any Alverstoke parish records (birth, baptism, marriage or death) of the 19th C. The notion that his parents had arrived there by sea from Ireland, not from Somerset, is no more than a guess based on his popularity in youth on the Dublin stage, and the tendency among Irish to emigrate; in any case the name James is rare among Irish Chutes. It is more plausible to suppose that the Chutes disappear from rural Combe after 1723 because they moved to where they could gain financially from the new Industrial Revolution - some going to Bristol, others to Exeter. We do not know what they did with the proceeds from selling Combe manor. But JHC was clearly a man of culture and moral uprightness, whose education will have cost money.

Sources. The Bridgwater Chute tree in the text is (with our minor additions) taken from Somerset Records Office (SRO) document DD/SAS c/795 HV66/2 (p.103 of album of genealogies) and from Robert`s 1615 Will naming his siblings and children. His Breach of Promise docs. are DD/HWY 3 c/1134. Nicholas C`s Will is dated 1581. SRO also holds Combe St N. parish records on microfiche; they show "Eliza Chute, gentlewoman" 1704, and the last is Dorothea Chute 1723. The 1672 Visitation of Somerset (Harl. Soc. 1992) confirms this genealogy, and attests their gentle status.

"Mediaeval Wills from Wells" shows the Maud Vermyn Will. Her siblings were William and Joan Chute, and her other legatees Julian, Robert and Elizabeth Chute. From their context , they were farmers of quite humble station. Miscell. Somerset Wills (noted in Taunton Library), like Maud Vermyn, not yet connected to any known lineage, show

cont./

- 1378 Margaret Chyte of Bridgwater; 1530 William Chute of Bridgwater; 1545 Agnes Chute of Chilton, nr. Yeovil, 1575 Margaret Chute of Shepton Mallet. Also <u>Somerset Gen. Records</u> show a Rachel Chute who 1596 m. J Clement.
A <u>State Paper dated 1 May 1553</u>, recording a major purchase of manors in Norfolk & Somerset, mentions in the context of Bridgwater: "grant of the 4 ac. land in the field called Horsey Felde and 3 ac. meadow in Bradney Meade in tenure of William Chute".. as formerly belonging to the late priory or hospital of St John in Bridgwater. (This William Chute is not otherwise known.)
<u>Records of Dean & Chapter of Wells 1626</u> Appoint Robert Chute Steward of the Dean's manors in Somerset, for life.
<u>Mormon records</u> show a George Chute of Bridgwater, married to Elizabeth Gilbert, emigrating to Shrewsbury, New Jersey c. 1630. **This would make him the first known Chute emigrant.** A George Chute Will of 31 March 1679 is on record in Shrewsbury NJ.
<u>Protestation Returns of Feb./March 1642</u> show:
- in Bridgwater - Mrs Chute, widow, taxed £1 on land;
      - George and John Chute (this John not otherwise known) - not taxed as property-owners;
- in the Liberty of Wells - Robert Chute, gentleman; taxed £3 on land. (Presumably this was the Dean's Steward; was
      he the same man who bought the manor of Combe ?)
<u>Guide to Combe St. Nicholas Church</u> mentions that in 1650 (when the Chutes bought the manor) the local priest was in prison by order of Cromwell, and only released at the Restoration. Had these Chutes now become Parliamentarians?

Bibliography.

"The Story of the Theatre Royal" (Bristol 1966) and other books/articles on the subject by Kathleen Barker
"The Prince's of Park Row" by Don Carleton (Bristol Branch of the Historical Society, 1982)
"The Bristol Stage - Its Story" by G Rennie Powell (Bristol Publ. Co. 1919)
"Fifty Years of an Actor's Life" by John Coleman (Hutchinson 1904, vol 2).
Scrapbooks of letters to JHC and his wife are kept in the library at Bristol Univ. Drama Dept. (Adrian Varcoe Coll.)
   Signatures include Charles Kean, Henry Irving, Clara Butt, Ellen & Kate Terry, Beerbohm Tree...
Father Desmond Chute figures large in all biographies of Eric Gill and Stanley Spencer. See, in particular:
   "Stanley Spencer, a Biography" by Kenneth Pople (Collins, 1991), and an article
   "Desmond Chute" by Walter Shewring in the Jan. 1963 edition of *Blackfriars*.
Pictures and memorabilia re Desmond Chute and Eric Gill can be seen in Sussex at the Gill Collection at Chichester Records Office, and at Ditchling Museum near Brighton, where some of Desmond's woodcuts are on display.
Some of Desmond Chute's letters are preserved at the Spencer Gallery in Cookham, Berks. His extensive library and wartime diary were left to the International Library of Rapallo in the Italian Riviera (Villa Tigullio, Rapallo).

Desmond Chute

    Described by Spencer's biographer Kenneth Pople as a "considerable personality", and brought to life in the article by Walter Shewring (Eric Gill's executor), Father Desmond Chute deserves much fuller treatment than we can give here. To be respected and remembered for one's integrity of life and thought is surely an enviable achievement. (His life is presently being researched by Mr D C R Manners.)

    His **art works** are much prized, especially **portraits,** which are still coming to light unexpectedly (e.g. in a private collection in Scotland). His **letters** will repay close study, as will the **diary** in Italian which he wrote throughout the 1939-45 War in Italy, during much of which he was given freedom to work as priest, until interned by the Germans at Bobbio. There he took over a run-down hospital, with the help of a captured Yugoslav communist sergeant, and ministered to the humblest needs of the sick, the wounded and the poor. When war ended, he returned to Rapallo and , now in financial straits, he gave English lessons for cash. Gradually conditions eased, and he stayed there for the rest of his life.

    But there was no post-war re-gathering of international talents, such as the galaxy who had gathered there in the 1920s/30's - Hemingway, W B Yeats, Max Beerbohm, Ezra Pound and the Tigullian Circle, Truman Capote, Thornton Wilder, Evelyn Waugh, Isaiah Berlin et al. They are still celebrated in Rapallo's local literature (now on Internet); see for example articles by Giuseppe and Massimo Bacigalupo, who rate Desmond highly in the circle of artists, musicians and writers who lived there, and remember affectionate details such as his daily visit to the public bath-house in visor and sun-glasses, wearing greatcoats over his "imposing corporation". Chute was then the town's main concert-promoter, helped by Ezra Pound's mistress, a cellist.

    (Pound himself, pro-fascist & anti-semitic, broadcast against America from Italy during the war. For this, the Americans jailed him at Pisa in 1945, and he only escaped public trial in the US by being declared insane. From charity, Desmond took care of Pound's child while he was in prison.)

NOTES ON THE CHUTE FAMILY IN IRELAND

The family tree shown on p.148, from Burke's 1900 ed., is broadly attested by independent documents. Further family data can be seen in *Kerry Families* by Hickson and *History of Kerry* by J. King. It is a pity that surviving records offer such fragmentary detail on this branch of the family, but research in Tralee/Listowel would surely be rewarding. There is not space here to list all the fragments we have on the Irish Chutes. The late Desmond Chute (d. 2002) had a trunk full of family miscellanea, which his sons may have inherited. A few background notes now follow.

Gerard Francis ('Jed') Chute of Listowel, the Chute centre in Ireland today, is the man to consult on family history. It would be enormously valuable if he would write a comprehensive history.

Oddities   King's 'History' does not explain the alienation of George/Daniel's original lands, nor the huge cash payment, some £1000, made by Daniel to John McElligott to enable him to inherit her family's Tullygaron estate when he married Johanna McElligott in 1630. (Tullygaron means: hill of a copse or shrubbery).

It is also odd that Daniel took so long to marry, and that his father had deserted him for England many years earlier.

Background   In 1600, English families formed only 2% of the population of Ireland. For the natives, to speak English was taken as an index of loyalty. In consequence *"O'Donnell, invading Connaught in 1595, spared no male between 15 and 60 years old who was unable to speak Irish"*.

For colonists out in the sticks (as against those who formed the brilliant intelligentsia in Dublin) life was perhaps comparable to that of early settlers in Kenya. By 1611, we read, Munster as a whole had 5000 English settlers; by 1640 the figure was 22,000; relations between them and the Irish were better than in Ulster. *"In Cork, unlike Ulster, the new English were so successful in convincing themselves that their future in Ireland was secure that they did not perceive themselves as an embattled minority."*

As Protestant land-owners the Chutes were ready to do their duty for the Crown, both civilly and in war (see list of Irish Chute army officers on next page). So much so, that during Charles II's exile, because of the close Stuart ties with France, several Irish regiments were formed to serve alongside the French; as one result of this, in 1653 an Irish Chute officer was in an Irish Regt. of Horse serving with the French against Spain in the Netherlands. (Compare Chaloner Chute III in 1684; p.25 above.)

The Chutes' refusal to engage in sectarian discrimination in Ireland is attested by an article "In the Penal Days" in a Co.Kerry newspaper of c. 1930-40 edited by a Catholic Sister, which says : "...This Chute family of Chute Hall was in the Penal days the protector of the parish priest of East Kerry; and ... although the Chutes were then Protestants, they had a "hiding hole" for priests who had a price on their heads."   (Ref: -irlker on Internet.)

Early Prominence of Chutes in Kerry   Daniel's son Richard Chute M.P. joined the governing hierarchy under Charles II, per these extracts from MSS in the Collection of the Marquis of Ormonde, Kilkenny Castle:-

Dec. 5th 1663 the Earl of Ormonde, protesting at rumours that he has been oppressive, writes to the Earl of Orrery :

"I have therefore required Mr. Crosby and Mr. Chute, who were recommended to me as Protestants and honest men, forthwith to attend your Lordship and give you an exact account of what they had done by virtue of the authority and instructions they had from me, whereof I think I will be able with this to send you copies. If not, they shall be ordered to produce them, and assure your Lordship any person, English or Irish, that shall be found to have suffered loss under the colour of commission from me shall have ample reparation..." (Vol 3)

As a commissioner for Kerry, Chute of Tullygaron wrote other letters to Ormonde's office during 1665-67. In Ormonde MSS, HMC, Vol 6, they are dated Feb 26, 1665 (2 letters), Mar 29 '65, April 24 '66, Sept 18 '66, Oct.23 '66, Oct 24 '66 and Feb 5 '67.

In Ormonde MSS HMC Vol.4 pp 554-5, are more letters from Chute - Feb 15, 1663 and May 18 1664; its page 565 records the existence of a "Statement dated May 31, 1664, from Ardfert, made to Earl of Ormonde by Richard Chute, Thomas Crosbie & James Nagle, Commissioners in Kerry, with respect to purchases there by Sir William Petty".

From Ormonde MSS Vol 3, p.171
THOMAS CROSBIE AND RICHARD CHUTE to JOHN WALSH.1664, May 31. Ardfert.
"Honoured Sir; when we received our commission and instructions from my Lord Duke for the dispose of his Grace's interest for the present year, we did propose unto ourselves, by the rules therein prescribed, that we should have been

able to have advanced his Grace's revenue to double the rents it was set for the last year, being resolved to have stuck to that rule of not setting above twelve ploughlands to any one man, but having since received his Grace's positive commands to let all the English have their respective holdings, even at the very same rent they were set for the last year, and they being possessed of the most considerablest part of his Grace's interest in this county, we cannot by reason thereof add any augmentation to my Lord Duke's revenue."

Crosbie, Chute and a James Nagle wrote same day to the Earl of Ormonde. Vol. 3 p.172.

Richard Chute (see p.148) had 2 Crosbie brothers-in-law - his wife's brother and his sister's husband; their father was Sheriff of Kerry.

Other Dignitaries

The family's continued importance can be seen from the list of High Sheriffs, etc

1633	Thomas	Chancellor of Ardfert		1829	Caleb	Provost for Tralee borough. He and
1697	Eusebius	High Sheriff of Kerry				Pierce were free burgesses of Tralee in 1833.
1820s	Pierce	published Western Herald newspaper		1856	Richard	High Sheriff of Kerry
1822	Francis	High Sheriff of Kerry		1865	Francis B	ditto

Locations apart from Tullygaron *(ref: Hickson, King and Griffith - op. cit.)*

In 1814 Caleb Chute owned Ballymullen and Castlemorris at Tralee, and Richard C owned Chute Hall.
There were Chutes in Kerry in 1831 at Springhill, Ballyheighe (where Rev James C was rector), Tralee, Caherciveen.
In 1833 "W. Chute Esq." owned Chute Hall *(per Lewis Topogr. Dict. of Ireland, 1837 Vol II)*.
A full list of Chutes at Tralee in 1852 appears in Griffith's Valuation Survey.
In 1876, Chute landowners in Kerry were:

			Rev. G T, of Market Drayton, Shropshire*	5,094	acres
Algernon, of Dublin	1,606	acres	Capt. R R of Tralee	406	
Charles, of Tralee	1,141		Richard, of Tralee	433	
Francis, of Chute Hall	10,328		Capt. Thomas, of Glenville near Camp	248	

[*Rev George & wife Maria, plus 3 sons, 2 dau. and 3 servants, appear in the 1871 Census for Market Drayton]

Military Tradition

Apart from Gen. Sir Trevor and Lieut. Challoner (see pp. 156-158 above) a long line of Irish Chutes served the Crown bravely in war, such as:

Falkiner Chute	Capt. Dragoons		Richard Chute	Lieut. 8th Foot
Caleb Chute ("Clab")	Capt. of 69th; active in the Peninsular War		Richard Trevor C	Ensign 66th Regt., killed at Maiwand 20 July 1880.
Rowland Chute	Capt. 52nd Regt.		Richard A.B.Chute D.S.O.	Major, East Surrey Regt,
Richard Rowland C	Capt. 26th Cameronians			then of Manchester Regt. (1914-18)
Francis Chute	Lieut. 70th Regt.; died serving in India.		Desmond (son of Challoner)	Major, Border Regt. (1939/45)
Arthur Chute	94th Regt.; served in Indian Mutiny; invalided out.			
Arthur Rowland C	Ensign 90th L.I.; died at Calcutta 23 Feb. 1858 from effects of Siege of Lucknow.			
Richard William C	Lieut. Royal Artillery; died in service at Gibraltar 1.5.1862.			

Col. Torrens, husband of Charity Chute of Cork, was another famous soldier, who in 1811 won a Sword of Honour for his defence of the island of Ansholt.   MP and newspaper owner in England, he dared to publish proposals for unconditional Catholic emancipation in Ireland. Chairman of South Australian Commission. A lake and a river in South Australia are named Torrens after him and his son.

Chute Hall

Jed Chute records that the first Chute Hall was rebuilt 1730/40 and there are no drawings or photos of it, but he gives a description: "3 storeys high, the house was built in a comparatively small open square. The stable yard was a large square encompassed by long rectangles. It was surounded by a Park, and there were Gardens, Plantations and a Gate Lodge." The house was sold in the 1920s to a Hickey family who lived there for a time. It was demolished in the 1950s. Nothing of it stands today but a few stones at one gable end (and Desmond Chute reported seeing some of its stones incorporated in local farm buildings).
There are descriptions of its site, and its Ogham Stones, in modern Kerry guidebooks and Internet.

GENERAL INDEX

FAMILY TREES

REGISTER OF CHUTES IN/FROM EUROPE*

Those born to the name and those who assumed it on inheriting
the estates (incl. Thomas Lobb Chute's children).
Identification Numbers e.g. 17.21 are as shown in "Leaves on the Tree".

* The living Wiggett-Chutes are largely outside the period of this book, but are listed on p. 74.

George	17C	Stock.; 17.4	=Style & Hussey	127, 191
George	17C.	Stock.; 18.1	= Joane St. John	127, 191
George	d.1664	Beth.; 18.5	= Cecilia Freke	127, 189
George (Sir)	1663-1721	Beth.;19.2	Baronet, last of the Kentish line	
				125, 127, 146, 190
George Macready	1851-88	Bristol	Theatrical manager	166
George Trevor (Rev.)	19C.	Ireland	In record as Kerry landowner; not in Burke's;	206
Georgina Fanny	1849-1906	Wigg.Chu/Vyne	unm.	63, 74
Gerard Francis ("Jed")	b. 1944	Irel. (Listowel)	= Pauline Henry	149, 205
Gillian	b. 1980	Irel. (Listowel)		149
Grace	c.1575	Sussex		
Helena Jane	19C.	Ireland	= Capt. F Fuller	148
Henry	c. 1420	Taunton; 8.(ii)	= Joane Baskerville	104, 181
Henry (Dr.)	1849-1927	Bristol		166
James	c. 1325	Taunton; 4(i)	= Miss Greenfield (or Grenville?)	104, 181
James	c. 1550	Beth.; 16.7	grandson of Philip	127
James	b. 1613	Dedham/US	s. of Lionel and Rose	160
James	20C.	Irel./Scot.	s. of John and Alice	149
James Henry	1810-1878	Bristol	actor/manager; = M Macready	166, 169,203-4
James Macready	1856-1912	Bristol	s. of the above; = A Hennessey	166, 176
Jane	b. 1595	17.19	sister of the Speaker	194
Jane (Lobb)	1760-1	Pick.	one of the twin dau. of TLC & Ann Wiggett	198
Jenny	19/20C.	Bristol		166
Joane	c. 1340	Taunton; 5(ii)	= Sir John Carminow	104, 181
Joanna	17C.	Stockwell	= Sir P Soames	125, 191
John	c. 1300	Taunton; 2(i)	= Jane Brumfield (or Bampfylde?)	104,181
John	c. 1500	Bridgewater	uncle of Nicholas C	166
John	c. 1675	Combe St. Nicholas		166
John	1701-1776	Vyne; 20.10	Architect	24, 28, 30-38, 83-88, 160, 197
John (Rev.)	19C.	Ireland s. of Arthur C & Frances Lindsay		148
John	20C.	Irel./Scot.	s. of Desmond & Elspeth Bell	149
John Chaloner (Ven.)	1881-1961	Wigg.Chu/Vyn	Archdeacon; =Mamie Durnford	64-66, 73-4, 201
Judith	c.1575	16.11	= John Adkinson	160,192
Julia	19C.	Bristol	d. of J H C & Mazarine Macready	166
Lawrence Vere	1878-1948	Wigg.Chu/E Anglia	= Norah Carruthers	74, 202
"Len" - see Edward Lennard				
Lennard Buckworth	1856-72	Wigg.Chu/Vyne	d. at school	63
Letitia	19C.	Ireland	= William Raymond	148
Lionel	1580-1645	E Anglia	Founder of American Branch;	
			= Rose Barker	103, 141, 160, 163, 192
Lydia	late 17C.	Beth.; 17.9		127
Lyonell	c.1500	Sussex; 13(iii)	= Miss Butler	104, 182
Lyonell	16C.	Sussex; 15.12	= Susan Greene	160, 192-3
Mabella	17th C.	Beth.	=F. Bettenham	127, 188
Marchette	20C.	USA	literary scholar; *outside the scope of this book*	
Margaret	d.1638	Stockwell	d. of Sir George & Ann (tomb @ Lamb.)	125, 145
Margaret	b. 1699	Vyne; 20.8	unm. sister of John	28, 160, 197
Margaret	18C.	Ireland	= George Rowan	148
Margaret	19C.	Ireland	unm.? (sister of Dorothea)	148
Margaret	19C.	Ireland	= Thomas Sandes	148
Margaret	b.1881	Irel.(Listowel)		149
Margaret	20C.	Bristol		166
Maria Esther	1851-1961	Wigg.Chu/Vyn	"Mynie"; unm.	63, 74

Mary	c.1550	Bridgwater	sister of Robert (of the Breach)	166
Mary	b.1619	Dedham/US; 17.17	d. of Lionel & Rose	160
Mary	c.1650	Combe St. Nich.	= Francis Tuthill	166
Mary	b.1693	Vyne	unm. sister of John	28, 160, 197
Mary (Lobb)	1760-1	Pick.	a twin dau. of TLC & ARW	198
Mary (born Lobb)	1762-1822	Pick./Vyne	= Wither Bramston	89, 198
Mary	19C.	Ireland	= Wm. Harnett	148
Mary Anne	19C.	Ireland	d. of Richard C & Rose Aremberg	148
Mary	b.1919	Irel.(Listowel)	= M. O`Connor	149
Maud	19/20C	Wigg.Chu/Vyne	d. of Rev. Devereux C; = H de R Walker	74, 202
Maude	d.1555/6	Somerset	=farmer Vermyn; will recorded; ?relationship	168
Melicent Agnes	19C.	Ireland	= Robert Leslie	148
Mervyn Lyde	1881-1961	Wigg.Chu/E Anglia	Lt. Col. Royal Engineers; High Sheriff;	
			=(1) Frances Armour; (2) Emerin Keene	74, 202

Nathaniel	b.1616	Dedham/US; 17.16	s. of Lionel & Rose	160
Nicholas	d.1583	Bridgwater		166
Norah Madeleine	1877-1966	Wigg.Chu/Vyne	unm. d. of Rev. Devereux C	74

Oliver	c.1500	Sussex; 13(i)	= Miss Redd	104, 182

Paula	b.1976	Irel.(Listowel)		149
Penelope	d.1863	Ireland		148
Philip `Choette`	1234	Somerset	?connection not proved	107
Philip	1332	Taunton	= Miss Britton	104, 181
Philip	d.1565/6	Appledore; 14(ii)	Standard Bearer. 16, 17, 104, 109, 122, 128ff,	182
Philip	c.1650	Beth.		127
Philip	c.1675	Beth; 17.1		191
Pierce	17C.	Ireland		148
Pierce	19C.	Ireland	Newspaper publisher; ?relationship	205

Rachel Eleanor	1876-1968	Wigg.Chu/Vyne	J.P.; unm d of Chaloner Wm. & Eleanor	
				65-6, 74,200-1
Randolph	20C.	Ireland/USA		149
Richard	c.1300	Taunton; 2(ii)		104, 181
Richard M.P.	17C.	Ireland	= Miss Crosbie	148, 205-6
Richard	17C.	Ireland	= Charity Herbert	148
Richard	18C.	Ireland	"of Roxborough"	148
Richard	18C.	Ireland	=(1) Agnes Bateman (2) Eliz. Maunsell	148
Richard	19C.	Ireland	= Eliz. Rowan	148
Richard	1811-1862	Ireland	= (1) Th. Blennerhassett; (2) Rose Aremberg	148, 205-6
Richard Trevor	19C.	Ireland	s. of Richard & Rose Aremberg	148
Richard Aremberg	b.1870	Ireland	= Anna Lowe	149
Richard	b.1867	Irel.(Listowel)	s. of Rowland & Margaret	149
Robert	fl.1425	Taunton; 8(iv)	(erroneously "Baron of Exchqr.")	104, 119, 182
Robert	1438	Taunton; 9(i)	= Alice Berkeley	104, 182
Robert	early 16C.	Sussex; 12	=Jane Lucas	104, 182
Robert	1564-1615	Bridgwater	he of the Breach of Promise case	166-8
Robert	16C.	Bridgwater	Deed of 1570	166
Robert	?1600-1650	Bridgw./Combe		166
Robert	b.1634	Combe St. Nicholas	= Eliz. Hobbs	166
Robert	1663-1720+	Combe St. Nicholas		166
Robert	d.c.1759	Devon	1759 Will recorded; ?relationship	203
Roland	b.1918	Irel.(Listowel)		149
Rosa	19C.	Ireland	d. of Richard & Rose Aremberg	148

> **This Register is, at best, the result of your editor's personal research, and makes no claim to completeness. He will gladly remedy errors and omissions in any future re-print, if readers are kind enough to point them out.**

---

* The <u>American Chutes</u>, being thousands in number, cannot figure in this book for reasons of space.
William E Chute`s , **"Genealogy and History of the Chute Family in America"**, published in 1894 in Salem, Mass., was a comprehensive record of the family up to that date.
It is currently being updated by his great-granddaughter Jacqueline Chute of New York, who has instituted a worldwide database of Chutes and their relations (visit "Chute" on Internet).

GEOGRAPHY OF THE PRINCIPAL FAMILY BRANCHES

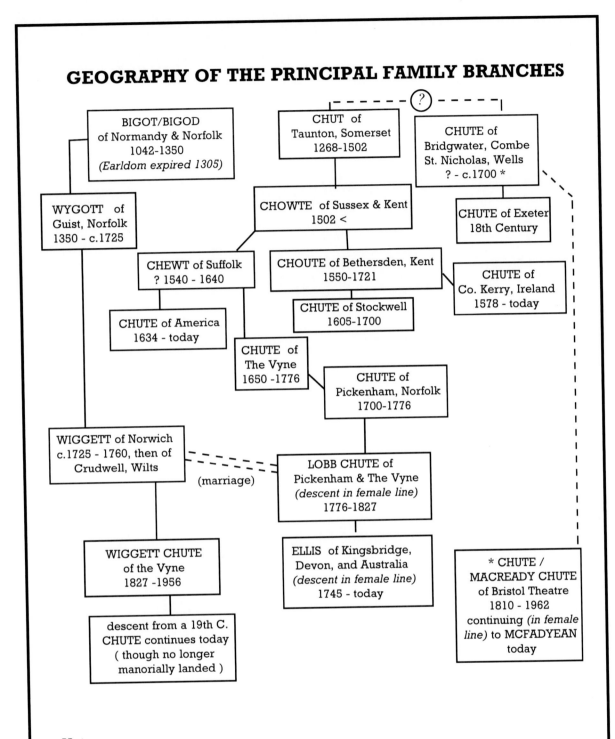

Notes:

(i) * For the `junior` branch of Somerset Chutes, there is a gap in records (1700-1810 approx.) needed to prove conclusively the genealogical connection between the lineage at Bridgwater/ Combe St. Nicholas and the lineage of Bristol.

(ii) From c.1900 onwards, the Irish Chutes gradually dispersed, some migrating to USA, England and Scotland; Chute Hall has gone, but a substantial number remain established in Kerry.

(iii) Much the largest membership of the family now lives in America.